PARENTS' GUIDE TO SCHOOL SELECTION

in San Mateo and Santa Clara Counties

Sixth Edition

Nancy Ginsburg Gill

Brendan Pratt

THE PRATT CENTER, LOS ALTOS, CALIFORNIA

ISBN: 0-9772835-0-X

Published by

The Pratt Center
Four Main Street, Suite 210, Los Altos, CA 94022
Phone (650) 949-2997, Fax (650) 949-2442
www.prattcenter.com

Page Layout and production by

Bonnel Photography & Imaging
221 G Street, Suite 202, Davis, CA 95616
Phone (530) 758-2142

TABLE OF CONTENTS

FORWARD

By Brendan Pratt, Ph.D.

Five years ago, I completed a doctorate in clinical psychology and a post-doctoral fellowship in neuropsychology. I naively thought that I was prepared for my career in private practice. Although I had excellent theoretical training and treatment experience, I had learned little about running a business. I discovered that developing a practice begins with knowing yourself well. Rather than trying to be good at everything, I have sought to excel in one area. I have focused on providing comprehensive psychological evaluations of children and adolescents. Educational success is the primary reason that parents seek evaluations of children, and an appropriate school placement is often the most important recommendation I can make. In a few short steps, I concluded that my knowledge of local schools was critical to my business.

I immediately began a quest for knowledge about local schools and was delighted to discover Nancy Gill's book, *Parents' Guide to School Selection in San Mateo and Santa Clara Counties.* I read about each school and over time visited more than half of them. Several times I called Ms. Gill for further information about a school. Over the years, Ms. Gill and I have consulted with each other frequently. I have contacted her about school selection, and she has called me regarding the psychological needs of children. I have come to respect Ms. Gill's knowledge, professionalism, and expertise. For these reasons, I asked to collaborate with her on the sixth edition of her book.

Ms. Gill and I have worked together to completely revise the guide. We wrote letters to every public school district and private school in Santa Clara and San Mateo Counties. We also wrote to every private high school in San Francisco. We then called every school and interviewed many administrators by phone. We gave school personnel the opportunity to edit information about their school through our online database. Finally, we read school brochures and websites for nearly every school. In short, we made every attempt to gather objective and comprehensive information about schools. We hope that parents will find this book helpful in making informed educational decisions for their children.

I would like to take a moment to thank Ms. Gill for her guidance, support and dedication to this project. Thank you also to Hannah DuVon and Tuan Dao for their tireless work in data entry and follow-up with schools. This project also would not have been possible without technical assistance and computer programming from my brother, David Alves. Finally, I owe a great debt to my wife Kristen and our children, McCain and Evan, for their love and patience with me.

INTRODUCTION

By Nancy Gill

When I was growing up in the old section of Los Altos in the 1950s, the neighborhood children went to either the local public school or a nearby Catholic school. In 1979, my husband and I moved back to the same neighborhood with two children of our own and discovered that the children living within a three block radius of our home attended twelve different elementary schools, five public and seven private.*

Talking with friends and neighbors about schools, I saw how the great increase in school choices, both public and private, had created confusion and often panic among many parents. Fears of violence, teacher strikes, budget cuts, and declining academic standards had made parents leery of sending their children to the neighborhood public school. Highly publicized national studies lamenting the state of public education intensified these concerns.

In the winter of 1980, after writing "Choosing a Private School" for *Parents* magazine, I decided to use my experience teaching in public and private schools, the research I had done as an education writer, and my interest in education issues to help local parents through the baffling and often frightening process of finding a school for their children. After four years of working as an education consultant, I wrote the first edition of *Parents' Guide to School Selection in San Mateo and Santa Clara Counties.*

When the book came out in 1985, I received positive responses from many parents and educators. The fact that both private and public school educators liked what the book had to say made me feel that I had achieved my primary goal: to give parents an unbiased and balanced picture of their school options and offer guidelines that would help them make the best choice for their children.

When I wrote the first edition, most public school districts had been facing shrinking enrollments for a decade. Districts were closing campuses and letting go of teachers with the least seniority, in some cases tenured teachers with many years of experience. Young teachers had great difficulty finding jobs except as substitutes or in private schools, most of which paid far less than their public counterparts. At the time many of the families who sought private education did so because of a perceived lack of accountability and standards in the public school system.

My, how times have changed. Now many schools, especially those in poor urban areas, have difficulty finding and retaining qualified teachers. And while the growth in the school age population of the 1990s has ended and many districts are again seeing a decline in enrollment, teachers who started teaching in the 1960s and 70s are retiring, and therefore the need for new teachers continues.

While the economic boom of the late 1990s has ended, runaway inflation in the housing market has not. The disappearance of affordable housing has created a nightmare

*In this book, for the sake of simplicity, we use the term "private school" to refer to all non-public schools--parochial and secular.

for both public and private schools as each year hundreds of young teachers, frustrated with the impossibility of paying for a home, either leave the profession or leave the area. One local superintendent described the challenge of retaining teachers: "We feel like we have become the training ground for the central valley schools. We train newly credentialed teachers, they work for us for a few years, and then they go to Fresno or Stockton where they can afford a down payment on a house."

School administrators, in both public and private schools, are doing all they can to stem the teacher exodus and attract new teachers to the profession. However, the on-going state budget problems and rising health care costs ensure that raising teachers' salaries enough to allow them to compete for housing with higher paid private sector workers is unlikely in the near future. While most private schools have substantially raised tuition to keep their salaries competitive with public school salaries, they know that if they raise fees too much they will lose all but their wealthiest families.

In fact, private elementary schools have already seen the effect of increased tuition. Applications to private elementary schools have in general declined at both parochial and independent schools; therefore, parents seeking a private education are more likely to find an opening than they were in the late 1990s. However, private high schools report an increase in applications, perhaps a reflection of the concern parents have with the ever-increasing competition to get into both the University of California and prestigious private universities. Some also worry that budget cuts prevent large public high schools from giving students the kind of individual attention, college counseling, or enrichment opportunities that private high schools can offer.

The education picture has shifted most dramatically in the debate over accountability and standardized testing. In the early 1980s, many parents and educators were concerned that a decade of experimentation had led to excessive amounts of what was often referred to as "touchy-feely" education. Neither the states nor the federal government held the schools accountable for ensuring that students were actually learning important basic skills and made little attempt to measure academic success among all elements of the school population.

Now many educators, parents, and students argue that we have accountability run amok. Critics of high-stakes testing contend that nationally normed tests, the state's standards tests, Advanced Placement (AP) tests, and school exit exams are transforming our schools into test-taking factories. They argue that time spent preparing for and taking all these tests leaves little room for critical thinking, in-depth exploration of subject matter, the arts, or any topic no matter how interesting that won't be covered by a high-stakes test. The No Child Left Behind (NCLB) mandate by the federal government has fueled this concern as it requires districts to close the testing gap between their most disadvantaged and their wealthiest students. Educators also grumble that they are expected to achieve this difficult goal without receiving enough extra funding to do so. While politicians and some parents and teachers applaud these tests and NCLB as the only way to make our schools and teachers accountable, a growing number of people are wondering whether the testing mania may be doing more harm than good. Many of these critics of our obsession with testing argue that performance based assessments, such as portfolios and oral presentations, are a better way to gauge what students have learned and prepare them for the demands of the modern workplace.

Another concern among educators and psychologists is the high stress level found at many high schools—public and private. The competitive frenzy to look good on their college applications has created an epidemic of stressed-out students who worried themselves sick, taking every available AP class and filling every free moment with extracurricular activities and volunteer work. While programs like Stanford's Stressed Out Students Project are working with public and private high schools to help students achieve a more balanced and relaxed experience, the competitive climate that produces the stress is proving difficult to change.

One of the most positive changes in the last two decades is the increase in public school options available to families. Over thirty charter schools have opened in the area covered by this book, and educators involved in the small school movement are successfully lobbying school districts to offer smaller, personalized schools to students who don't usually succeed in large schools. Middle college programs offer further options to high school juniors and seniors who are bored or unmotivated at traditional high schools.

Whichever way the current education and economic winds are blowing, wise parents will avoid succumbing to hysteria. Despite the challenges educators face, this area is blessed with many fine teachers and administrators in both the public and private sector. Happy, well-educated kids continue to come out of many different public and private schools.

This edition, like those before it, is designed to clarify some of the issues that can make the school selection process so confusing and stressful. After using the directory to identify the schools that meet your financial, philosophical, and geographical needs, you should evaluate schools for yourself, using the guidelines provided in the first part of the book. If you make an honest assessment of your child's needs and look for an environment full of enthusiastic, caring educators, chances are your search for the right school for your child will be a successful one.

For the sixth edition, I have been pleased to collaborate with licensed psychologist Brendan Pratt, Ph.D. We have worked together periodically for the past five years to help families meet the educational needs of their children. In his Los Altos clinic, Dr. Pratt specializes in educational and psychological evaluations of individuals from kindergarten through college. Many of the people he evaluates have learning disabilities, attentional problems, anxiety, and depression. Dr. Pratt received his doctorate in psychology from the California School of Professional Psychology in Alameda, which has full accreditation from the American Psychological Association (APA). He then completed an APA-accredited internship and a two-year post-doctoral fellowship in pediatric neuropsychology. Dr. Pratt is currently the president of the Santa Clara County Psychological Association.

HOW TO START THE SCHOOL SEARCH

Make an honest assessment of your child's interests, strengths, and weaknesses.

Many children will do well wherever they go. For their families, the school selection process is primarily a matter of finding the school that best meets parental expectation, practical needs, and education values. However, parents should first assess their child's personality, strengths, and weaknesses. Some parents feed their own egos and need for status by pushing their child into prestigious schools that may not serve the child's needs at all. No one school is right for all children. A child who is easily distracted might need a structured learning environment, whereas a creative, self-motivated child would flourish in a more open, unstructured school. Children with low self-esteem often need a small school with a low student-to-teacher ratio, a place where they can feel important. More confident children often thrive on the variety and stimulus a large school can offer. Teachers who have worked with your child can be of great help in assessing the class size, amount of structure, and degree of academic pressure that will be best for him or her. If you have difficulty deciding what kind of school will be best for your child, you can also use the services of an education counselor.

Before you start visiting schools, decide what you want in a school.

You will have an easier time evaluating schools if you combine your assessments of your child's specific needs with your own practical requirements (e.g., on-site day care cost, distance from home) and the qualities you think a good school should have. Some parents want structure, discipline, and lots of homework. Others want a more open learning environment that allows children to learn at their own pace. The better sense you have of what you want in a school, the easier it will be to recognize the right school when you visit it.

You should also decide how involved you want to be in your child's school. Most public schools and some private schools welcome parental involvement in the classroom and on advisory committees. A few public and many private schools even require participation. Some private schools restrict parent participation to fundraising efforts and write into their philosophies that volunteer aides are not used in the classroom. If you have the time and inclination to participate, look for a school that will welcome your involvement.

CONSIDERING A PUBLIC SCHOOL

In spite of the many challenges facing public education, the San Francisco Bay Area has many excellent public schools. Unless you want a school that offers religious instruction or a special program that public schools can't offer, start your school search by evaluating for yourself the education your child can receive free of charge.

To obtain more specific information about a public school than this book can provide, you should request from the school district the annual accountability report card that each school must make available to the public. These report cards provide information about different aspects of the school, including demographics, test scores, instructional materials, class size, and support services. You may be able to get this information from your district's website or from one of several websites which provide detailed reports on California public schools. (See the website page in the appendix for a description of these resources.)

You should also investigate the health of a school beyond what these report cards and websites reflect. Talk to your public school administrators, teachers, and especially parents of current students. By following the "How to Evaluate a School" guidelines, you can get a good feeling for the kind of education available in your assigned public school. You may find good teachers and exciting programs. Even if you are not satisfied with the public schools available to you, taking the time to evaluate them will give you a better idea of what you want in a private school.

FUNDING

Several decades ago financing of public education in California was relatively simple though inequitable; it was determined for the most part by the assessed value of local property and the extent to which communities were willing to increase their property taxes for schools. However, in 1976, the State Supreme Court ruled in *Serrano v. Priest* that unequal funding among school districts is unconstitutional. In response to the Court order, the Legislature passed a law to redistribute property taxes to reduce inequities. In 1984, the Court declared that sufficient compliance with the *Serrano* decision had been achieved, and indeed, compared to many other states, there is relatively little disparity in how much tax money each school district in California receives for each child.

Most districts are "revenue limit" districts, i.e., they rely on the state for most of their funding. Fifteen districts in the area covered by this book are currently "excess tax" districts,* which means their property tax revenues exceed what the state would normally pay per student. These districts, formerly known as Basic Aid districts, tend to have more money per student than other districts, and they are less vulnerable to the state's budget crises than other districts. However, if these districts face a sudden downturn in tax revenues, they too can face the same budget problems that revenue limit districts experience.

* Belmont, Hillsborough, Las Lomitas, Menlo Park, Portola Valley, San Mateo Union H.S., Sequoia, Woodside Elem., Fremont Union H.S., Los Gatos-Saratoga H.S., Mountain View-Los Altos H.S., Palo Alto, Santa Clara, and Sunnyvale.

Because excess tax districts no longer receive the basic aid amount of $120 per student from the state, they are less likely than other districts to accept out of district students.

The shift of school finances to state control became virtually complete in 1978 when Proposition 13 limited property taxes. It also made it much more difficult for local communities to add to the state contribution by requiring a two-thirds, instead of a majority, vote to pass local school bonds and parcel taxes. In 2000, the state's voters approved a proposition that allowed bonds to pass with only 55% voter approval.

While *Serrano* mandated relative equity in what each district receives to educate each child, it did not cover all sources of funding. Therefore, as the list in the appendix shows, per pupil spending can vary greatly district to district. Some districts receive substantial funding for special programs or categories of students. Many districts have established foundations to raise money to maintain programs that would otherwise have to be cut. A few districts that serve affluent families like Hillsborough, Palo Alto, Woodside and Los Altos raise more than a million dollars annually to hire specialists, buy new textbooks and equipment, and reduce class sizes.

The biggest contributor to the difference in per pupil spending is the ability of some districts to pass large parcel tax measures. Since 1995, twenty-two districts in Santa Clara and San Mateo Counties have been able to win the required two-thirds vote to raise extra money to improve or maintain instructional programs and/or reduce class size. While most districts must keep these tax requests modest, typically at below $100 a parcel, districts, like Menlo Park, Hillsborough, Palo Alto, and Los Altos, that serve affluent families have been able to get their communities to approve taxes over $300 a parcel. In the last decade, more than forty districts have passed general obligation bonds to build, renovate or improve facilities. (The appendix lists the districts that have passed these tax measures.) A district's success at passing parcel taxes and bond measures demonstrates broad-based community support for the local public schools. A few very small districts get extra money because they qualify as necessary small schools and require extra money per child to run a complete school program. For a more comprehensive explanation of public school financing and policy issues, contact EdSource of Palo Alto (650-917-9481; www.edsource.org).

CURRICULUM FRAMEWORKS

California has developed curriculum frameworks that establish state-wide standards for what children should learn at each grade level in reading/language arts, mathematics, history/social studies, and science. These standards are widely viewed as among the most rigorous in the nation. The Department of Education lists these content standards by grade level on its website, www.cde.ca.gov/be/st/ss.

STATEWIDE TESTING PROGRAM

In 1999, California passed the Public Schools Accountability Act to hold students, schools, and districts accountable for meeting the standards established by the curriculum frameworks. Since 2000, the state has published an annual Academic Performance Index (API) to track academic performance and improvement of the state's public schools.

The API scores are based on the results of the state's Standardized Testing and Reporting Program (STAR), of which the two main components are the California Standards Tests and for grades 3 and 7 the nationally normed California Achievement Test (CAT/6). Results from the California High School Exit Exam (CAHSEE) are also used to determine the API scores of high schools. Schools receive a number on a scale of 200 to 1000, with 800 as the eventual minimum goal for all schools. Schools scoring under 800 that fail to meet their target growth goals several years in a row may face state intervention. The appendix contains the most recently available API scores for schools in the two counties covered by this book.

While STAR tests and API rankings can be useful in helping parents determine which schools adequately cover the skills tested by the CAT/6 and the Standards Tests, parents should realize that many important aspects of education—e.g., critical thinking and creativity—are not assessed by the STAR exam. Don't assume that the school in your district with the highest test scores is the best school for your child. Test scores are closely correlated with demographics and therefore don't necessarily indicate which schools have the best teachers and principals. Even when schools serve a similar demographic pool, the difference in test scores may reflect a difference in educational philosophy. For example, in districts that offer parents a choice of both a traditional "back-to-basics" program and one that has an open, hands-on approach that emphasizes critical thinking and creativity over rote learning, the traditional schools invariably have substantially higher test scores because those schools focus on the skills measured by standardized tests.

Research a school's or district's general attitude towards testing. If teachers are focusing too much classroom time on teaching to the test, many important aspects of a quality education may be ignored. Beware of schools that pressure teachers to spend weeks of classroom time prepping for the statewide tests. Most educators understand that while raising test scores will make their school look good, spending too much time teaching to the tests can cheat children out of the kind of educational experiences that make learning really exciting.

In some cases, it's not the school staff but the parents who become obsessed with test preparation. Private afterschool tutorial centers are thriving. However, many of their clients are not children who are struggling academically and need extra help but children whose parents want to do all they can to ensure their children get top scores on standardized tests. If you don't want that kind of pressured environment for your child, look for a school where most of the parents want their children to spend weekends and afterschool time playing or participating in sports or the arts.

High School Exit Exam: In its attempt to strengthen standards and make a California high school diploma more meaningful, the State Department of Education now requires that students pass an exit exam as well as fulfill course requirements to graduate from high school. The test is based on California's statewide academic content standards and has language arts (reading and writing) and mathematics (up to basic algebra) sections. Schools give the tests several times each year, and students who do not show progress in passing the test are offered special tutoring and summer school programs. Disabled students graduating in 2006 may graduate without passing the exam if they have fulfilled all other graduation requirements.

INTERDISTRICT AND INTRADISTRICT TRANSFERS

In the summer of 1993, the California Legislature passed AB 19 and AB 1114, which allow parents to send their children to any school within their district or in another district as long as space is available. However, if the transfer would have a negative impact on desegregation or if a school has already lost one to three percent of its students in a given year, the resident school district can prevent the transfer.

Even before AB 1114 was passed, many districts had an open enrollment policy, allowing parents to choose any school within the district as long as space was available. But by the early 1990s, districts were finding it increasingly difficult to honor these requests, since many schools, especially those deemed "the best," were packed with students from the school's attendance area.

In 1986, the state passed the Allen Bill, which allows parents to place children in kindergarten through eighth grade in the school district in which their workplace is located. Districts are only required to grant such transfers as long as space is available and as long as such a transfer does not negatively impact a district's desegregation plan or cost the accepting district more money to educate the child than it would receive from the state in additional aid.

Although the Allen Bill, AB 1114, and AB 19 are well-intended efforts to give parents more choice in public schools, they have had little impact. Over the last decade, most school districts experienced a population spurt among their own residents and thus have been able to grant few transfers under these bills. However, parents who feel their children can receive a better education in another district should inquire about an interdistrict transfer as provided by these bills. Now that some districts are seeing an enrollment decline for the first time in many years, these transfers may become easier to get. Basic Aid districts, now referred to as "excess tax districts," rarely take out-of-district students even if their enrollment declines as they do not receive extra funding from the state for additional students.

ALTERNATIVE SCHOOLS

Some districts operate alternative schools that have a different focus or philosophy than the neighborhood schools and are open to all families residing in the district. If your district offers such schools, start investigating them as soon as possible. If you are interested in such a program, find out when the registration period is. Most districts give priority to siblings of students already enrolled in the school. Schools that have more applicants than spaces—and most do—usually hold a lottery in late winter or early spring to determine which children will get places in these alternative schools. The most common types of alternative schools are listed below.

Back-to-Basics Schools generally have a teacher-directed, textbook approach to learning with a minimum amount of individualization. They often have a dress code and clearly defined homework and discipline policies. Grade levels are rarely combined, and parents are generally not used as classroom aides. Students and parents are often required to sign a written agreement to follow the rules and philosophy of the school. These schools appeal to parents who want a traditional, highly structured program for their children. They are especially effective for children who are most comfortable and productive with firm guidelines and a quiet environment. While the test scores in these schools are typically among the highest in the state, profoundly bright or creative children may find the structure and textbook orientation of these schools too confining.

Bilingual Immersion Programs: While the passage of Proposition 227 (the Unz Initiative) ended most of the state's bilingual programs, some districts still offer language immersion programs designed to help both Spanish-speaking and English-speaking children become bilingual and biliterate. (Cupertino offers a Mandarin-English bilingual program.) Typically, these programs are magnet schools open to all children in the district and—if space is available—to children from districts that don't offer this option. Children must usually enter the program in either kindergarten or first grade. In the primary grades, most instruction is in Spanish. The amount of English gradually increases each year until fourth or fifth grade when instruction is evenly divided between the two languages. Advocates of bilingual immersion cite studies that show that younger children learn a second language much more easily than do adolescents or adults.

Magnet Schools are used by some large school districts to help balance the ethnic distribution of the district's schools. These schools emphasize one of a wide variety of areas, such as performing arts and technology, and integrate the specialty throughout the curriculum.

Open Education Schools are characterized by student initiated activity, independent study, and freedom of movement in the classroom. Open schools are less textbook-oriented than most schools and instead emphasize an interdisciplinary and hands-on approach to learning. These schools often mix age groups and may require parent participation to achieve the low student-to-adult ratio necessary for individualized education. Open schools usually do not give graded report cards, but instead evaluate students through written comments and conferences. They generally work best for creative, self-motivated children who thrive on freedom of choice, and they appeal to parents who want to be actively involved in their children's education. They are not appropriate for children who are easily distracted, who are overwhelmed by too many choices, or who have learning styles that require systematic and sequential instruction to grasp basic skills.*

* Most public schools belong in the middle of the educational spectrum between open schools and back-to-basics schools. In the 1970s, many schools moved towards the open end of the spectrum with an emphasis on student-generated activities; in the early 1980s, public schools in general moved back towards a more structured model. In the 1990s, many educators, driven by the desire to strengthen critical thinking skills and prepare students for the modern workplace, embraced some of the ideas—e.g., an integrated curriculum and collaborative learning—that typify "open" schools. However, the current emphasis on raising test scores has led many schools, especially those in lower income areas, to emphasize scripted, rote instruction. All of this illustrates what is referred to as "the pendulum swing" in public education.

You may also have available to you some other public school options:

Charter Schools: California allows school districts to abandon the 11-volume, 7800 page Education Code and create whatever kind of school the community wants, as long as its curriculum meets basic state education requirements. Charter schools vary greatly. Some embrace a specific educational philosophy, and many target the needs of a specific student population—most often, students who have historically failed to succeed in traditional schools.

Some charter schools—especially those operated by for- profit companies and those that serve home schooled and independent study students—have been the subject of heated debate and legislative investigation. Others have been short-lived because they failed to produce promised outcomes or maintain the support of parents and staff. However, many educators and parents see the alternatives offered by charter schools as a healthy way to serve students whose needs are not addressed by traditional public school programs. A few districts have transformed their neighborhood schools into charter schools because doing so gives them a flexibility they do not have with non-charter schools. For example, it is easier for out-of-district families to get approval from their home district to transfer to an out-of-district public school if that school is a charter school.

Charter schools can be started by parents, teachers, or community members but must be sponsored either by a school district, the county office of education, or the State of California. They must choose students by lottery and must offer appropriate instruction to students with learning differences. The biggest challenge faced by many charter schools has been locating a site; however, now, according to the provisions of Proposition 39 passed in 2000, if a charter school enrolls at least 80 students, the school district in which the charter school is located must find a site reasonably equivalent to other district sites.

Continuation Schools: Almost every high school district offers a continuation program designed for students who have difficulty adjusting to regular school programs, who fail to attend classes according to district criteria, or who have already dropped out of regular high school. These schools' academic programs are often individualized according to students' needs, and the student-to-teacher ratio is lower than that of the comprehensive high school. Some districts also offer Opportunity Programs directed at middle school students who have been evaluated as potential dropouts. An increasing number of districts are implementing other programs to identify potential drop-outs and offer specialized programs to motivate these students to stay in school.

The International Baccalaureate Organization Diploma Program was created in 1968 to meet the needs of geographically mobile students, especially those moving from one country to another, by establishing a common curriculum and university entry credential. The curriculum leads students to take exams in six subject groups. To earn the IB Diploma, students must score 24 or higher on the exams (max. score is 45) and complete several other demanding requirements. Several public high school districts and one private school in this area offer this rigorous course of study to high school students.

Middle College Programs are established as partnerships between public high school districts and local community colleges. While these programs may vary slightly from campus to campus, they typically allow high school juniors and seniors residing in the district to complete their high school education in a small supportive program on a college campus while getting a head start on earning a college degree. The programs are designed for students who feel disconnected from the traditional high school environment, are capable of handling a rigorous academic program, and will thrive at a supportive school in an enriched and flexible educational setting.

The Small School Choice Movement is based on the recognition that many students, especially those from low-income families, are not well served by large public schools. A growing number of these new small schools, such as Aspire and KIPP schools, are operated as part of regional or national non-profit organizations. Unlike charter schools, they are part of the school district whose students they serve but have been newly designed, often with input from the community. These new small schools have philosophies that may differ in degree of structure or specific curriculum focus. However, they share in common the belief that small schools in which teachers know all of the school's students, have high expectations for their students, and are willing to put in extra time to make sure no one falls between the cracks can help disadvantaged students complete high school and be successful in college and the world beyond.

Year-Round Schools: Over the last two decades, some districts have started operating year-round schools. Students in these schools attend school the same number of days (about 180) as children in schools with traditional calendars, but instead of a three-month summer break, vacation and instructional periods are spread more evenly throughout the year, (e.g., 60 days of instruction followed by 20 days of vacation). When year-round schools are single-track, all students are in school at the same time. Multi-track schools divide the students and staff into three to five tracks, so that one track is always on vacation. This system allows districts to save on school construction costs as each school site can serve 20% or more students.

Proponents of year-round schools argue that eliminating the obsolete, traditional school calendar improves academic achievement; reduces teacher, student, and parent burnout; and makes more efficient use of school facilities. However, the implementation of year-round schools has not spread as quickly as many predicted because they can cause inconvenience to parents with children on different school calendars and because operating schools throughout the summer months requires many districts to install air-conditioning, an expense few can afford. No area high schools have changed to a year-round schedule because of logistical problems (e.g., running athletic programs when students and other schools are on different calendars) and because many high school students rely on summer jobs to help them save money for college.

Education for Children with Special Needs: Every public school district provides special education programs for students with disabilities. Resource specialist programs (RSPs) serve students who qualify for special education services but are able to spend

9

most of the school day in regular classrooms. Specialists provide individual and small group instruction, conduct educational assessments, and coordinate the child's educational program with classroom teachers and parents. School districts and county offices of education offer other programs for the more severely disabled.

Under federal and state laws, public funding can be used to pay for sending children with disabilities to specialized private schools. These laws state that if a resident school district is unable to provide an appropriate program for a disabled child, that child may be funded at a non-public institution if it has been certified by the California State Department of Education and can appropriately meet the needs of the student. For more information on these laws, inquire at your public school district or the State Department of Education, or contact the Community Alliance for Special Education (CASE) at 408-998-5200. CASE offers free consultations about special education rights and services. It also provides legal support, representation, and educational consultations to parents whose children need special education services.

Schwab Learning Center (650-655-2410; www.schwablearning.org) in San Mateo provides information for parents of students with learning differences. Resources include a special library, information/referral services, educational programs, guidance, and a parent newsletter.

Gifted and Talented Education Program (GATE) is a state-funded program designed to offer special instruction to children identified as mentally gifted or talented. The method used to identify these students varies greatly from district to district. Districts usually use a combination of teacher or counselor recommendations, performance on intelligence tests, and demonstrated potential in leadership or performance art to identify children they think need more stimulation and challenge than they are receiving in the classroom. Some educators advocate integrating GATE programs into the regular classroom because they believe that all students deserve the kind of stimulating, enriching activities that typify instruction for the gifted. However, many advocates for the gifted argue that gifted education must provide a differentiated curriculum that enables the gifted student to learn in greater depth and complexity with greater acceleration. While most of today's educators proclaim a commitment to differentiation, the level of success with which they actually meet different students' needs varies greatly from school to school and teacher to teacher.

The specific programs offered to GATE students vary from district to district. Sometimes students are pulled out of their regular classrooms once or twice a week and given special instruction or are offered afterschool enrichment activities. Some districts use GATE funds to hire specialists to help classroom teachers keep their exceptional students challenged. A few districts offer cluster programs, in which gifted students are placed together in self-contained classes designed to meet the needs of especially bright students.

Once students reach junior high or middle school, clustering of gifted children occurs more naturally, as these children tend to be the ones taking foreign languages and advanced math and science classes. In high school, this natural clustering of the gifted increases as bright students —at least the academically motivated ones—group together in honors classes and Advanced Placement classes. Some community colleges and universities also offer summer programs designed for gifted students.

The California Association of the Gifted (CAG; www.CAGifted.org) is an advocacy and information organization for teachers and parents of gifted children.

LOOK INTO THE HEALTH OF YOUR PUBLIC SCHOOL DISTRICT

Learn how well the components of your public school district work by reading local newspaper coverage of school board meetings and attending a board meeting. Try to answer the following questions:

- Do board members work well together and with the superintendent for the good of the schools and the children, or are factions on the school board and within the administration working against each other? Do superintendents leave soon after they are hired?

- Are teachers constantly threatening to go on strike? Do they seem distrustful of the administration and school board?

- Are teachers, administrators, parents, and the board working together to solve problems and improve the schools?

- Are parents and teachers given the opportunity to offer input when difficult decisions must be made regarding the future of the schools?

- Do hostile accusations and bickering characterize the communication level within the school community, or is there a feeling of mutual respect?

- Have administrators and teachers in your district improved the educational programs in their schools through joint ventures with local businesses and grants from private foundations?

WARNING TO NEWCOMERS

If you are buying or renting a home specifically because you like a certain school in that neighborhood or like the idea of living close to your child's school, don't assume that the real estate agent is correct when she or he tells you what school your child will attend. Check with the school district to verify what school your child will attend. Some newcomers find out that the only school with space for their children is across town or discover that the house they have bought is not in the school district or attendance area they thought they were moving into. To save yourself this kind of disappointment and frustration, contact the school district before you commit to housing.

CONDUCTING A PRIVATE SCHOOL SEARCH

One advantage private schools have over public institutions is that they don't have to be all things to all people. A private school can say, "These are our objectives, these are the methods we use to reach them, and these are the kinds of children we want to educate. If this is what you want and your child meets our qualifications, you are welcome to apply. Otherwise, go elsewhere." Therefore, parents searching for a private school should take special care in evaluating their child's needs and their own educational values.

By carefully reading the descriptions of schools' philosophy, curriculum, and facilities in this book's listings of schools, parents can identify the ones that are most likely to provide the kind of education they are looking for. However, at times schools that are actually quite different can have philosophies that sound very similar: "We offer a sound academic program while we develop in our students responsibility, self-confidence, and a concern for others." Visiting a school and talking with parents will help you determine whether you are comfortable with the school's environment and the methods it uses to achieve its goals. While some schools might work toward responsibility and academic excellence by offering a traditional classroom environment and stressing homework and test-taking abilities, other schools seek to achieve the same goals by promoting collaborative efforts among students and offering an interdisciplinary, project-oriented curriculum.

INQUIRE ABOUT THE CREDENTIALS AND BACKGROUNDS OF THE FACULTY

Many private schools hire only credentialed teachers; some do not. However, parents should not select a school purely on this basis. Many weak teachers have credentials; many excellent ones do not. Some private schools, especially high schools, look for staff with a variety of interests, previous teaching experience, advanced degrees, and practical experience in their subject matter, and consider the possession of a credential relatively unimportant. However, parents considering a school that does not require teaching credentials should carefully assess the caliber of teaching through parent and student evaluations and, if possible, class visits. Beware of schools staffed almost completely by young, inexperienced teachers who have no formal training in how to teach.

CHECK THE FACULTY TURNOVER RATE

While some private schools have now matched or even surpassed public school salaries, many private schools still pay less than their public school counterparts. However, many teachers who could get public school jobs prefer to work in private schools for a number of reasons: small classes, close personal relationships with students, fewer disciplinary problems, less pressure to "teach to the test," more control over curriculum, or, in the case of religious schools, the opportunity to teach in a religious environment.

Most schools in the Bay Area have lost teachers because of high housing costs. But if teachers are constantly leaving a private school to teach at public or other private schools in the area, it may indicate that the school does not offer enough of the above advantages or that the salaries are dismally low.

CHECK ON THE SCHOOL'S FINANCIAL SOLVENCY

Few private schools can operate on tuition revenue alone. Most parochial schools are subsidized by their supporting church and therefore can offer private education at a relatively low cost to parents. Older schools often have substantial endowment funds and annual alumni fundraising drives. Many schools rely on parents' fundraising efforts to pay for special programs, scholarships, and improvements. Almost all private schools publish some sort of annual financial report. If you are concerned about a school's financial solvency, ask to read this report.

Proprietary schools operate under private ownership as profit-making ventures. Consequently, they cannot qualify for tax-exempt donations and must pay property taxes. Some educators are skeptical of any school run on such a basis. However, many proprietary schools are operated by dedicated educators and provide excellent programs. If you are interested in a proprietary school, check carefully to determine whether the school provides necessary services and materials to its students, sufficiently small classes, and adequate salaries to maintain a strong faculty while still making a profit for its owner.

ASK ABOUT THE PERMANENCE OF THE SCHOOL SITE

During the last ten years, many private schools that leased sites from public school districts lost their leases when the sites were reopened as public schools. Now some districts are again closing sites and leasing them out to private schools. If you are attracted to a private school because of its proximity to your home or workplace, find out whether the school can assure you that it will be located in the same site for the time your child attends it.

UNDERSTAND THE DIFFERENCES IN PRIVATE SCHOOLS

Carden Schools were started in the 1930s in New York City by Mae Carden and soon spread throughout the country. The curriculum is highly organized and stresses continuity from grade to grade. Reading, language, and grammar instruction begins in kindergarten. The textbooks are privately printed and designed so that skills are taught in clear sequence. Emphasis on written and oral communication in a structured environment characterizes Carden schools. Carden teachers do not have to be credentialed by the state, but they must go through special Carden training and attend instructional seminars twice a year. Each Carden school runs independently—some as non-profit and some as proprietary institutions—but all must be accredited by the Carden Foundation. The degree of academic acceleration varies from school to school, depending on the abilities of the school's students.

Christian Schools. The label "Christian School" applies to schools that have an evangelical or fundamentalist approach to theology and integrate the Bible in almost all aspects of the school curriculum. Most are operated by churches that adhere to a literal interpretation of the Bible, but only a few require that students' families belong to a specific church. Christian schools usually use *Abeka* or other Christian texts; most use them along with secular textbooks, but some use Christian materials exclusively. Many of these schools offer specialized programs for students with learning disabilities.

Some schools with Christian church affiliations are not considered "Christian Schools" in the above sense because they do not take an evangelical approach to religion, and they teach academic subjects in a secular manner.

Daycare Originated Private Schools. In the last three decades, there has been a great increase in the number of schools that started out as preschool/day-care centers and have responded to working parents' needs by expanding into elementary programs. These schools are generally owner-operated, stay open year-round, and include extended daycare as part of the tuition. They vary greatly in quality and philosophy.

Independent School is a term generally used for non-church affiliated, non-profit private schools, but some schools that belong to the National Association of Independent Schools (NAIS) and the California Association of Independent Schools (CAIS) do have religious affiliations. While independent schools may include the teaching of religious values and traditions in their philosophy, they teach academic subjects with a secular approach.

Independent schools tend to be more expensive than other private schools but usually have much smaller class sizes and are generous with financial aid. They are governed by boards of trustees and usually list preparation for high school or college as their primary goal. Because they are independent, these schools vary greatly in philosophy, structure, and academic programs.

Montessori Schools. In the early 1900s Maria Montessori, an Italian physician and educator, developed her ideas on education from observing slum children in Rome. Her belief that children have a great capacity for mental concentration, a desire to repeat activities, and a love of order led her to write influential books on education, which formed the basis for the Montessori method. Montessori schools stress the importance of a rich environment to provide children the opportunity to understand the world through sensory experiences. The Montessori teacher generally keeps a low profile, allowing children to move from one set of carefully designed materials to another as they wish. Montessori education stresses self-motivated learning and strives to develop self-discipline and self-confidence. Because any school can use "Montessori" in its title, Montessori schools vary greatly in quality and approach.

Catholic Schools are committed to teaching the principles of the Roman Catholic Church while offering a strong academic program. However, Catholic schools can vary in their educational philosophy, structure, and overall flavor. Some are highly structured and traditional; others are more relaxed, open, and innovative. Catholic schools often use state-adopted texts, and usually educate the same spectrum of children as are found in public schools. While most Catholic schools do not feel equipped to educate seriously learning-disabled children, some offer programs for those with mild learning differences.

Most Catholic elementary schools are parish (parochial) schools operated under the sponsorship of a specific church. Tuition at these schools is relatively low compared to the fees charged by other non-public schools, and the tuition discounts for siblings are substantial. A few Catholic schools are operated by religious orders. These independent Catholic schools are usually more expensive than parish schools but tend to have smaller class sizes.

All Catholic schools give admissions priority to qualified Catholic applicants and most charge a higher tuition to non-Catholic and out-of-parish Catholic families. They welcome non-Catholic students when space is available but expect all students to participate in the school's religious instruction.

Waldorf Schools, started in Germany in 1919 by Rudolf Steiner, stress the relationship between the physical, psychological, and spiritual. Steiner believed that children pass through distinct stages of development, and the Waldorf curriculum and teaching methods reflect these stages. In Waldorf schools, the core teachers continue from grade to grade with the same children and are responsible for their main subjects. Other teachers teach foreign languages, music, eurythmy (movement), crafts and games. Waldorf schools do not use traditional textbooks in the early grades and eschew the use of television, video games, and computers; instead the curriculum relies on oral presentations by the teachers and lesson books created by the children for each subject studied. Administrative decisions are made collectively by the faculty, who work from consensus.

Other Schools. Some private schools listed in this book do not fall into any of the above categories. Most of these are either proprietary schools or are affiliated with a particular religion, e.g., Jewish, Episcopal, Islamic, Seventh Day Adventist. Parents can learn about the philosophy and curriculum of these schools by reading the entries listed in the directory and contacting the schools.

HOW TO EVALUATE A SCHOOL

ASSESS THE LEADERSHIP QUALITIES OF THE PRINCIPAL (called the head of school or director at many private schools).

Your child's education will certainly be shaped largely by the quality of individual teachers; however, a strong principal can create an atmosphere that inspires staff members to put more energy into their jobs and fosters the high morale and family feeling that create a sense of community among teachers, parents, and students. To assess the quality of leadership in a school, talk to parents, students, and teachers, and if possible arrange a meeting with the principal to help you answer some of the following questions:

- Do parents feel comfortable telephoning the principal when a problem arises that teachers cannot or will not handle? Are calls returned and, when necessary, conferences arranged?

- Does the principal support the staff but still respond to legitimate complaints when parents feel teachers are not doing their jobs?

- Does the principal take the time to know the students? Does he or she make appearances on the playground, in the lunch area, and in classrooms, and participate in activities with students?

- Do students and teachers respect, but not fear, the principal?

- Can the principal clearly describe the school's curriculum, and is he or she excited about the school's programs?

- When discipline problems arise in the classroom or on the playground, does the principal respond immediately and effectively?

If you get affirmative answers to most of these questions, then you have found a place with one of the most important elements of a healthy school—strong leadership. (Parents should note that at large private elementary schools and most private high schools, their initial contact with the school is most likely to be with an admissions director and not the principal or school head. However, it is useful to try to determine how students, parents, and faculty feel about the administration.)

EVALUATE THE TEACHERS

In evaluating the quality of teaching at any school, parents should realize that no teacher is perfect for all children and that no school has only "star" teachers. Some children do best with hard-nosed disciplinarians who stretch students with demanding assignments and run a tight ship in the classroom. Others wilt under pressure and are happier and more productive with warmer, more nurturing teachers.

A lot of your information will come from talking with parents, but you should remember that tastes in teachers can be like tastes in movies—the reviews can be so different that you will wonder if people are talking about the same person. Unfortunately, many schools have at least one or two "lemons"—teachers who are incompetent, burned-out, or just plain mean or indifferent. Schools usually also have at least as many stars—teachers praised by parents and students for their extraordinary teaching abilities. Avoid schools that have a large number of lemons and look for one that has at least one or two stars.

Class visits can help you judge the caliber of teaching at a school. Most public schools and some private schools welcome such visits as long as prior arrangements are made with the school office. However, many schools do not allow such visits. Some schools, especially large private ones with many applicants, consider class visits disruptive and logistically impossible, but give parents a chance to meet some teachers at informational events for prospective families. If a school does not allow classroom observation, you might ask to attend an open house or back-to-school night. Such a visit may give you an opportunity to hear about and see the results of what goes on in the classroom.

Many private schools allow—and sometimes require—that applicants spend at least a day at the school. Children entering kindergarten or a primary grade may be asked to spend part of the day at the school so a teacher can assess whether the child will be a good fit academically and socially. At the high school level, applicants can usually make an appointment to "shadow"—to spend a day attending classes—so they can decide whether they feel comfortable at the school and are excited by the teachers and curriculum.

Through classroom visits, attendance at open houses, discussions with parents and current students, and the impressions of your child after a visit, try to answer the following questions:

- Do teachers explain material clearly and respond to questions without putting down students?

- Is the degree of discipline and control in the classroom what you want for your child? If you want a structured classroom, be sure that control is not achieved through fear or intimidation. If you want an open learning environment, be sure that freedom does not result in chaos.

- Do teachers discipline children without cruelty or sarcasm?

- Do teachers seem to enjoy their jobs and bring energy, enthusiasm, and empathy into the classroom?

- Are teachers willing to spend extra time—recess, lunch, or afterschool time if necessary—to explain material a child did not understand in class?

- Do teachers clarify class rules and the consequences of breaking the rules, and follow through with consistency and fairness?

- Do teachers combine solid instruction in basic skills with projects and study units that generate excitement and intellectual curiosity? Even if you are primarily interested in a "basics" school, do not forget that stimulation of intellectual curiosity is probably the most important element of a good education. Ask parents if their children ever come home excited about what they are learning. When visiting classrooms, do you see only math dittoes and spelling tests covering the walls? Or is there evidence of more interesting assignments as well—creative writing samples, social studies projects, and science experiments?

You will probably never find a school where every teacher is wonderful, and it would be virtually impossible to answer all of the above questions for every member of a school's faculty. But talking to members of the school community and spending time at the school should give you a good sense of how enthusiastic, caring, and competent a school's teachers are.

ASK ABOUT THE CREDENTIALS AND TRAINING OF NEW TEACHERS

Because of the retirement of teachers who started teaching in the 1960s and 70s, most schools have new teachers in the classroom. Find out what percentage is fully credentialed. If these teachers are inexperienced, ask what the school does to mentor and train them. Does the school have enough classroom veterans to act as mentors to new teachers?

LOOK AT THE CURRICULUM

The adoption of statewide grade-level standards has in theory made the curriculum far more uniform among public schools than it used to be. And even though private schools are under no obligation to teach according to those standards, many do use them as guidelines for the material their teachers cover. However, in practice, schools and individual teachers may have very different approaches to covering the curriculum. Some believe the best way to ensure that all students learn what they're "supposed to know" is to adopt scripted curriculum packages like Success for All and Open Court that spell out exactly what teachers should cover and how they should cover it. Other schools view such programs as too confining and instead use materials that give teachers more freedom and flexibility. Some schools teach subject matter as discrete disciplines while others take a more interdisciplinary approach. Some schools embrace direct instruction in which subject matter is taught directly by the teacher while others combine direct instruction with hands-on activities and collaborative projects in which students work together and teachers spend much of their time serving as "the guide on the side" instead of the "sage on the stage." Asking questions and making observations about the curriculum can help determine whether a school will meet your expectations and be appropriate for your child.

- Are the textbooks up-to-date?
- Is there a healthy balance between development of basic skills and the exploration of ideas and thinking skills?

- What ability level is the school geared toward? (This question is especially important if the school stresses group instruction as part of its philosophy.) If your child seems to fall above or below the ability norm of the general student body, ask how ability levels and different learning styles are handled. Do teachers understand and apply the principles of differentiation so that the needs of all children are met? Are brighter children allowed to move ahead at a faster pace and given more challenging assignments? Or are they merely given 40 math problems instead of the normal 20 to keep them busy? Are slower students given extra help and more time to grasp concepts and complete work?

In specific areas, consider the following:

Reading. At the elementary level, look for schools that use a mixture of materials and techniques to stimulate interest and improve competency in reading. Literature assignments, oral reading by the teacher and students, and regular outside reading assignments should be used in combination with traditional reading textbooks. Also ask whether teachers actually know how to improve their students' reading skills by not only teaching phonics but also developing inference and comprehension skills. To promote the concept that reading is a relaxing, enjoyable experience, many schools, public and private, set aside a specific time of day for school-wide silent, sustained reading

At the high school level, an examination of required reading lists and syllabuses will help you determine whether the school's curriculum is appropriate to your child's abilities and your values and expectations. While a few high schools still pride themselves on assigning only classics—e.g., Shakespeare, Dickens, Hawthorne—most are committed to a multicultural approach that reflects the rich diversity of our population and history. Whatever a school's philosophy about literature, the English classes should generate enthusiasm for reading and promote the ability to discuss and write about literature beyond the purely literal level of book reports.

Math. Of all the areas of the curriculum, changes in math instruction have probably generated the most controversy in recent years. Teachers who embrace the reform or "standards-based" movement believe that the best way to prepare students for the modern workplace is not to just lecture as a "sage on the stage" and explain the correct way to solve math problems; instead they encourage students to apply their math skills to real-life situations, teach that there are usually numerous ways to solve a problem, and ask students to work in groups to construct mathematical ideas and processes. This new approach to math is often taught in classrooms in which much of the instructional time is spent with students working in groups of mixed abilities.

Some parents and math traditionalists are concerned that what they refer to as the "new, new math" slights instruction in basic math skills; they also argue that the use of collaborative learning wastes a lot of class time, especially when the groups are heterogeneous, as group work merely holds back more advanced students and frustrates slower students.

No matter what philosophy reigns at a specific school, parents would be wise to investigate whether a school's math teachers are properly trained and enthusiastic about what they are doing and are able to challenge the mathematically gifted and help those who struggle with math. If students seem to be positive about their math instruction, the math program is probably an effective one.

Whether or not a school is traditional, math programs in the early primary grades should use manipulative materials to emphasize an understanding of concepts. Beware of schools that rely almost completely on rote learning of number facts without stressing mathematical concepts. Also look for programs that stress problem solving, logic, and real-life applicability without ignoring the importance of learning number facts and basic computation skills.

Several decades ago, all but the most gifted math students waited until high school to take algebra. Now many schools, public and private, expect the bulk of their students—at least the college-bound ones—to take algebra in 8th grade so that they are ready for calculus or statistics in their last year of high school. A growing number of schools offer algebra to seventh graders who demonstrate special proficiency in math. While the goal of most schools is to encourage greater numbers of students to take at least three years of college preparatory math classes, the debate continues about the best way to achieve that goal. Some educators argue that homogeneous grouping before high school, also known as tracking, stigmatizes the lower level students as failures before they even enter high school, while critics of heterogeneous grouping argue that the needs of all students, especially in math classes, cannot be met when students of vastly different abilities are taught together in one math class.

Unfortunately, many middle and high schools still assign their weakest math teachers to the weakest students and reward their "star" teachers with the accelerated classes. If you have a child who struggles with math, ask parents as well as administrators about the school's policy regarding this issue. If you have a child entering high school who is exceptionally gifted at math, find out how far a school can take him or her and whether the school has provisions for students to take advanced classes at a local community college or university if the school doesn't offer those classes.

Spelling. Spelling, like math and reading, generates a lot of debate. To encourage children to want to write and express themselves freely, many public and private elementary schools have de-emphasized the importance of correct spelling in the primary grades. Proponents of what many call "creative spelling" argue that this technique works because children who love to write will want to learn to spell words correctly and will improve their spelling as they progress through school. They believe that just as we shouldn't criticize the pronunciation and grammar of toddlers learning to talk, we shouldn't dampen young students' eagerness to write by pointing out all their mistakes.

Critics of this approach argue that children who are praised for essays rife with misspellings are taught that correct spelling is unimportant. They also believe that the absence of traditional spelling books and drill in the curriculum means that many students never learn basic spelling rules and never memorize the irregular spellings of of many commonly used words. Look for teachers who are able to generate enthusiasm for writing while at the same time use a variety of techniques to help their students become good spellers.

Composition. Look for a school that has defined expectations in the quantity and quality of writing it expects from students. A good writing program not only stresses the mechanics required for clear expression but also teaches the process of how to write, exposes students to different kinds of writing, and inspires students to want to write. Beware of programs that focus almost completely on grammar, spelling, and sentence diagramming with little emphasis on actual composition. When evaluating high schools, ask parents and students how much writing is assigned, and whether the assignments require analysis and synthesis and are not merely plot-reciting book reports. Find out if compositions are returned in a timely manner with meaningful teacher comments.

Science. A good science program gives children the opportunity to observe, experiment, and use problem-solving techniques—in other words to experience the methods and tools that scientists use. A purely textbook approach to science, especially one that emphasizes memorizing facts, is one of the surest ways to stifle a child's natural curiosity about the world. Recognizing that most classroom elementary school teachers were not science majors, many private schools and a few public school districts hire science specialists to enrich the science curriculum.

At the middle and high school level, ask whether the science teachers have training in the field they're teaching. Some schools are so desperate for science teachers that they assign any warm body to teach the class by staying one page ahead in the textbook. The best high school science programs are those that offer courses for all levels of students, both AP and non-AP courses, including classes like marine biology, electronics, and astronomy. Also, look for programs that demonstrate to students that understanding modern science and all the ethical dilemmas it presents is of increasing importance to all of us, no matter what field we enter.

A growing number of high schools are flipping the traditional sequence (biology/chemistry/physics) around and offering new electives like biotechnology and forensics that reflect the new careers and applications of modern science. If your child aspires to continue at a competitive private college or a UC campus, make sure that the science courses he or she takes fulfill the entrance requirements for those schools. If your child struggles with science, ask if the high school offers tutorial help in this subject. If your child is especially interested in a science career, ask if the school supports extracurricular activities like robotics and engineering competitions and if instructors or counselors help place students in summer science or engineering internships.

Computer Education. In the 1970s and 80s, many schools enthusiastically invested in computers and then discovered their teachers didn't know what to do with them. Furthermore, much of the early educational software was disappointing because it was primarily limited to games and computerized workbooks and drills. In the last decade, educators have begun to realize the extent to which technology can revolutionize the classroom. The quality of software has improved, and younger teachers entering the profession are much more computer literate and therefore more comfortable incorporating technology into the curriculum than were previous generations of teachers. With the advent of interactive computer programs, schools that have invested in computer technology are finding exciting new ways to engage even reluctant learners, stimulate critical thinking, and create successful collaborative learning experiences. By plugging into the information highway, educators can break the isolation of the classroom as students communicate with other students across the globe and bring the resources of libraries and museums into the classroom.

Currently the hottest trend in private and public schools is to give all students their own wireless laptop to use both at school and at home. Advocates believe that giving every student a computer is the only way to close the computer gap between wealthy students who have access to all the latest technology tools at home and students whose parents may not be able to afford a computer or internet connection. They also point out that constant access to a computer and the Internet leads students to become more engaged in school, allows them to get and sometimes turn-in homework assignments on-line, and prepares them for the modern work place.

Skeptics of this new trend argue that the money spent on buying a laptop for every student and hiring technology experts to deal with breakdowns would be better spent reducing class size, restoring arts programs, or raising teacher salaries. Furthermore, they point to the danger that students will misuse the computers by spending time tapping into inappropriate websites, playing games, or chatting with their friends.

While most educators now accept that computer literacy and wired classrooms are an essential part of a student's education, many are concerned that today's children are already overly "plugged in" to computers and TVs at home. They contend that schools need to focus on the human element of the classroom as the dominant instructional medium.

If a school appeals to you because it incorporates computers into the curriculum and offers state-of-the-art technology, you would be wise to investigate the degree of enthusiasm teachers express for using computers as an educational tool and the ability of the staff or district advisors to select high-quality software that enhances the quality of instruction throughout the curriculum. Find out what the school does to monitor whether students are using school time on-line for legitimate educational activities and whether it teaches students doing research on the Internet how to differentiate between reputable sources and cyberjunk.

Social Studies and History. By the time children complete the sixth grade, they should have a strong background in key events in American history, respect for other cultures, and familiarity with world geography. Look for schools that teach these basic areas while generating interest in the subject matter by assigning historical fiction and using non-textbook activities like special projects, simulation games, interactive computer software, field trips, movies (but beware of teachers who rely too much on movies to keep students entertained), guest speakers, and research papers.

At the high school level, history classes should not be merely exercises in regurgitation. Look for programs that emphasize thinking, study, and research skills. A good history class should also include essay questions on exams. Also look for schools that have realized the value of coordinating English and history instruction so that while students are studying American history, they are also reading American literature of the period.

The Arts. Some parents consider a strong arts program merely a frill; others view the arts as an essential part of a good education. If you are one of the latter, certainly ask about a school's art, music, and drama programs. When public school districts were hit by the budget crunch of the 1970s, many of the first cutbacks came in the arts curriculum. Instrumental and choral music teachers found their jobs cut or completely eliminated, and art specialists were relegated to volunteer status. In fact, many districts have come to rely on volunteer help using music and art volunteer docents to run programs formerly taught by paid specialists. These docent-run programs are often excellent, but many districts don't have a stable group of non-working parents to volunteer their time for the programs.

Some elementary schools are blessed with classroom teachers who have a strong background in the arts, and thus, despite a shortage of art docents and the lack of funds to pay specialists, their students continue to get enriching exposure to the fine arts. Some innovative districts have won grants from the California Arts Commission to establish artists-in-residence programs that bring working artists to the schools to offer art education to both students and teachers.

Many private schools hire specialists to teach art, music, and drama. (In fact, having these specialists is often a draw that keeps teachers who aren't comfortable teaching this part of the curriculum in private schools. They are willing to work for lower pay because they are not responsible for teaching all aspects of their students' education.)

Often in high schools, both public and private, the success of a specific arts program is determined by a single individual. For example, on the San Francisco Peninsula, one public high school has an extraordinary chorus, another a nationally known jazz band, and another an award winning marching band. One private school has an exceptionally strong public speaking program, another has an outstanding drama department, and a third has an excellent visual arts program. Each of these programs is generated by the energy, enthusiasm, and expertise of one specific teacher. If your child has demonstrated talent or interest in a specific area of the arts, look for a school known for its strength in that area.

TUTORIAL HELP

Ask whether the school has ways to help students who need extra help understanding material that is difficult for them. Extra help can be especially important when class sizes are large, and the classroom teacher just doesn't have time to give students a lot of individual attention. At the elementary level this help is often provided through the use of paid or volunteer classroom aides or cross-age tutors. Many high schools provide tutorial centers staffed by faculty, para-professionals, or community volunteers.

EVALUATE THE SCHOOL ENVIRONMENT

Walking around a campus during school hours can be a helpful way of determining whether you will be happy with a school. (However, be sure to make an appointment with the school office before you show up.) Take note of the following:

Recess and lunch periods. Are recesses well supervised? Do children wander around aimlessly, or do most seem involved in games and playground activities? Are playground fights very common, and when they occur, are they handled effectively? Do children toss litter around, or do they show a sense of pride in their school by using trash cans? Are the restrooms clean? Is there graffiti on the walls? Do children seem relaxed and happy?

Library. Few elementary schools, public or private, can afford a full-time professional librarian, and instead rely on para-professionals or parent volunteers. Whoever oversees the library should be warm, enthusiastic, and knowledgeable about children's literature so that students want to use the library and seek out that person's advice. Do students treat the library with respect? Is the library open enough hours so that students can drop in and do work or just browse? Do the classroom teachers schedule visits to the library so that students can learn how to use the library? Is there evidence on the bulletin boards and walls of staff efforts to stimulate students' interest in reading? Are the books current, and is the collection appropriate to the size and age level of the student body? Is the library automated so that the school research capabilities are greatly expanded beyond its own collection of materials, and do those who staff the library patiently explain to students how to make use of the computers and how to find reliable sources of information? If a school cannot afford a librarian or a well-stocked library with Internet access—and some small ones cannot—ask how the school stimulates interest in reading and teaches research skills.

Sounds of a school. When you walk by classrooms, is the dominant sound a teacher yelling at unruly students, or do you hear encouragement, lively class discussions, and occasional laughter? Do students speak to each other with kindness or with teasing and cruelty? Whether you want a highly structured school, an open one, or something in between, look for a school that engages its students in a calm, safe atmosphere.

Safety. With the highly publicized tragedies of schoolyard bullying and shootings in recent years, safety is of great concern to all parents. As the Columbine tragedy illustrated, even high-scoring schools serving high-priced neighborhoods can breed alienation and vio- lence. Angry, disturbed children can also show up in private schools, as was illustrated recently when an elementary school student threatened to bring a gun to school and shoot his classmates at a local, highly academic private school.

Look for a school that doesn't tolerate bullying or teasing and trains its staff to be attuned to signs that a student may be alienated, angry, and in need of counseling.

SPECIAL POINTS TO CONSIDER WHEN LOOKING FOR AN ELEMENTARY SCHOOL

- **If you need all-day care for your child, closely examine what the before and after school activities involve**. Parents should be certain that the school's childcare program doesn't just mean sitting children in front of a television set or a video game or turning them loose on a playground with minimal supervision. Look for a program that provides enriching activities provided by a trained, enthusiastic, and *stable* staff. Some childcare operations pay employees so little that there is a constant turnover of employees.

- **If you are thinking of sending your child to a school some distance from your home, consider your child's social needs and your own sanity**. In their zeal to give their children the best education, parents sometimes forget to include neighborhood friends as an important factor in the school selection process. If you choose a school far from home and there aren't many other children in your area attending the school, sign your child up for neighborhood athletic teams or scout troops to give him or her the opportunity to make friends to play with during weekends and vacations. Furthermore, don't commit yourself to long drives unless you can do so without disrupting your home and work life, and you are confident that the stress of a long school commute won't adversely affect you or your child.

- **Ask about a school's homework policy and consider whether it matches your needs and your child's abilities.** If you want evening and weekend time to spend on family activities, a school that gives several hours of homework a night might be inappropriate. Inquire about the nature as well as the quantity of homework. Homework is useful if it broadens a child's interest in and understanding of classwork while developing good study habits. It is meaningless and potentially damaging if it is merely busy work or if the quantity is inappropriate to the age and ability of the child.

POINTS TO CONSIDER WHEN LOOKING FOR A MIDDLE SCHOOL

In the late 1980s a California study group issued a report that defined sixth, seventh and eighth grades as the "neglected grades." The concerns and recommendations of this group were echoed in the spring of 1989 in the "Carnegie Report on the Education of Young Adolescents." This report pointed out that "the guidance [students] needed as children and need no less as adolescents is withdrawn" just as pressures to try drugs, alcohol, and early sex intensify. Responding to the recommendations of these reports, many districts moved their 6th graders out of the elementary schools into what became known as middle school.

Supporters of the three-year configuration believe that a three-year school can more successfully meet the very special needs of this age group. However, many parents worry that eleven and twelve year olds are not well served at large middle schools because they lose the sense of importance and community that they had in elementary school. They also believe that when sixth graders are surrounded by older adolescents, they feel more pressured to grow up fast. In response to those concerns, many schools keep the sixth grade program separate and provide teams of teachers who share the same students. A few districts, following the model of many private schools, now offer families the option of K-gr. 8 schools. Others give families the option of keeping their sixth graders in elementary school or sending them on to middle school.

Private school programs for this age group are typically small, with only 30 to 90 students per grade. However, some students who have spent their elementary years in a kindergarten through grade 8 private school switch to public middle schools because they are eager to attend a, bigger school that can offer more electives, social choices, and athletic opportunities. Conversely, some families who have been happy with their public elementary school but are uneasy with the size of their public middle school switch their 6th graders to private middle schools where the school and class sizes are smaller.

In choosing a middle school, parents should consider their child's academic and social needs. Confident children may love the novelty and stimulus of a large school that offers a full spectrum of electives, extensive athletic and extracurricular programs, and a broad range of social choices. Others may continue to need the security of knowing the principal and most of their classmates and teachers.

Middle schools also differ in their approach to the curriculum. Some embrace heterogeneous grouping with an interdisciplinary, hands-on approach and encourage collaborative projects; others are more discipline specific and most class time is teacher directed in the traditional lecture/whole group discussion format. If you are interested in the former make sure the instructors know how to manage a classroom of high-energy adolescents without the group work becoming chaotic or mere socializing sessions. If you are interested in the latter, make sure the teachers don't stifle critical thinking skills and creativity by focusing solely on rote learning and testing outcomes.

Whatever the configuration or pedagogy of the middle school you are considering, look for schools staffed by people who understand and enjoy young adolescents and know how to make the subject matter relevant to their students' lives. Great middle school teachers are a special breed because working with eleven to fourteen year olds successfully requires a high level of energy, patience, and humor. Since children at this age can be very cliquish and cruel, also look for schools that have strict rules about bullying and faculty who are tuned in to enforcing those rules and tending to the kids who may need extra attention and support in this most insecure time of life.

POINTS TO CONSIDER WHEN LOOKING FOR A HIGH SCHOOL

- **Consider what size high school would be best for your child**. Many students thrive in large high schools. They love the stimulation of broad course offerings, a diverse student body, and a full menu of extracurricular activities. Such students usually find their niche through special interests: sports, school government, music, or drama. However, public school educators are beginning to realize what has long been clear to those who work in small private schools—many students get lost in large comprehensive high schools. They cut classes and fail to do assignments because they are convinced no one cares, and they feel no connection to the teachers, administrators, or their peers. To give students the opportunity to feel like an important part of a community, many school districts across the nation are establishing "schools within a school" and, when possible, small, self-contained public high schools. In this area, a few districts are following this trend; if such an option isn't available to you, and your child seems to be one who won't find a niche in a large high school, you might want to consider a small private or charter school.

- **Ask to see representative class syllabuses, textbooks, and reading lists to determine whether the school's academic requirements are appropriate to your child's needs and abilities.** If your eighth grader struggles through Jack London short stories, you probably should have second thoughts about sending him or her to a school that assigns Conrad and Hawthorne to all ninth graders.

- **Look for a school that offers extracurricular activities that appeal to your child.** Teenagers actively involved in extracurricular activities are more likely to be happy and stay out of trouble than those who merely go to classes and come home. Look for a school that not only offers programs in your child's special interest areas but also encourages and allows broad participation in extracurricular activities so that he or she can develop new interests. (The segment on Bruce Cohn in "Four Families" at the end of this section illustrates why extracurricular involvement can be so important to a high school student's success and happiness.)

- **Find out how many periods are in the school day.** Students attending high schools with only a six period day may have difficulty fitting in a full academic load and having time for classes like band, drama, or journalism—classes that may not be required but address their special interests.

- **Ask about the school's college counseling and career guidance program.** Many public high schools have been forced to make drastic cutbacks in their counseling programs. If you choose a high school that offers little or no counseling, consider using a private counselor to help your child make college or vocational decisions. (Avoid those who make extravagant promises about their ability to get their clients into the most competitive colleges.) Private high schools generally provide thorough and personalized college counseling—check to see that they do.

- **Ask to see the list of colleges and universities attended by recent graduates, and ask what percentage of students meet the minimum qualifications for acceptance (referred to as the A-G requirements) to the University of California.** When students are surrounded by peers who are serious about preparing for college, they are more likely to take high school seriously. However, do not select a school because you think it is a feeder school to certain colleges. Parents should also realize that many students attend two-year colleges, not because they aren't qualified to go to a four-year school but because family finances necessitate the bargain education community colleges provide. If a public high school serves a low socioeconomic level and thus has a relatively small percentage of students going on to four-year colleges, find out if it has a strong college preparatory program for its motivated students.

Two other indicators of the strength of a high school's academic program are the pass rate of students enrolled at the University of California on the Subject A Exam and its students' performance on Advanced Placement (AP) examinations. Grades of 3, 4, or 5 on these tests qualify for credit at most of the nation's colleges. Through the California Department of Education website (www.data.cde.ca.gov.dataquest), you can obtain figures on the percentage of each public high school's senior class that take these exams and how well the students perform.

While a broad offering of AP classes has long been considered a mark of an excellent college prep school, some educators have started questioning the value of these courses. They contribute to the stress experienced by many of today's high school students, especially juniors, and lock AP instructors into teaching to the test. In fact, some very prestigious private prep schools have stopped offering these courses, and a few universities will no longer give college credit to students who have passed the tests. While AP classes will probably continue to be an important part of most high schools' college preparatory programs, many counselors are encouraging students to limit the number they take so students don't set themselves up for mental or physical breakdowns.

- **Look for a school whose faculty and counselors are sensitive to the danger of students becoming obsessed with college acceptance**. Educators should not feed such obsessions by exaggerating the importance of getting into a prestigious university or encouraging students to take a too-heavy load of AP classes.

- **Ask about the school's policy towards ability grouping**. For years, educators have debated the pros and cons of ability grouping, sometimes referred to as tracking. Currently, many influential educational researchers argue that all students should be exposed to the kind of challenging, stimulating curriculum typical of honors classes. Many school districts maintain heterogeneous grouping in an attempt to give all students a rigorous, academic experience. They have also made their honors programs and AP classes less exclusive by opening the classes to all students willing to do the extra work. However, some teachers and parents believe that opening these courses up to all students leads to a watering down of the curriculum and sets up students of average abilities for failure and frustration.

  - If you have a high-achieving child and a school mandates heterogeneous grouping in most or all subjects, try to ascertain whether instructors implement the goals of differentiation by successfully challenging all their students by taking into account the range of abilities and interests within the classroom. Just giving the highly gifted students more work (e.g., three pages of math problems instead of two) and slower students less work (e.g. one page of math problems instead of two) is not a sign of effective differentiation.

- If your child doesn't shine academically and a school does track, find out if the school adequately stimulates its average and struggling students. Try to ascertain whether these students get stuck with uninspiring instructors who expect little of their students.

ASK WHETHER THE SCHOOL IS ACCREDITED

Accreditation certifies to other educational institutions and to the general public that a school meets established criteria and standards and has been evaluated by an official review board. Private schools that receive public funds to educate handicapped children must be certified as meeting certain standards by the California Department of Education, but California does not accredit private schools. If a school claims it is "accredited by the State of California," inquire further. Legally, private schools are merely required to register with their county office of education. This simple registration procedure is in no way a form of accreditation, but some schools try to make parents believe it is.

The Western Association of Schools and Colleges (WASC) is one of six regional agencies authorized by the U.S. Department of Education to accredit public and private schools. Accreditation by this private agency is especially important for high schools because students from unaccredited schools may have difficulty getting into some colleges. In 2002, the University of California announced that as of 2006, it would approve classes meeting its A-G entrance requirements only from schools—public or private—that were accredited by WASC or in the process of receiving WASC accreditation. To obtain WASC accreditation, a school must complete a thorough self-study, which is followed by a three-and-a-half-day visit by a team of educators. The visitation committee evaluates the school on the basis of whether the school is accomplishing its stated objectives. Once full accreditation is granted, a review occurs at least every six years. If you are considering an accredited school, feel free to ask to read the accreditation report. A school is under no obligation to show it to you, but a refusal to do so should cause you some concern. WASC reports include a section commending the school for what the school does well and a section recommending what areas the school should work at improving. If the areas of recommendation are not merely trivial and address some concerns you have, ask the school what it is doing to implement the recommendations. For more information about accreditation, go to the WASC website at www.acswasc.org.

While nearly all public comprehensive high schools have WASC accreditation, public elementary and junior highs rarely apply as they are already subject to a high degree of accountability under state guidelines and controls. However, because there is virtually no state control over private schools, a growing number of private elementary and middle schools are applying for WASC accreditation. The accreditation process helps them evaluate and improve their programs while also assuring the public that the school meets established standards and provides a program that successfully implements its goals and philosophy. Accreditation is not a guarantee of excellence, and a lack of accreditation does not imply an inferior program. Accreditation is a time-consuming and expensive process, and thus many good private elementary schools, especially new ones operating on a tight budget, do not choose to apply for it.

Other accreditation or certifying organizations mentioned in this book include:

- **The California Association of Independent Schools (CAIS)** was established in 1939 to promote high academic and professional standards for its member schools. Most CAIS schools are secular, but some have a religious affiliation. High schools seeking CAIS membership must be accredited by WASC. All member schools are required to undergo a thorough self-evaluation every six years, followed by a visit from an evaluation committee. To be considered for provisional membership in CAIS, a school must have been in operation for at least five years and be incorporated as a not-for-profit institution.

- **The Western Catholic Education Association (WCEA)** has an evaluation procedure very similar to that used by WASC. The San Francisco Archdiocese, which oversees the operation of San Mateo County parish schools, and the Santa Clara County Archdiocese have chosen to certify their schools jointly with WASC.

- **The Association of Christian Schools International (ACSI)** offers to its members an accreditation program similar to the WASC instrument. Many area ACSI schools obtain accreditation from both organizations.

Several other religious and educational organizations accredit their member schools. In most cases, the accreditation process involves a self-study and a visit by outside educators.

PSYCHOLOGICAL EVALUATIONS

Most parents do not need psychological evaluations of their children to make informed educational decisions. They enroll their children in a local public or private school based on their own educational values, research, and information from other parents. Some children, however, have special needs that make school placement more complex. No one school is a good match for every child, and it can be a challenge to understand some children's educational needs. The purpose of a psychoeducational evaluation is to understand a child's strengths and special needs, and then apply that knowledge to educational decisions. Common areas of evaluation include intelligence, academic achievement, attention, and emotional functioning.

A standardized intelligence test is central to a psychoeducational evaluation. Some children have an extremely high intelligence, and they may be well placed in a program for gifted students. There are also academically accelerated programs for students who are not gifted but are smart and hardworking. Other children need a school with age-appropriate expectations for intellectual development, and there are those who need a slower pace. Therefore, considering a child's intelligence should be a major factor in finding a school that is a good match and that will allow for appropriate growth.

For most children, academic achievement is on par with intelligence; however, some children have learning disabilities that affect just one area of learning. They may have lower skills than expected in reading, writing, or mathematics. It is important to select a school that provides enough challenge but is not overwhelming. If a child has a learning disability, parents should find out if the school has learning specialists or special programs. They also need to explore needed educational accommodations for that student.

Every child is inattentive at times, but some children have persistent and severe attentional problems that can affect both academic performance and behavioral management within the classroom. Class size, teacher rules, and environmental distractions all play a critical role in school selection. Some schools are extremely strict and structured, and other schools have few deadlines and rules. Choosing the most appropriate school will depend on a variety of factors, including the child's attentional problem and his or her attitude toward school.

Some children struggle with social anxiety, depression, or other emotional issues that can influence success in school. An appropriate school placement can make a critical difference in meeting a child's emotional and behavioral needs. Some teachers are well-versed in working with children with emotional problems, and others have little experience with these issues. Within a school, an evaluation can help to create an effective behavioral management plan.

Once parents decide to proceed with an evaluation, they often begin by contacting their child's school and meeting with a school psychologist. School psychologists are professionals who generally have a master's degree and have completed training in educational testing. Their evaluations focus on academic skills and determining whether a child needs special education services. The evaluation is free, and the services they recommend are generally free as well. As an integral member of the school staff, the evaluator has the opportunity to observe the child in the classroom, consult frequently with the teacher, and attend school meetings. Continuity also helps a school psychologist evaluate the child's progress. If parents are not satisfied with the results, they are often entitled to a free second opinion.

A school evaluation has several limitations that should be considered. First, a parent does not choose the evaluator and often does not have any control over the processes. Second, an evaluation can take a long time to complete, and all testing is done during the school day. Third, the evaluation only focuses on the educational needs of the child, so the scope may be limited. For instance, there is generally no formal testing of attentional abilities or emotional functioning. School psychologists do not generally give diagnoses of any kind because their role is just to determine educational needs. Fourth, school psychologists generally focus only on strategies that are directly related to education. They do not usually discuss other treatments parents might need to consider, such as medications or psychotherapy. Although parents generally appreciate it when school staff respect these boundaries, parents also may need advice on how to meet the full range of their child's needs. Fifth, at times school psychologists receive considerable pressure to recommend few services due to the financial constraints of the school; for example, they rarely recommend placement in a private school because the public school would then have to pay for it. Finally, an evaluation by the school is automatically in the child's record, and there is no way to keep the results from school personnel even if it contains negative information about the child.

Some parents prefer to have a private evaluation conducted by a licensed psychologist. A psychologist has completed a doctoral degree and may have specialized training as a neuropsychologist. Psychologists evaluate intelligence, academic achievement, attentional abilities and emotional functioning. A psychologist can diagnose a learning disability, attentional disorder or emotional disorder. A psychologist will give comprehensive recommendations regarding special education accommodations, educational interventions, parenting strategies, and other professional services. Private evaluators can also help parents understand the range of public and private school options and can also act as advocates for the child's needs once the child is in a program. A parent needs to sign a release of information form for the evaluator to send the report anywhere and to anyone. As with all medical records, parents have the right to deny school personnel access to the records.

Private evaluations have several disadvantages as well. Investment of time and money can be considerable, and insurance does not generally pay for an evaluation that is primarily educational. Although competent evaluators strive for professional objectivity, they can sometimes be perceived as biased toward the parent's views. If an evaluator does not develop rapport with school personnel, it may limit the psychologist's usefulness to the child.

In conclusion, parents should carefully consider if they have the information to make informed educational decisions about their children. Many children will succeed at almost any school; however, some children have an unusual learning profile. If there are concerns with intelligence, academic skills, or attention or emotional functioning, an evaluation can help clarify a child's educational profile. This book can then help to match that learning profile with specific local private schools and public school districts.

ANSWERS TO FREQUENTLY ASKED QUESTIONS

When should I start investigating schools?

Although you can't start talking to friends, neighbors, and preschool teachers too soon about school choices, the fall term of the year before your child enters school is usually the best time to start visiting schools and evaluating your public and private school choices. If you decide in October that you do not want what your public school district has to offer, you will have plenty of time to visit and apply to other districts or private schools. Few private schools, at least in this area, are interested in taking applications more than a year in advance. Certainly, an early start will maximize your options, but don't despair if you start later. While some private schools won't consider any student who applies after the application deadline (usually in January or February), some have openings up until—and even after—the school year starts.

There are two important exceptions to this schedule. Private schools with preschool programs usually give priority to children coming from their pre-kindergarten program and therefore may not have many spaces left for children applying the winter or spring before kindergarten starts. For the same reason, some parents feel that to maximize their child's chances of getting into a private high school, they must enroll their child in the 6th grade if the school has a middle school program.

How much research should I do when deciding on a public school?

When I wrote the first two editions of this book, parents had difficulty finding much information about public schools other than results of statewide tests. The Internet has changed all that, and several excellent websites (see listing in the appendix) allow parents to find out almost anything they might want to know about a given public school: test scores, percentage of credentialed teachers, and percentage of English learners and students on free lunch programs. In fact, so much information is available that parents can become overwhelmed with statistics and feel even more confused when deciding on a school. Remember that many of the aspects that will make school a positive experience for your child cannot be measured by numbers or rankings. Talking to current parents and getting a sense of the philosophy, leadership, and quality of the teaching staff at schools you are considering will probably be far more helpful than basing your decision purely on the reams of information you can find on the Internet.

What should I do if a school recommends that my child wait a year before starting kindergarten?

A child must be five years old on or before December 2 to enter a California public school kindergarten. Many private schools use a similar cut-off date, but a few will allow younger children to enter their kindergartens if they feel the child is mature enough to handle the class work. A growing number of private schools require that entering kindergartners be five by September. Most schools give a kindergarten readiness assessment to determine a child's level of developmental maturity. On the basis of that test, the school may recommend that a child wait a year before entering kindergarten or that the child go into a transitional kindergarten, a pre-kindergarten program offered by many private schools and a few public school districts. These programs typically have a smaller student-to-teacher ratio than the regular kindergarten classes and take into account the shorter attention span and less developed motor skills of their students.

It has become very common, especially in affluent areas where parents can afford an extra year of preschool and where schools pride themselves on running academic kindergartens, to start children with fall birthdays a year later even if the child appears to be developmentally ready for kindergarten. This is especially common with boys because they tend to develop fine motor skills later than girls do and because parents often are apprehensive about their son being the smallest or youngest boy in the class.

Children who are developmentally, emotionally, or socially immature should be given an extra year to mature before starting school. If there is any doubt about your child's readiness, wait a year. Later, it will be far less painful to skip a child who is too advanced for his grade than it will be to have him repeat a grade.*

How important is it that reading is taught in kindergarten?

Many educators in both public and private schools do not believe formal reading instruction should begin until first grade because they feel kindergarten should be a year for developing social skills, building self-confidence, and working on reading readiness. These educators point to research that shows a significant catch-up factor in reading ability. In studies of children with similar intelligence, those who aren't taught to read until first or second grade (or even later) catch up and often surpass in enthusiasm and ability those who were taught formal reading in kindergarten.

Experienced kindergarten teachers realize that some of their students are ready to read and others aren't. A good program doesn't hold back those who are eager and ready to read, but doesn't pressure those who aren't. If you are considering a kindergarten that promises to teach all its students to read, be sure your child is developmentally ready for the tasks expected. Too much pressure on children early in their school careers can cause frustration and insecurity that might result in negativity towards school in general.

*Because the need to meet state curriculum standards has put pressure on kindergarten teachers to make their programs more academically rigorous, many educators argue that the cut-off date for kindergarten should be in September, as it is in most states. Changing the cut-off date has been proposed many times in the California Legislature, but the law has not been changed, primarily because of concern that raising the school entry age will place an economic burden on poor families who can not afford high quality preschools or daycare.

Can a child who starts out in public school change to a good private school later?

In most cases, yes. All private schools experience some natural attrition. Because of family moves, changes in family finances, or transfers to other schools, even the most competitive schools have occasional openings in the upper grades. And many private schools increase their class sizes in the upper grades, creating more openings. Therefore, a child who has done well in public school has an excellent chance of transferring to a private school.

Even parents with a child who has not done well in public school (a reason many parents consider making the switch) can find private schools willing to try to turn the child around. Some private schools are especially effective at taking underachievers or "diamonds in the rough" and turning them into successes. However, some schools that take students with low test scores or grades make summer school attendance or the repetition of a grade a condition of acceptance.

Many parents are happy with public school for their children's elementary school education but wish to enroll them in private schools for their middle and high school years. In most cases, secular private high schools accept students on the basis of test scores, grades, interviews, extracurricular interests and talents, and recommendations. To most admissions people, a good student is welcome, and past schooling is of relatively minor importance. The most competitive (i.e., most applicants for number of places) independent schools on the Peninsula all report that close to half or more of their entering students come from public elementary schools.

Acceptance to area Catholic high schools can be more difficult for the non-Catholic child who has attended a public elementary school because Catholic high schools give priority to Catholic children and graduates of feeder parish schools. However, these schools also accept large numbers of public school products.

Should I forget about sending my child to a private school if the tuition is more than I can afford?

While some small private schools cannot afford to give scholarships, many of the large and well-established schools do. Parochial schools, where fees are relatively low anyway, usually give sibling discounts, and some try to set up a certain percentage of their budgets for scholarships for parishioners. Independent schools, which tend to charge the highest tuition, are usually quite generous in granting financial aid. According to recent National Association of Independent Schools (NAIS) figures, 18% of students at member schools receive some financial aid. Proprietary schools and new schools struggling to make ends meet tend to give few scholarships.

To what extent should I involve my child in the school selection process?

With children just starting elementary school, this is usually not much of an issue. Five or six year olds are generally pretty amenable to whatever their parents think is best. However, once you've done your research it might be useful to involve your child in the final decision if you are torn between two or more schools, especially if the schools you are considering allow or require prospective students to visit for a day or two. Such a visit can allow you to consider your child's reaction to the teachers, the other students, and the playground environment.

Allowing older children to be involved in the school choice decision is much more important but also can be more complicated. Adolescents are more likely to try to do well in school if they feel that their desires have been considered. If you are comfortable with several schools, arrange for your child to spend a day shadowing at each one and let him or her make the final decision. However, if, for example, you believe your fourteen-year-old needs the structure and small classes of a private high school, but she wants to go to the public high school with all her friends, you may want to strike a bargain. Explain why you think a private school would be best and ask her to try it for a year. Chances are that once she makes new friends and sees the advantages of small classes, she will want to stay. If she doesn't, then maybe the public high school will be a better place for her. (See the story of the Stark family in "Four Families.")

Are the best teachers in public or private schools?

Good and bad teachers can be found in all kinds of schools—public and private, traditional and open. Some private schools save money by hiring young uncredentialed teachers who are not as qualified as their public school counter-parts. On the other hand, because it's difficult to fire a tenured teacher, public schools have more difficulty getting rid of weak teachers than do private schools. However, private schools also have their share of "lemons." Because of the teacher shortage, especially in science and math, and the high turnover rate among young teachers, private school administrators are less likely to let go of a mediocre teacher than they would have been two decades ago.

Ideally, a school should balance the experience and wisdom of older teachers with the energy and enthusiasm of younger ones. In the early eighties, public school hiring of new teachers had been virtually nonexistent for almost a decade, so few had that healthy balance. Now the pendulum has swung as veteran teachers are retiring and many schools have a preponderance of young teachers.

Often, especially at the high school level, it is easier to be a good teacher at a private school than a public one. In schools with fewer students per class, teachers can assign more written work and respond more thoroughly. Private school teachers don't have to put up with as many discipline problems or as much red-tape as do their public school counterparts. And private school teachers can expect more support from home because when parents are paying a hefty sum for tuition, they're more likely to make sure their children complete assignments and attend classes. Despite the extra challenges public high school teachers face, area public high schools are blessed with many energetic, inspiring teachers who make a huge difference in their students' lives.

Why are the public schools that score the highest on the statewide tests always in areas most people can't afford to buy a house?

High-priced neighborhoods have a concentration of well-educated professionals, and there's an obvious correlation between the academic achievement and values of the parents and their children's ability to do well in school and on standardized tests. Furthermore, these areas have few rental units, and therefore the turnover rate of students during the school year is relatively low. Another explanation for the expensive housing/high test score correlation is that when children of affluent parents struggle academically, their parents have the financial resources to send them to specialized private schools or pay for extensive tutoring.

Another aspect of the high-priced neighborhood that helps improve the schools is the availability of energetic, capable volunteers—parents who have the luxury of not working full-time and can serve as classroom, music, art, and library aides. These parents also have the time to be active members of their Parent Teacher organizations. Furthermore, districts serving affluent families have passed generous parcel tax measures and set up foundations to raise money for the local schools. The extra revenues generated by these taxes and contributions are typically used to reduce class size, hire specialists, and purchase library books, computers, and equipment.

Should I believe people when they tell me that a certain school or district is good or bad?

Unfortunately, when people talk about good and bad schools, they usually are referring to the population a school serves and not the quality of the teachers, principals, and programs. Certainly, the good schools described above offer many advantages because they are working with children who may be easier to teach and are blessed with parents who support the schools in countless ways.

However, many schools that look bad when judged by standardized test scores are excellent if they are judged by the caliber of their programs and staff. An administrator in one local district described in glowing terms the best school in his district: a school full of committed, imaginative, dynamic teachers led by a wonderful principal. But he admitted that few people would describe this school as the best or choose to send their children there because it serves the poorest, most transient segment of the district. On the other hand, he told me that the school that is considered the district's best (i.e., has the highest test scores) is actually one of the worst in that it has a weak principal and many burned out teachers. Before ruling out what everyone says is a bad school or district, you would be wise to investigate for yourself in what ways a specific school is good or bad.

How much do test scores and other statistics tell me about how good or bad a school is?

Since schools tend to teach to the student norm, those that consistently score in the 90th percentile are apt to have a more accelerated and demanding program than those with much lower scores. However, parents should not choose a school purely on the basis of high scores. In many cases, high test scores tell more about the socioeconomic make-up of a school than the quality of teaching.

Parents should also realize that fluctuations in test scores do not necessarily mean a decline or improvement in the caliber of teaching. All schools experience years when they are blessed with especially gifted classes and years with students of more average abilities.

Schools that serve a low socioeconomic population operate under clear disadvantages. Parents are less likely to have the time or background to help children with homework or serve as classroom aides, and teachers may have to spend much of their time giving extra attention to English learners—students who don't speak English at home. On the other hand, having a child in a high-testing school district can be a mixed blessing. While these schools are apt to be filled with many gifted students and offer a challenging curriculum, children of average intelligence or those with learning disabilities often have difficulty keeping up with their peers and thus can suffer from poor academic self-esteem.

Don't assume that the school in your district with the highest test scores will be the best school for your child. Several years ago I worked with a family who was moving back to the area after several years in Asia. Their home was in the attendance area of the highest scoring school in their large district, but there was no space for their son when they moved back. For a year, they sent him to the next closest school, which had respectable but lower test scores. Although they were initially disappointed, their son had wonderful teachers and they were delighted with the principal. When a spot at their neighborhood school opened up the following year, they jumped at the chance to get him into the district's "best" school, assuming it would be even better than the school he had been attending. They were greatly disappointed. While the test scores at the school continued to be the highest in the district, this family found that the leadership qualities of the principal and the level of instruction and intellectual passion generated by the staff were far lower than what they had experienced at the lower-testing school.

Neighbors tell us that our local public school, where we plan to send our children, is quite good, and its state API scores are high. But now we see that it is on the list of schools that did not meet the Adequate Yearly Progress requirements of the No Child Left Behind Act. Should we be concerned?

Probably not. Many schools that do quite well by the state's standards do not meet the NCLB's requirements for closing the achievement gap among all students. States all over the nation have become frustrated with some of the rigid demands of NCLB that make some very good schools look as if they are underperforming.

Where can I find an objective ranking of private schools?

You can't. While the state mandates that public schools must give their students the same tests, and the results of these tests are public information, private schools are free to use whatever tests they want. Some do not give normed tests at all.

Even when private schools give system-wide tests, they are under no obligation to make the scores public. For example, students in parish Catholic schools all take nationally normed achievement tests so parents and teachers can assess how individual students are progressing. However, the Diocese does not make the results public because the Board of Education wants to encourage parishioners to support their parish school or to choose a school because it meets specific needs—not because the school is perceived as better because of high test scores.

This lack of accountability often frustrates parents, for they have no way of knowing if a private school's claim that "our students are way ahead of the public school kids" is in fact true, and parents can't compare students' scores from one private school with scores from another.

A lack of a reliable ranking system might lead to fraudulent claims by a few private schools. However, overall the absence of school-to-school testing data is probably healthy because the lack of statistical comparisons forces parents to look at more important indicators of whether the school will be right for their child: educational philosophy, class and school size, enthusiasm of the students for learning, passion and competence of the teachers, leadership style of the school's head, and academic and extra-curricular opportunities.*

What kind of school will be best for my exceptionally bright child?

Many area public and private schools have excellent programs for gifted students, usually defined as those who score above 130 on an IQ test. If you have a child who is exceptionally gifted (IQ above 160) or profoundly gifted (IQ above 175) look for either a specialized school for the gifted or one that has flexible and imaginative teachers who can keep your child intellectually stimulated while encouraging social interaction with peers. Also look for schools that encourage students to participate in science fairs and other activities—e.g., the Odyssey of the Mind Program at the elementary level, the Academic Decathlon and Robotics competitions at the high school level—that allow the intellectually curious to explore intellectual interests at a deeper level while collaborating with like-minded classmates. Avoid placing an exceptionally gifted or profoundly gifted child in a highly structured school that emphasizes group instruction, uses a scripted curriculum with little freedom for the teacher to deviate, and focuses primarily on teaching to standardized tests.

Is there anything special I should do to increase the chance that my child will get into a highly competitive private school?

Apply before the application deadline, do your homework so you understand the school's philosophy and academic expectations so that it is clear it is a good fit for your child, and don't annoy the admissions people by bombarding them with unnecessary phone calls.

---

*It's a little easier for parents who want quantifiable numbers to compare private high schools with public high schools because many do make public their students' SAT scores, performance on Advanced Placement exams, and college acceptance records.

Most highly competitive schools want a diverse population of students who will enrich the school in a variety of ways and succeed in the environment the school offers. They don't want to deal with parents who will be constantly making extra demands on the school. Several admissions directors have told me that if they have to choose among several qualified applicants, the one with the too-pushy parent is more likely to be rejected.

Promising large donations to the school or pulling strings through influential acquaintances will not ensure an acceptance if your child is not as qualified as other applicants. Yes, private schools do rely on extra donations from parents for building projects and scholarship funds, but most pride themselves on not letting parents buy their way into a school. Admissions offices will take into account recommendations from board members, but influential connections won't ensure your child a space.

Many parents try to prep their children for the admissions test by paying for private testing tutorials or by having them take practice exams that can be obtained from books or the Internet. While such preparation may help your child do a little better on the admissions exam, such prepping can also increase your child's level of anxiety. Parents should also remember that performance on these tests is only one part of the admissions process at most schools.

Many parents also coach their children on what to say and how to behave during interviews. Admissions people are usually adept at detecting the child who has been coached and tend to respond negatively to applicants who seem to be parroting what their parents have told them to say.

What are the advantages of single-gender schools?

Proponents of single-gender education argue that students at these schools stay more focused on academics and develop deeper friendships than do students in co-ed schools. Advocates of all-girls schools claim that without the presence of males, girls are more likely to develop leadership skills and maintain their confidence and interest in advanced science and math, which have traditionally been viewed as male-dominated disciplines. Some parents also like single-sex middle and high schools because they feel there is less pressure on students at these schools to grow up too fast.

Many parents and educators who are opposed to single-sex schools point out that since men and women will end up working with the opposite sex in the workforce, they are better off learning how to interact and develop friendships with them in the classroom.

If a family can't afford a private school, what options are available for adolescents who hate high school because they feel invisible or are just turned off to the big high school environment?

In recent years, many educators have recognized that the large comprehensive public high school is not a suitable learning environment for some students. In response many new small public high schools have opened. These schools typically offer students small classes in an environment that ensures personal attention from a dedicated faculty, who have high expectations of their students. Most of these schools also feature an extended school day with afterschool tutorials.

Middle College programs offered at many local community colleges in cooperation with local high school districts provide an excellent option for bright, motivated juniors and seniors who are unhappy in the large high school environment. Students complete their high school graduation requirements while also taking college credit classes. These programs are small and personal and usually staffed by energetic, committed teachers who want to teach in an environment that allows them to know each of their students well and give them the kind of support it is difficult to offer when a teacher has 120-150 students a day.

Who should consider a boarding school?

Sending children to a boarding school for their high school education is less common in California than it is on the East Coast. However, parents might consider boarding school if:

- Family problems interfere with a child's academic and emotional well-being;

- A child needs a change of environment to get a second chance academically or socially;

- They cannot find an acceptable school in their own community; and

- A child seems to need the close interpersonal relationships and total school environment offered by good boarding schools.

If you are considering a boarding school, you can save yourself time, money, and disappointment by using the services of an educational counselor, an expert who specializes in matching students with appropriate schools. Avoid counselors who charge schools a commission for each student they place.

What school will give my child the best chance of getting into a prestigious college like Stanford or Harvard?

Admissions people from the most competitive private colleges assert that students with good grades, high test scores, and impressive talents and extracurricular activities have a good chance of acceptance no matter what high school the student attends. Some area high schools, public and private, consistently have a high percentage of students accepted at highly competitive colleges. However, these students are generally accepted because of their abilities and achievements, not because of any special influence their schools have.

Private high schools and public schools that serve wealthy communities also have a higher proportion of their top seniors applying to (and therefore being accepted by) expensive private colleges than do schools serving families of more moderate means. After all, if parents are already spending $16,000 or more a year on private school tuition or live in multi-million dollar homes, they are more likely to be able to afford the $35,000+ price tag of universities like Stanford or Yale.

Parents who place their child in an academically competitive high school may find that because the competition is stiffer and the courses are more demanding, the child's grades are lower than they would be in a school with a more average spectrum of students. Consequently, selecting a high school with a good track record in college admissions can backfire if the school is chosen primarily because parents think it will be a stepping stone to a prestigious college. Parents should select high schools on the basis of philosophy, course offerings, quality of teaching, and the ability of the school to meet the student's needs and not because of the expectation that attending the school will ensure acceptance to an elite university.

FOUR FAMILIES

The following experiences of four Bay Area families illustrate important aspects of the school selection process. The names of the families and schools involved have been changed.

The Thompsons' Story

Madeline Thompson is an endearing girl with highly educated and emotionally supportive parents. Her father, a software engineer and small business owner for twenty years, retired young and became a stay-at-home father. Her mother is a partner at a law firm; however, she manages to leave work early several days per week to spend time with the family. Madeline's parents both attended high-pressure private schools and excelled academically. However, they both felt that some of their childhood had been lost to constant studying and worrying about grades.

For their child, they wanted a school with reasonable academic expectations that would allow her to enjoy childhood. When Madeline was five years old, her parents enrolled her in a small kindergarten program at a supportive private parent-participation school. Both parents worked in the classroom several hours each week, and they helped on field trips frequently. They liked the school's emphasis on seeing all students as individuals and helping them to develop areas of strength. The school has few tests, places little emphasis on grades, and encourages children to develop skills at their own pace. Although all of the teachers have some experience with learning disabilities, no learning specialist is on staff.

By the end of Madeline's second grade year, the Thompsons had become concerned with her lack of academic progress. She was having difficulty sounding out words that her peers could read easily, and she was starting to avoid reading. Her teacher had no concerns and, in fact, admonished her parents for placing too much pressure on their daughter. However, Madeline's parents decided to consult a pediatrician, who referred Madeline for a psychoeducational evaluation to assess her academic progress.

A licensed psychologist conducted the evaluation and began by observing Madeline at school. There were ten students, one teacher and two parent volunteers in her classroom. The students were cheerful, polite, and socially mature. Madeline interacted comfortably with her peers, and she spent most of her time working on a joint art project. When students were asked to read aloud, Madeline clearly was embarrassed about her lack of skills and read quietly and self-consciously to the class. On a standardized test, Madeline had overall intellectual abilities at the 75th percentile. Academically, mathematics was at the 80th percentile, written language was at the 27th percentile, and reading was at the 12th percentile. In essence, she had the intellectual abilities of a 9 year old but the reading abilities of a 6 year old. She showed signs of low self-esteem and anxiety in activities that involved reading. The psychologist diagnosed her as having a reading disorder (dyslexia) and recommended that her parents place her in a school that specializes in learning disabilities.

Madeline's parents had a difficult choice. They loved her school and knew that she was happy there. She had a strong group of friends, and she had known nearly all of them since kindergarten. Her social skills and creativity were also blossoming. At the same time, her parents realized that she was not making sufficient academic progress to warrant continuing there. They also knew that her confidence was declining. The Thompsons tried intensive private tutoring focused on reading, but Madeline continued to fall further behind. They finally placed Madeline at a small private school that specializes in learning disabilities. After a period of adjustment, Madeline settled into her new school, and she received the specialized reading instruction that she needed.

Madeline is now 10 years old, and she was recently re-evaluated. She beamed with pride when discussing her school performance, and formal testing confirmed reading abilities at the 55th percentile. The Thompsons are quite happy with their decision, and she will continue at her present school for next year. It is critical to note that both schools in this scenario were excellent overall. They both placed a strong emphasis on customizing education to an individual child's needs, and they both had excellent academic resources—but the first school was not equipped to help Madeline learn the skills she needed to make her a happy and successful student.

The Starks' Story

Jim and Pat Stark learned years ago the importance of matching a child with the appropriate school. Their older son Dave decided when he was in the eighth grade that he wanted to attend St. Mark's, a boys' prep school known for its strict discipline, rigorous academic demands, and competitive sports program. Although his family is not Catholic and had always been public school oriented, Dave chose to go to St. Mark's because he wanted the academic challenge and because several of his public school friends were also going.

Dave worked hard and did well, so when his brother Phil, two years younger, completed junior high, he too decided to leave the public school system and enter St. Mark's. Reflecting on that decision, Phil states, "I wanted to succeed and be admired. My brother was successful there, and so I figured I would be too. My parents left the decision to me, but I knew they were pleased when I decided to follow Dave." Jim and Pat acknowledge that the two boys had always been different. "Dave was much more self-motivated academically and things came easily to him. Phil was more social and athletic, and he was always more interested in girls than his brother was."

Despite these differences, the Starks assumed that St. Mark's would offer Phil the same positive experience it had given Dave. However, several months into Phil's freshman year, the family began to realize that he was having a difficult time. Pat recalls, "He was so anxious to please us. He studied with intense diligence, but with a joylessness that gave us the feeling he was doing it for us rather than himself. That year he had a terrific amount of work and just seemed overwhelmed." Despite the effort he expended, Phil's grades the first semester hovered in the low C range, a real shock since he had always earned A's and B's in public school.

As Phil struggled with his studies, his family witnessed a troubling personality change. "Phil had always been a real charmer, very open and easy to be with. But he began to lose his self-confidence. He became very quiet and withdrawn. He would stay hunched over his desk for hours until we called him for dinner. As soon as he finished eating, he would go right back up to study."

Phil and his parents now realize that academic pressure was not the sole cause of his unhappiness. While Dave's best friends had joined him at St. Mark's, Phil's had remained at Pierce, the public school across the street from his house. However, Phil's inability to participate in St. Mark's highly competitive athletic program was probably the most demoralizing aspect of his freshman year. "I loved basketball, but I didn't make the team. That was tough for me. I really needed that outlet. By the spring my grades had improved, and I knew I could make it through academically. I was proud of that, but overall I had a bad feeling about school and myself. I knew St. Mark's was teaching me good study habits, and the teachers were dedicated and caring, but all that didn't make up for what was missing for me."

The summer after his ninth grade year, Phil saw a family counselor who specializes in working with troubled adolescents. Phil's parents feel those visits helped him make the decision to return to public school. His mother recalls, "Once he made that decision, he could relax again."

Both parents note, somewhat sadly, that Phil never worked very hard at Pierce and maintained a B average with minimum effort. Despite their realization that Phil wasn't being academically challenged in the public school, Pat stresses, "I felt much better about the whole Phil. He played basketball, had girlfriends, and was much easier to get along with." Jim adds, "He had more time to spend time at our ranch, which he'd always loved but had little time for that year at St. Mark's."

Phil, now a graduate of a state university and a successful marine biologist, knows that he would have been more academically prepared for college had he stayed at St. Mark's. But he also believes that public school offered him broader educational experiences than were available at a private school. "Because Pierce's student body was predominantly minority, I was exposed to other cultures and backgrounds. St. Mark's was just too narrow for me. I wasn't comfortable with academics taking over my whole life. When I tried to go that route, I just moved inside myself and was a pretty miserable human being."

The Cohns' Story

Like the Starks, Mimi and Larry Cohn also have two very different children. Their older child Jenny has always been a bright, self-motivated student, and school choice for her was never a problem. "Adams, our public high school, was perfect for her. She was in all the honors classes, had fabulous teachers, and received an excellent education. Even if we were very wealthy, I never would have considered a private school because I can't imagine her getting a better education anywhere else."

Jenny's younger brother Bruce is also bright and was placed in the gifted program in junior high school. "But," notes Mimi, "he was a gifted child who didn't want to work. His teachers, recognizing his laziness, did not recommend him for the honors classes at Adams." Bruce's grades were good his first year of high school, but his parents were displeased with how little effort he expended. "The school just doesn't challenge the kids much if they're not in the honors group. However, Bruce seemed happy enough that first year, so we accepted his lack of academic motivation with resignation."

At the end of Bruce's freshman year, the Cohns' school district closed one of its three high schools. Mimi describes that year as traumatic for everyone. "There was a huge influx of new students and staff, and the transition was tough on everyone." Because Bruce had always been shy and overly sensitive, his mother believes he was especially affected by the confusion. "Bruce sat in the back of his very large classes and did nothing. He became less social and wasn't involved in any extracurricular activities—even sports, which he had always loved." Bruce's parents became most concerned when they discovered he had been cutting history, and the school had never let them know. "He was getting an A just by copying his friends' notes. When I contacted the school about his cutting classes, the teachers and counselors kept telling me they would do something, but they never did."

By the end of his sophomore year, Bruce's parents realized their son needed a different school. "At home we were having constant battles, and the tensions created by Bruce's problems affected us all." The private day schools in the area were either full or didn't seem right for Bruce. At that point, Bruce told his parents he was willing to try a boarding school, and so Mimi contacted an educational consultant. After interviewing the Cohns and Bruce, the consultant recommended three schools that still had openings and would serve Bruce's needs. In retrospect, Mimi is very glad that they spent the money to get professional advice. "I had no idea how to start looking for a good boarding school. We would have dragged Bruce around for weeks and spent far more money trying to find the right school on our own."

The Cohns selected Shannon School, a small prep school in Southern California, which, according to the consultant, did a good job motivating underachievers. The school, impressed by Bruce's test scores, accepted him for the eleventh grade and gave him a partial scholarship. Even with financial assistance, the Cohns had to dip into savings intended for Bruce's college education. "But," Mimi says, "we realized that if he stayed in public school, he might never even make it to college."

Bruce's performance his first year at Shannon surpassed his parents' expectations. He received all A's and B's, partly, his mother admits, because "as a new student that first grading period, he was required to spend his evenings in a supervised study hall." But Bruce and his parents were also pleased that attending a small school allowed him to star in athletics. At Adams, he hadn't even tried out for a team, but at Shannon he made varsity soccer, basketball, and baseball. The most unexpected dividend of Bruce's boarding school experience was his involvement in the arts. Bruce had taken a little piano and trumpet when he was younger but hadn't done anything musically for years. He had a free period, so the school put him in the band. Then, on his own, he started taking piano lessons from the music teacher, who soon had him composing his own music. "Music," states his mother, obviously pleased, "has now become an important part of his life. He still composes music to relax. What's even more remarkable," continues Mimi, "is that Bruce was in a play his senior year. That would never have happened at Adams."

Mimi feels one of Shannon's greatest strengths is its college counseling. "If Bruce had still been at home, I would have gone mad trying to get him through his applications. The public school counselors just have too many students to give much individual aid. Shannon's counselor not only made sure the students completed their applications correctly and promptly but also did a good job recommending appropriate colleges. Knowing Bruce's past, the school steered him towards small schools where he would have a chance to shine."

Mimi acknowledges that her son did have some difficulties during his two years at Shannon. "Despite his success that first year, he almost didn't return for his senior year because he missed the freedom and social life of home. But he went back because he wanted to go to a good college and knew returning to public high school would be a real risk." During that second year, some of Bruce's old habits reappeared. "When he had a teacher he didn't like, he just refused to work, and his grades dropped. However, the staff helped him pull through, and he was accepted by all the colleges he applied to."

In trying to assess why Shannon was so good for Bruce, Mimi attributes much of its success to its size. "Because he had an opportunity to succeed in several activities, his self-esteem naturally improved. And with small classes, students couldn't get away with cutting or slacking off without the teachers knowing." Mimi doesn't think Shannon's teachers are necessarily better than those at Adams, although they tend to be younger and more energetic. "Small classes allow the faculty to be more effective with kids like Bruce. It's easier to be a better teacher with only 15 students, instead of 30 or 35, in a class. The public school teachers have so many students that they quite understandably focus on the ones like my daughter who want to learn." Mimi also believes that boarding school was good for Bruce because it allowed him to get away from his high achieving sister. "It was healthy for all of us to be off his back. When he came home for vacations, we were all more relaxed, and he and Jenny began to get along for the first time in years."

Mimi is still grateful that the public high school gave her daughter such an excellent education. But she knows that Bruce's experience there was not unique. "Our public school serves two levels well—the top and the bottom. But not enough is done for the average or unmotivated kids. I'm not sure what the answer is, but I'm afraid a lot of them fall through the cracks as Bruce was doing."

The Martins' Story

Even though they aren't especially wealthy, Audrey and David Martin's early decision to send their children to private schools made perfect sense considering their own school history. Audrey had attended what she describes as "unchallenging" public schools where she had often been bored. Even though her excellent grades and impressive test scores got her into Stanford, she felt way behind her college classmates who had gone to private schools. "I didn't know how to write a research paper, my writing skills were weak, and I had lousy study skills. And many of my Stanford classmates had already read in high school books by writers and philosophers like Virginia Woolf and Aristotle that I hadn't even heard of." David, on the other hand, has always been grateful for the top-rate education he received in private schools. At these schools, he had a "hands-on" learning experience with an enriched curriculum. So when Kendra, the oldest of their three children, was ready to start kindergarten, they enrolled her in a highly respected private school in their community, hoping their children would feel as positive about their schooling as David had about his.

Before it was time to re-enroll Kendra for the first grade, Audrey became concerned about the school's one-size-fits-all philosophy in the primary grades. She worried that her daughter, who was clearly very bright and intellectually curious, would be bored in a school that assumed that even the children who were already reading would benefit from the basic phonics instruction that the non-readers needed. So Audrey found another private school that billed itself as especially good for gifted children as it embraced the Montessori philosophy of individualized and self-directed learning. She was also drawn to the school because it offered several foreign languages in the elementary grades.

By the middle of Kendra's second year at this school, Audrey started having some concerns. Most of the teachers were young and inexperienced, and the faculty turnover rate was high. The lack of structure and experienced faculty made the school day often seem chaotic and disorganized; moreover, she wanted to be involved in the classroom and on field trips, but the school didn't welcome this kind of parent participation. The foreign language program turned out to be mere exposure with little depth. But what concerned Audrey the most was that Kendra just wasn't very happy. While the school was a good fit for many families, it clearly wasn't the right school for Kendra. She rarely came home excited about what she was learning at school and complained about bullying by some of the kids. The lack of direction from the instructors left the Martins feeling that their daughter wasn't progressing in this unstructured environment.

Having been disappointed twice, Audrey decided to go ahead and try her neighborhood public school, which most of her neighbors praised. This decision made even more sense because with their second child entering kindergarten, the tuition bill would double if they stayed in private school. In the three years since they made that change, Audrey hasn't had a moment of regret. In fact, she now considers herself an advocate for public schools—particularly those that have the kind of parent support and strong leadership and staff that her children's does.

Audrey's fear that Kendra would be bored as she herself had been was unfounded. In fact, Kendra has thrived academically and socially since she left her previous school. Even though the district uses a scripted reading program, Audrey feels that the teachers are experienced and imaginative enough to make differentiated education work so that all children are engaged and challenged. She was especially impressed when this year's second grade classes performed "Geology Rocks," a musical based on the science they had been studying, an experience that has given her eight year old daughter a real interest in geological formations.

Audrey and David also worried that the public school tenure system would mean that the school would have a number of lazy or weak teachers who couldn't be fired. However, they have been delighted with the eight teachers their two daughters have had so far. She admits that the school might have a few mediocre teachers that her children have not had, but she also realizes that "sometimes teachers who aren't popular with the parents can turn out to be great."

For Audrey and her children, the greatest reward of public school has been the sense of community they wouldn't have had had they stayed at the private school. Audrey volunteers in her daughters' classrooms and leads a Brownie troop. She knows the parents of her children's friends. And the children love the ease with which they can play with friends on the weekends, vacations, and after school.

David and Audrey still recognize some of the problems and limitations that public schools face. When David receives alumni literature from his old school, he is reminded of how much enrichment he had that public schools have neither the money nor time to provide. And Audrey knows that the first private school Kendra attended can pay for more specialists—in areas like art, PE and drama—than the public school can. They have also seen how the mandate to mainstream special needs children puts a strain on administrators' budgets and places an extra burden on classroom teachers. Audrey admits she has concerns about what she has heard about the social pressures and bureaucracy of the public high school in her community and therefore may again look for a private school when Kendra is in the eighth grade. But for now Audrey knows she and her children are in the right place—a warm, exciting school environment with involved parents and professional and caring educators creating a real community of learners.

REFERENCE MAPS

San Mateo County Map
San Mateo County District Boundaries
Santa Clara County Map
Santa Clara County District Boundaries

SAN MATEO COUNTY

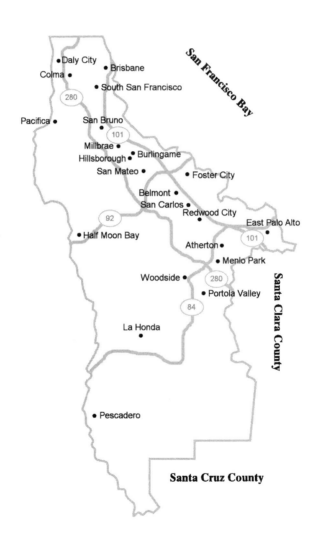

DISTRICT BOUNDARIES
SAN MATEO COUNTY

ELEMENTARY, HIGH SCHOOL & UNIFIED SCHOOL DISTRICTS

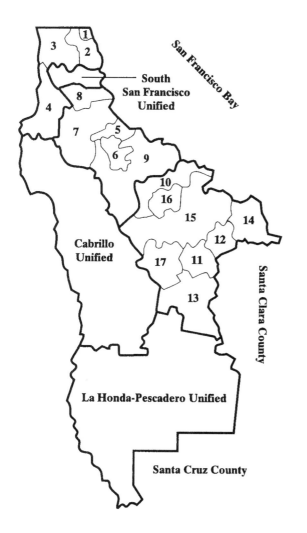

Jefferson Union High School District
1. Bayshore
2. Brisbane
3. Jefferson
4. Pacifica

San Mateo Union High School District
5. Burlingame
6. Hillsborough City
7. Millbrae
8. San Bruno Park
9. San Mateo-Foster City

Sequoia Union High School District
10. Belmont-Redwood Shores
11. Las Lomitas
12. Menlo Park City
13. Portola Valley
14. Ravenswood City
15. Redwood City
16. San Carlos
17. Woodside

SANTA CLARA COUNTY

DISTRICT BOUNDARIES
SANTA CLARA COUNTY

ELEMENTARY, HIGH SCHOOL & UNIFIED SCHOOL DISTRICTS

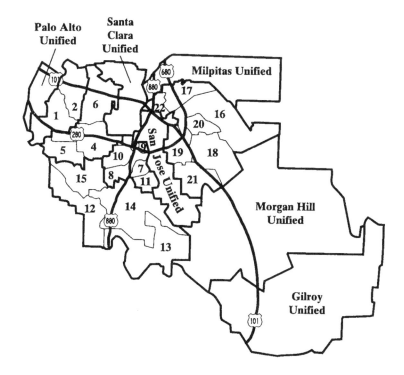

Mountain View/Los Altos High School District
1. Los Altos
2. Mountain View/Whisman

Fremont Union High School District
4. Cupertino
5. Montebello
6. Sunnyvale

Campbell Union High School District
7. Cambrian
8. Campbell
9. Luther Burbank
10. Moreland
11. Union

Los Gatos/Saratoga Joint Union High School District
12. Lakeside
13. Loma Prieta
14. Los Gatos
15. Saratoga

East Side Union High School District
16. Alum Rock
17. Berryessa
18. Evergreen
19. Franklin McKinley
20. Mount Pleasant
21. Oak Grove
22. Orchard

DIRECTORY OF PUBLIC SCHOOL DISTRICTS

Grade two, Hillview School, Los Altos, 1955

EXPLANATORY NOTES
FOR PUBLIC SCHOOL LISTINGS

In the summer of 2005, every school district in San Mateo and Santa Clara Counties was asked to complete a questionnaire for the sixth edition of this book. Some districts filled out these questionnaires completely and took advantage of the opportunity to share with the public a description of the programs offered in their schools. Others provided only basic information. The authors also made every attempt to describe every public charter and alternative school in the two counties covered by this book. Every reasonable effort has been made to see that the listings in the directory are accurate. The authors assume no responsibility for inadvertent errors.

The information about public school districts was compiled from a number of sources: the school district offices, the Ed-Data website (www.ed-data.k12.ca.us), and the County Office of Education directories.

School districts are listed alphabetically within each county. If you live in Santa Clara County and do not know what school district you reside in, go to www.sccoe.org/resourcesfamilies/districtlocator. If you live in San Mateo County, phone the San Mateo County Office of Public Works at 650-599-1440. To obtain more information about individual public schools, use the school district's website or one of the websites listed in the appendix of this book.

Class size and teacher student ratio: The teacher-to-student ratio is calculated by simply dividing the number of students by the number of teachers the district employs. Many public schools use paid and volunteer instructional aides, thus making the teacher-to-student ratio lower than the average class size. The average class size in middle and senior high schools varies greatly from course to course; academic classes usually have fewer students than do physical education and performing arts classes.

Teacher experience and percent who are credentialed: Districts were asked to indicate the average years of teaching experience of their teaching staff and the percent fully credentialed. Some districts provided this information; others did not. However, several of the websites in the appendix provide statistics regarding the number of fully credentialed teachers in the state's public schools.

Extended day care: Districts were asked to indicate which of their schools have on-site day care and whether these programs are available to parents during school (non-legal) holidays. On-site day care is offered by a variety of providers: non-profit agencies such as the YMCA and city recreation departments, and proprietary day care centers. Some districts indicated which providers serve their schools, but most did not. Principals often have a list of licensed day care homes and centers that serve children attending their schools.

Transportation: During the budget crisis of the 1980s, bus service was one of the first items slashed in most districts. A few districts, especially those in which students live great distances from school campuses or in which children must take dangerous routes to school, have retained transportation services. All districts must by law provide transportation for handicapped students.

Alternative programs: Districts were asked to describe alternative programs in some detail. Some high school districts did not describe programs, such as independent study or work study, because they do not operate as alternative schools.

GATE: Programs for students designated as gifted or talented vary greatly from district to district. School districts were asked to indicate how their schools serve their GATE students.

Open/Closed Campuses: Many of today's high school campuses are open—i.e., students are free to come and go during lunch and their free periods. Other districts, in response to parental and community concern, have maintained or reinstated closed campuses and forbid students to leave campus during the school day without permission. Some districts have a modified form of the open campus—e.g., students may leave campus only during lunch or only if they are seniors.

Counselor to student ratio: High school districts were asked if they have a counseling staff serving their student body and to indicate the ratio of counselors to students.

College preparatory: Districts with high schools were also asked the number of Advanced Placement (AP) classes offered, the percentage of graduates attending four year and two year colleges, and the percentage of their graduates who fulfill the course requirements for the University of California.

Programs cited by the districts—e.g. AP classes, music programs, foreign languages—may not by available at all schools within the district. Please contact specific schools for more details about what they offer.

The appendix lists school districts which have won voters' approval for general obligation bonds and parcel taxes to build and renovate facilities and improve instructional programs. State and national awards won by each public school are also listed along with API and SAT scores. There is also a table of expenditures per student.

PUBLIC SCHOOL DISTRICTS IN SAN MATEO COUNTY

San Mateo County Office of Education
(650) 802-5300
www.smcoe.k12.ca.us

BAYSHORE ELEMENTARY

1 Martin Street, Daly City, CA 94014. Phone: 415-467-5443. Fax: 415-FAX-1542. www.bayshore.k12.ca.us. Superintendent: Stephen J. Waterman. Gr.K to 8. 423 students. Avg. class size: 24.

One elem. school (K-4). Enrollment: 200. 1:18 teacher to student ratio. Max class size K-gr.3: 20. Aides in all grades. 4 students per computer. One mid. school (4-8). Enrollment: 225. 1:25 teacher to student ratio. Max class size for upper grades: 26. 4 students per computer. Extended care through Bayshore Child Care, 7 AM - 6 PM, open during school holidays. Uniforms at both schools. Automated libraries and computer lab at both schools. Band and choir. Afterschool tutorials 4 days/wk. Healthy Start school-based program. Counselor. 100% of teachers credentialed. Avg. yrs. teaching exp: 21. Enrichment and remedial summer programs.

BELMONT REDWOOD SHORES ELEMENTARY

2960 Hallmark Drive, Belmont, CA 94002. Phone: 650-637-4800. Fax: 650-637-4811. www.belmont.k12.ca.us. Superintendent: Josh McIntosh. Gr.K to 8. 2,460 students. Avg. class size: 24.

Five elem. schools (K-5). Avg. enrollment: 325. 1:20 teacher to student ratio. Max class size: K-gr.3 20; gr.4-5, 26. 3 students per computer. One mid. school (6-8). Enrollment: 825. 1:20 teacher to student ratio. 3 students per computer. Extended care at elem. sites, open during school holidays. Spanish and French. Computer labs and vocal and instrumental music at all sites. GATE: afterschool program at elem.; clusters and advanced placement for gr.6-8. Four new science labs at middle schools. 99% of teachers credentialed. Avg. yrs. teaching exp: 12. School Foundation raises approx. $320,000/yr. Partnership with City of Belmont for afterschool sports and summer recreation programs. Adopt-a-School programs at all schools. Summer school academic core and enrichment classes.

BRISBANE ELEMENTARY

1 Solano Street, Brisbane, CA 94005. Phone: 415-467-0550. Fax: 415-467-2914. Superintendent: Stephen J. Waterman. Gr.K to 8. 659 students. Avg. class size: K, 20; gr.1-3, 19; gr.4-8, 28-29.

Two elem. schools (K-5). Avg. enrollment: 200. 1:19 teacher to student ratio. 5 students per computer. One mid. school (6-8). Enrollment: 250. 1:20 teacher to student ratio. 7 students per computer. Extended care at both elem. schools, 3 PM - 5 PM, open during school holidays. Homework center at mid. school 4 days wk., 3 PM - 4 PM. Panorama Elem.: classical, fine arts program. Brisbane Elem.: math, science, technology. All schools use integrated thematic approach to instruction, inquiry-based science. Outdoor ed. for gr.5; service learning required for gr.6. Afterschool algebra for 8th graders. Chorus, Spanish, drama, computer lab, Adopt-a-School, Quest, journalism, humanities, art. GATE: pull-out for gr.3-8. Afterschool tutoring. ESL programs. 98% of teachers credentialed. Avg. yrs. teaching exp: 13. District foundation raises money for outdoor ed. and library. Summer school programs in thematic math for K-gr.8.

BURLINGAME ELEMENTARY

1825 Trousdale Drive, Burlingame, CA 94010. Phone: 650-259-3800. Fax: 650-259-3820. www.burlingameschools.com. Superintendent: Dr. Sonny H. Da Marto. Gr.K to 8. 2,100 students. Avg. class size: 27.

Five elem. schools (K-5). Avg. enrollment: 300. 1:19 teacher to student ratio. Max class size: K, 20; gr.1-3, 20; upper grades, 27. 4 students per computer. One mid. school (6-8). Enrollment: 875. 1:21 teacher to student ratio. Max class size: 27. 4 students per computer. Extended care at all elem. schools, 7 AM - 6 PM. Music programs for gr.3-8. Computer labs at all schools. 99% of teachers credentialed. Avg. yrs. teaching exp: 11. District foundation raises $500,000/yr. Summer programs for at-risk and GATE students.

CABRILLO UNIFIED

498 Kelly Avenue, Half Moon Bay, CA 94019. Phone: 650-712-7100. Fax: 650-726-0279. www.cabrillo.k12.ca.us. Superintendent: Dr. John Bayless. Gr.K to 12. 3,592 students. Avg. class size: 28.

Four elem. schools (K-5). Avg. enrollment: 400. 1:20 teacher to student ratio. Aides in K-gr.3. 5 students per computer. One mid. school (6-8). Enrollment: 825. 1:24 teacher to student ratio. 5 students per computer. Extended care at all elem. sites, open during school holidays at Farallone, El Granada, and Hatch. Spanish/English immersion program at Hatch. Computer labs at all schools and computers in all classrooms. GATE program integrated into the classroom. Boys and Girls Club, homework centers at mid. and high schools. District has migrant education and bilingual programs. 99% of teachers credentialed. Avg. yrs. teaching exp: 12. District foundation. Summer programs at all levels.

Half Moon Bay H.S. (9-12): Avg. enrollment: 1,175. 1:24 teacher to student ratio. 5 students per computer. Open campus. Six period day plus "early-bird" classes. Spanish and French. Bilingual tutorial center, bilingual program, integrated language arts/social studies, AP classes, school-to-work program, technology emphasis, peer counseling. One counselor/415 students. 43% students fulfill UC req. 30% of grads attend 4 yr. colleges; 50% attend 2 yr. colleges.

King's Mountain Alternative School offers smaller classes and individualized instruction in a unique rural setting.

HILLSBOROUGH CITY ELEMENTARY

300 El Cerrito Avenue, Hillsborough, CA 94010. Phone: 650-342-5193. Fax: 650-342-6964. www.hcsd.k12.ca.us. Superintendent: Marilyn Loushin-Miller. Gr.K to 8. 1,365 students. Avg. class size: 22.

Three elem. schools (K-5). Avg. enrollment: 300. 1:15 teacher to student ratio. Aides in K-gr.5. 3 students per computer. One mid. school (6-8). Enrollment: 450. 1:16 teacher to student ratio. 4 students per computer. Classroom music in K-gr.5, instrumental music gr.3-8, band gr.6-8. All schools have extensive multimedia centers and computer labs. All classrooms have computers and are networked. TV studio at Crocker Mid. School. Spanish offered K-8; French in gr.6-8. Enrichment specialists focus on critical thinking skills though math and science. GATE programs integrated into total program. Crocker Mid. School cited by Royal Academy of Sciences in Sweden as one of the best schools in the world. 99% of teachers credentialed. Avg. yrs. teaching exp: 14. District foundation raised $2.1 million in '04-'05. Enrichment four-week summer program.

JEFFERSON ELEMENTARY

101 Lincoln Avenue, Daly City, CA 94015. Phone: 650-991-1000. Fax: 650-992-2265. www.jsd.k12.ca.us. Superintendent: Barbara Wilson, Ph.D. Gr.K to 8. 5,600 students. Avg. class size: 28.

Eleven elem. schools (three K-5, eight K-6). Avg. enrollment: 360. 1:21 teacher to student ratio. Aides in all grades. 8 students per computer. Three mid. schools (one 6-8, two 7-8). Avg. enrollment: 550. 1:24 teacher to student ratio. 7 students per computer. Extended care 7 AM - 6 PM at Edison, Columbus, Kennedy, Wilson, Roosevelt, and Webster; open during summer. Computer labs, chorus and instrumental music at all sites. Business partnerships at most schools. Afterschool tutoring at all schools. GATE: one day a week pull-out for elem.; advanced courses for mid. school. 99% of teachers credentialed. Avg. yrs. teaching exp: 13.

JEFFERSON UNION HIGH

699 Serramonte Boulevard Suite 100, Daly City, CA 94015. Phone: 650-550-7900. Fax: 650-550-7888. www.juhsd.k12.ca.us. Superintendent: Michael J. Crilly. Gr.9 to 12. 5,300 students. Avg. class size: 28.

Four high schools (9-12). 1:23 teacher to student ratio. All freshmen English and mathematics classes have class max. of 20 students. 5 students per computer. One counselor/ 550 students and additional special services counselors. All schools are closed campus. Six period days. All district schools are open enrollment. All students served by the Daly

City Youth Health Center. 37% students fulfill UC req. 25% of grads attend 4 yr. colleges, 60% to 2 yr. 37% fulfill requirements for UC entrance. 95% of teachers credentialed. Avg. yrs. teaching exp: 13.

Jefferson High School: 1,275 students. Comprehensive high school supported by academic partnerships with San Francisco State University, Step to College Program, double literacy class at freshman level, award winning band, AP classes.

Oceana High School: 650 students. Member of the Coalition of Essential Schools. 100 hrs. of community service required. Personalized approach to learning, with emphasis on interdisciplinary curriculum. Teachers serve as advisors and meet on a regular basis with small groups of students. Block scheduling with classes meeting 100 minutes on alternating days. Senior exhibition of learning required for graduation.

Terra Nova High School: 1,450 students. Comprehensive high school with emphasis on college preparation. Uses a rotating schedule. AP classes, strong athletic program.

Westmoor High School: 1,820 students. Comprehensive high school with elective emphasis on technology, business, fine arts and science. Special programs such as AVID and AP courses.

Thornton High School: 170 students. Seven continuation classes and the Community Environmental Education Program for the re-integration of at-risk students into educational, social and community activities.

LA HONDA PESCADERO UNIFIED

620 North Street, P.O. Box 189, Pescadero, CA 94060. Phone: 650-879-0286. Fax: 650-879-0816. www.lhpusd.k12.ca.us. Superintendent: Timothy Beard. Gr.K to 12. 365 students. Avg. class size: 18.

Two elem. schools (K-5 and K-8). Avg. enrollment: 150. 1:18 teacher to student ratio. 4 students per computer. Extended care at La Honda elem. from 3 PM - 6 PM, open during school holidays. Music program. Computer labs at elem. sites. GATE program. Interdistrict transfers welcome. 100% of teachers credentialed. Avg. yrs. teaching exp: 11. District foundation raises money for extra staffing, programs. Summer school.

Pescadero High School (9-12): 90 students. 1:9 teacher to student ratio. 2 students per computer. Open campus. Part-time counselor. Environmental studies, honors world literature, Spanish. 100 service hrs. req'd. 53% students fulfill UC req.

LAS LOMITAS ELEMENTARY

1011 Altschul Avenue, Menlo Park, CA 94025. Phone: 650-854-2880. Fax: 650-854-0882. www.llesd.k12.ca.us. Superintendent: Mary Ann Sommerville. Gr.K to 8. 1,007 students. Avg. class size: 20.

One elem. school (K-3). Enrollment: 450. 1:16 teacher to student ratio. 3 students per computer. One mid. school (4-8). Enrollment: 550. 1:16 teacher to student ratio. 3 students per computer. Extended care open during school holidays. Classroom aides and math lab aide. Las Lomitas League afterschool sports run by volunteer parents. 100% of teachers credentialed. 50% of teachers have adv. degrees. Avg. yrs. teaching exp: 13. District foundation raises about $850,000/yr. Summer academic program.

MENLO PARK ELEMENTARY

181 Encinal Avenue, Menlo Park, CA 94027. Phone: 650-321-7140. Fax: 650-321-7184. www.mpcsd.k12.ca.us. Superintendent: Kenneth Ranella. Gr.K to 8. 2,019 students. Avg. class size: 23.

Three elem. schools (K-2, K-5, 3-5). Avg. enrollment: 450. 1:16 teacher to student ratio. Aides in K-gr.3. Extended care at all elem. sites, open during school holidays. 4 students per computer. One mid. school (6-8). Enrollment: 675. 1:17 teacher to student ratio. 3 students per computer. Computer lab at each site; reading specialist in K-8. Hillview Mid. School: foreign languages, woodshop, music, band. GATE programs designed and implemented by classroom teachers and director of curriculum. 100% of teachers credentialed. Avg. yrs. teaching exp: 13. District foundation raises about $1.5 million/yr. Summer remedial programs.

MILLBRAE ELEMENTARY

555 Richmond Drive, Millbrae, CA 94030. Phone: 650-697-5693. Fax: 650-697-6865. www.smcoe.k12.ca.us/msd. Superintendent: Karen K. Philip. Gr.K to 8. 2,096 students. Avg. class size: 24.

Four elem. schools (K-5). Avg. enrollment: 300. 1:20 teacher to student ratio. 4 students per computer. One mid. school (6-8). Enrollment: 875. 1:22 teacher to student ratio. 5 students per computer. Extended care at all elem. sites, 6:30 AM - 6 PM. Internet, music programs, computer labs, automated libraries at all schools. Spanish in MS. 96% of teachers credentialed. Avg. yrs. teaching exp: 13. Summer programs: literacy, proficiency, enrichment, GATE.

PACIFICA ELEMENTARY

375 Reina Del Mar Avenue, Pacifica, CA 94044. Phone: 650-738-6600. Fax: 650-557-9672. www.pacificasd.org. Superintendent: Dr. Michele Garside. Gr.K to 8. 3,200 students. Avg. class size: 25.

Two educational paths: Single school (K-8) and dual school (K-5 + Middle School). Two K-5 schools, avg. enrollment 455, 1:23 teacher to student ratio. Three K-8 schools, avg. enrollment 480 students. One middle school (6-8), 500 students, 1:21 teacher to student ratio. 5 students per computer. Home School Program, enrollment varies. Extended care at all school sites, open 6 am-6 pm. All classes equipped with high fiber optic network.

Completely modernized schools. The Rob Schneider Music Foundation supports instrumental music throughout the district. Each school promotes district adopted character traits: Compassion, Honesty, Integrity, Respect and Responsibility. 99% of teachers credentialed. Avg. teaching exp: 15 yrs. Site specific summer programs.

The following options are open to students throughout the district:

Ortega School (K-5): emphasis on literacy, mathematics and visual and performing arts. High degree of family and community support. Enrichment includes technology, performing and visual arts, and music. Concepts based mathematics curriculum and balanced literacy across grades.

Sunset Ridge School (K-5): emphasis on literacy/language arts and mathematics. Partners with the Noyce Foundation in the "Every Child a Reader and Writer Initiative." Curriculum is enhanced by fine arts and technology. Hosts many community programs.

Cabrillo School (K-8): emphasis on the visual and performing arts. Many arts classes are parent taught and teacher assisted. Program fosters a sense of responsibility for older students who interact regularly with younger students. Extended field trips for gr.5-8 students.

Vallemar School (K-8): "Back-to-Basics" with emphasis on academics and citizenship, one grade level per class (no combination classes) and teacher directed instruction. Parents support the concepts of the structured school, and students adhere to a behavior and dress code. Frequent reporting to parents. Extensive afterschool programs in foreign language, science, arts, and music.

Ocean Shore School (K-8): By utilizing the talents and labor of its parent body (95 hrs/ yr; 145 hrs. for two or more children), the school is able to provide a wide variety of enrichment activities such as field trips, hands-on learning experiences, theme-based projects, small group instruction, art and music. Competition minimized.

Ingrid B. Lacy Middle School (6-8): Open to all students from K-5 schools and by lottery to other students. 6th grade students in separate wing and each classroom stays together. Curriculum taught by credentialed specialist teachers. Science labs, an arts complex, a full media/library center, a state of the art gymnasium, and an applied technology lab are part of the school's design. School offers advanced placement/honors and support classes in math and language arts as well as a full sports program. This school is community-based with "dawn to dusk" opportunities for students focused on providing a well-rounded educational foundation and an easy transition to high school.

Home School Program (K-8): Flexible program to assist parents in creating lesson plans that motivate each student and best fit the child's learning style. Parents meet with teacher regularly to monitor student progress and obtain learning materials. Attendance certified by district and state. Learning program conforms to district and state requirements for admission to high school. Access to district and county support, including instrumental and vocal music. Experienced Home School Instructors work closely with families.

PORTOLA VALLEY ELEMENTARY

4575 Alpine Road, Portola Valley, CA 94028. Phone: 650-851-1777. Fax: 650-851-3700. www.pvsd.net. Superintendent: Anne Campbell. Gr.K to 8. 677 students. Avg. class size: 21.

One elem. school (K-3). Enrollment: 325. 1:15 teacher to student ratio. Aides in some classrooms. Max class size: K, 20; gr.1-3, 20. K hrs: half year half day, half year full day. Extended care from 12:30 PM - 6 PM, open during school holidays. 3 students per computer. One mid. school (4-8). Enrollment: 375. 1:13 teacher to student ratio. Max class size: 23. 3 students per computer. Computer labs at both schools. State-of-the-art networked computers. Middle school afterschool sports program- flag football, soccer, basketball, tennis, track and field, volleyball. Specialists teach art, Spanish, science, and music. GATE: differentiation, enrichment, individual learning plans. 100% of teachers credentialed. Avg. yrs. teaching exp: 10. avg. Foundation raises $750,000/yr. Academic Summer School.

RAVENSWOOD CITY ELEMENTARY

2160 Euclid Avenue, East Palo Alto, CA 94303. Phone: 650-329-2800. Fax: 650-329-6778. www.ravenswood.k12.ca.us. Superintendent: Maria Delavega. Gr.K to 10. 5,019 students. Avg. class size: 25.

Nine elem. schools (two K-3, seven K-8). Avg. enrollment: 450. 1:19 teacher to student ratio. 3 students per computer. Two mid. schools (4-8, 5-8). Avg. enrollment: 350. 1:25 teacher to student ratio. 4 students per computer. Extended care avail. at Green Oaks, Flood, Willow Oaks, and Belle Haven, open until 6 PM, closed on school holidays. Uniforms at all sites. Every school adopted by a business. GATE: cluster and afterschool programs. Computer labs, Micro Society Program and Mid-California Science Implementation Program. Extensive cooperation with community agencies, corporations, foundations, Stanford University. 60% of teachers credentialed. Avg. yrs. teaching exp: 9. Summer programs avail.

Belle Haven (K-8). 819 students. Newcomer school, focuses on academic and social success for all students.

Cesar Chavez Academy (K-8), 683 students.

Costano. (K-8). 561 students. Strong parent participation in planning multicultural experiences.

Green Oaks (K-3), 326 students. Emphasis on language and literacy and parent involvement.

Flood Math/Science Technology School (K-8), 318 students.

Menlo Oaks Visual and Performing Arts School. (4-8), 214 students. Well-equipped science lab; GATE program integrated into curriculum.

The 49er Academy (5-8), 122 students. Intensive academic program for "at risk" kids.

Willow Oaks Microsociety School (K-8), 679 students. Focus on literacy and language arts.

School of Wisdom and Knowledge College Preparatory Academy (K-8), 77 students.

East Palo Alto Charter School (K-8), 346 students. Strong focus on math and science and proficiency in two languages.

Edison Brentwood Academy (charter) (K-3), 599 students. Emphasis on technology, parent and community partnership.

Edison McNair Academy (charter) (4-8), 533 students. Integrated, thematic instruction; partnership with NASA-Ames Research.

REDWOOD CITY ELEMENTARY

750 Bradford Street, Redwood City, CA 94063. Phone: 650-423-2200. Fax: 650-423-2204. www.rcsd.K12.ca.us. Superintendent: Dr. Ronald F. Crates. Gr.K to 8. 8,647 students. Avg. class size: 23.

Thirteen elem. schools (seven K-5, six K-6). Avg. enrollment: 550. 1:18 teacher to student ratio. 4 students per computer. Two mid. schools (6-8). Avg. enrollment: 675. 1:18 teacher to student ratio. 3 students per computer. Year-round programs at 9 elem. schools. Uniforms at some sites. GATE: pull-out at most schools; cluster program at Northstar for gr.3-8; honors program for gr.7-8 at other schools. Peer counseling, "Quality Education Program," Bilingual Newcomer Center. 93% of teachers credentialed. Avg. yrs. teaching exp: 11. Summer school programs include programs for preK-gr.8, Stanford Math Institute for gr.6-7, Woodside Priory math program for gr.8.

All district schools are magnet schools, and all have a technology component. Unless otherwise indicated, all schools are K-gr.5. All schools except Northstar, Orion, Adelante, Garfield, and McKinley give priority to students in their attendance area. For further info, call the Magnet Schools Office at 650-423-2237.

Northstar (3-8), extensive enrichment program; admission based on a number of criteria including intelligence and academic testing.

Adelante (K-8), Spanish immersion.

Clifford (K-8), marine science.

Fair Oaks, literacy and fine arts.

Hawes, connections through science.

Hoover (K-8), math.

Garfield (K-8), communication and performing arts.

MacKinley, Institute of Technology, a small (400 students) middle school that operates on a year round calendar; parent participation requested.

Cloud (K-8), communication arts.

Gill, performing-visual arts and communication.

Kennedy (6-8), provides opportunity to take advanced math.

Roosevelt, social science.

Selby Lane (K-8), air and space science.

Taft, and Ford, literacy.

Orion Alternative has a flexible, non-competitive classroom structure that encourages self-motivation, self-discipline and self-evaluation. Students use a hands-on approach to learning and learn problem-solving, decision-making, and communication techniques. Parent participation required, 8 hrs/month.

Garfield Charter School, biliteracy and communication magnet. Class size limited to 25 students (20 in K-3). Parent participation encouraged; full day K. 200 day school year.

SAN BRUNO PARK ELEMENTARY

500 Acacia Avenue, San Bruno, CA 94066. Phone: 650-624-3100. Fax: 650-266-9626. www.sbpsd.k12.ca.us. Superintendent: David Hutt, Ph.D. Gr.K to 8. 2,900 students. Avg. class size: 25.

Seven elem. schools (K-6). Avg. enrollment: 300. 1:22 teacher to student ratio. 4 students per computer. One mid. school (7-8). Enrollment: 617. 1:22 teacher to student ratio. 6 students per computer. Uniforms at Belle Air and Parkside. Extended care at all elem. sites, 6:30 AM - 6 PM, open on school holidays. Computer labs at all sites. Music at some schools. Spanish for gr.7-8. 99% of teachers credentialed. Avg. yrs. teaching exp: 11. Summer school with separate programs for GATE students.

SAN CARLOS ELEMENTARY

826 Chestunt Street, San Carlos, CA 94070. Phone: 650-508-7333. Fax: 650-508-7340. www.sancarlos.org. Superintendent: Dr. Patricia Wool. Gr.K to 12. 2,696 students. Avg. class size: 26.

Five elem. schools (four K-4, one K-8). Avg. enrollment: 320. 1:20 teacher to student ratio. Max class size: K, 20; gr.1-3, 27. 3 students per computer. Two mid. schools (5-8). Avg. enrollment: 500. 1:25 teacher to student ratio. Max class size: 27. 4 students per computer. All schools except for Central Middle are charter conversion schools, allowing for more flexibility in use of state dollars. All elem. schools have day care from 2:30 PM - 6 PM. Spanish offered at both middle schools. GATE: differentiated instruction; some special classes. Instrumental music in gr.5-8. Vocal music specialist for gr.K-8. All schools have business partnerships, computer labs, renovated libraries, Noyce partnership in math

K-8, Noyce training K-4 in writing, Rite of Passage Experiences, outdoor ed. for gr.5; Yosemite trip for gr.7; trip to Washington D.C. for gr.8. Afterschool enrichment programs in technology, arts, foreign languages. 100% of teachers credentialed. Avg. yrs. teaching exp: 10. Education Foundation raises $350,000/yr. Remedial summer classes.

San Carlos Charter Learning Center (K-8);. 650-508-7343. info@scclc.sancarlos.k12.ca.us 260 students. Multi-age classrooms; instruction based on thematic units. Enrichment blocks and personalized learning plans allow students to choose their own experiences. Emphasis on science, multiple intelligences, arts/humanities, social-emotional learning and technology. Many field trips. Parent participation required: 80 hrs/yr for one child; 120 hrs/yr for 2 or more children (50% participation may be bought out @ $10/hr). Acceptance based on lottery. Extended care avail. from 7:30 AM - 6:30 PM, includes computer club, guest speakers, cooking class, chess, gymnastics, field trips, study hall, outdoor ed.

SAN MATEO - FOSTER CITY ELEMENTARY

51 West 41st Street, San Mateo, CA 94403. Phone: 650-312-7700. Fax: 650-312-7779. www.smfc.k12.ca.us. Superintendent: Dr. Pendery Clark. Gr.K to 8. 10,069 students. Avg. class size: 26.

Fifteen elem. schools (K-5). Avg. enrollment: 450. 1:20 teacher to student ratio. Max class size: K, 20; gr.1-3, 20. 5 students per computer. 4 mid. schools (6-8). Avg. enrollment: 850. 1:22 teacher to student ratio. Max class size: 33. 7 students per computer. District operated extended care offered at all elem. sites from 7 AM - 6 PM, open during school holidays. Choral music for K-gr.5; instrumental music for gr.4-5; band and orchestra for gr.6-8. Several schools involved in Adopt-a-School program. All middle schools have networked computer labs. Middle schools have site-based GATE programs. 95% of teachers credentialed. Avg. yrs. teaching exp: 13. District foundation raises over $400,000/yr. Enrichment and remedial summer programs.

Students in the district are assigned a neighborhood school based on their address. However, they may also apply for one of the magnet schools listed below or for a different neighborhood school. For more information about the magnet schools and procedures for applying, go to the district's website.

Fiesta Gardens, Parkside, and S.T.A.G.E. are year round schools; the calendar year at these schools starts in July or early Aug. and has 3 three week vacations during the year.

Bayside Middle School for the Arts and Creative Technology (6-8). The visual and performing arts and creative technology program at Bayside employs the arts—music, theater, visual arts, and dance—and creative technology to help students gain a better understanding of all areas of the curriculum. The Spanish-English Two-Way Immersion Program at Bayside is an extension of the Fiesta Gardens International School curriculum.

Fiesta Gardens International School (K-5) offers a Spanish-English Two-Way Immersion Program with an emphasis on Global Studies, providing a challenging curriculum through a global perspective. Native English speakers and Spanish speaking students study together in the same classroom. All students are bi-literate and bilingual by 5th grade graduation.

Horrall School Technology Integration Magnet Education Program (K-5) uses technology to enhance learning. Project-based learning approach so students are exposed to an in-depth exploration of real-life, open-ended problems. Video studio, iMac and mobile computer labs, networked computer workstations in each classroom; widespread access to digital cameras, scanners, and video.

Montessori Programs for K-5 offered at North Shoreview Montessori School and Parkside Montessori. The Montessori teacher "carefully constructs a classroom designed to challenge each student through the use of hands-on materials. Students encouraged to take responsibility for their own work and behavior and to develop a lifelong love of learning." North Shoreview enhances its Montessori curriculum with an emphasis on music and art. Orff and Suzuki instruction, dance and theater, artists in residence, band, chorus, and instrumental music. Parkside includes an integrated global curriculum.

San Mateo Park Math and Science Magnet School (K-5) offers an accelerated mathematics and science program, featuring "hands-on, minds-on" inquiry/research-based activities designed to challenge students' thinking while providing various venues for exploration. Living with Science Lab, an outdoor ecosystem and extra-curricular activities support the magnet theme.

School of Talented and Gifted Education (S.T.A.G.E.) at Turnbull (K-5) provides a rigorous, differentiated standards-based core academic program in the mornings; in the afternoons students participate in enriching activities in academic areas including reading and math empowerment programs, Mandarin, violin, Lego Robotics, art, music, drama, dance, applied algebra and geometry. The S.T.A.G.E. campus is the new home of the SMFCSD all day GATE program for highly gifted 4th and 5th grade students.

Sunnybrae Primary Years Prep Magnet School (K-5) is currently seeking status as an International Baccalaureate program. Sunnybrae provides a rigorous standards-based curriculum with an emphasis on the global community. Instruction organized around six themes that encourage critical thinking, arts integration and a global viewpoint. Students begin learning a foreign language in kindergarten.

SAN MATEO UNION HIGH

650 North Delaware Street, San Mateo, CA 94401. Phone: 650-558-2299. Fax: 650-762-0249. www.smuhsd.k12.ca.us. Superintendent: Samuel Johnson, Jr. Gr.9 to 12. 8,116 students. Avg. class size: 28.

Six high schools (9-12). Avg. enrollment: 1,350. 1:22 teacher to student ratio. 20 students in 9th gr. English and math classes. 4 students per computer. Six period day. Closed campuses. Two basic tracks: College Prep. and Honors/AP. One counselor/500 students. 19 AP courses. French, Spanish, Italian, Japanese, Chinese. Performing arts programs at each site. Extensive use of technology. District offers programs in biotechnology, food service and hospitality, fashion merchandising; active school to career program. Drug and Alcohol Abatement Program, proactive safety program. 55% students fulfill UC req. 40% of grads attend 4 yr. colleges; 55% attend 2 yr. colleges. 95% of teachers credentialed. Avg. yrs. teaching exp: 13.

San Mateo Middle College High School is a cooperative program between San Mateo Union High School District and College of San Mateo. The program allows motivated, mature high school juniors and seniors from any school in the district to complete their high school education while getting a head start on earning a college degree. Students may enter mid-year. The program is designed for students who are capable of handling a rigorous academic program and will thrive at a small, supportive school in an enriched and flexible educational setting. Students must have a good attendance record and at least a 2.0 GPA. For more information look at the program's website, www.smccd.net/accounts/smmchs or call 650-574-6101.

SEQUOIA UNION HIGH

480 James Avenue, Redwood City, CA 94062. Phone: 650-369-1411. Fax: 650-306-8870. www.seq.org. Superintendent: Pat Gemma. Gr.9 to 12. 7,484 students. Avg. class size: 29.

Four high schools. Avg. enrollment: 1,875. 1:21 teacher to student ratio. 3 students per computer. Seven period day. One counselor/350 students. Closed campuses. Business partnership with each school. Music, drama, and art programs at each site. The information technology program at Sequoia has received worldwide recognition. Web design and video production classes at Woodside H.S. Literacy Center. District is moving toward heterogeneous grouping but will continue to offer AP courses, honors and advanced standing classes. German, Japanese, Spanish, French and Latin. 10 AP classes. Academies Programs, Alternative Study Center, School-Age Mothers Program. 100% of teachers credentialed. Avg. yrs. teaching exp: 12. 45% students fulfill UC req. 50% of grads attend 4 yr. colleges; 40% attend 2 yr. colleges.

East Palo Alto Charter High School is operated by the nonprofit Stanford School Corporation (SSC), whose goal is to serve as a model for what other universities can do to train teachers and offer greater opportunities for students. The Early College Program at EPA, funded by the Gates Foundation and developed in partnership with Stanford and Cañada Community College, will give high school students an opportunity to accrue up to 30 credits of college coursework during the traditional four years of high school to promote a "college for certain" culture during high school, provide students access to college courses, and create a seamless transition to higher education. In 2006, the expanded school plans to enroll 80 to 100 kindergarten and first grade students and a of sixth graders. Students will be admitted through a community lottery system and the school will add new grades each year.

High Tech High Bayshore opened in the fall of 2003 as a public charter school, and is now located at a state of the art facilities at 890 Broadway, Redwood City. College preparatory program based on principles designed to immerse students in a rigorous learning environment that engages their interests. As a small school by design with a low student-teacher ratio, all students in the school are known well by their teachers. All students have an advisor who stays with them all four years. All students present their work to adult panelists, go on site visits to various workplaces, and complete a one semester long internship during their junior year. No ability grouping. All students participate in challenging work that prepares them for success in college, guided by project based curriculum. For more information, go to www.hightechhigh.org.

The IB Program at Sequoia High School offers juniors and seniors the opportunity to earn an International Baccalaureate (IB) Diploma. The rigorous, college preparatory program offers students college-level coursework from a global perspective as the courses focus on internationalism, critical thinking, and writing. Besides a traditional liberal arts core, students take Theory of Knowledge, an interdisciplinary course; write a 4,000 word independently researched essay; and meet the 150 hours of community service requirement. Freshmen and sophomores wishing to prepare for the IB program may enroll in the International College Advancement Program, (ICAP) a rigorous writing intensive program with an international focus. Students are self-selected but should be highly motivated, have good time management skills, competent in reading, writing, and speaking skills. Students enrolled in the program are encouraged to participate in other aspects of Sequoia's campus life, like the arts and athletics.

Summit Preparatory High School is a small, public, charter college preparatory high school temporarily located in downtown Redwood City. Founded in 2003, the school serves a diverse student population. The school's mission is to prepare each student for success in a four-year college and to be thoughtful, contributing members of society. 90% of teachers possess advanced degrees from Harvard, Stanford or Columbia. As one of three Stanford University School of Education high school partners, Summit prescribes to an approach for teaching and learning that is based on research and best practices. Max class size: 18. Long-term mentor guides a maximum of 18 students using a Personalized Learning Plan. Enrollment is open to all high school students in California. If the number of applicants exceeds the spaces available, admission is determined by a drawing. The school is scheduled to relocate to a permanent campus in the fall of 2006. For more information, visit the school web-site at www.summitprep.net or call 650-369-5851.

Cañada Middle College is a cooperative program between Sequoia Union High School District and Cañada College. The program allows motivated, mature high school juniors and seniors from any school in the district to complete their high school education while getting a head start on earning a college degree. Program designed for students who are group capable of handling a rigorous academic program and will thrive at a small, supportive school in an enriched and flexible educational setting. Students must have a good attendance record and at least a 2.0 GPA. Informational meetings held in March, placement test given in April and May. For more information, call 650-306-3120 or go to www.canadacollege.edu/middlecollege.

SOUTH SAN FRANCISCO UNIFIED

398 B. Street, South San Francisco, CA 94080. Phone: 650-877-8700. Fax: 650-583-4717. www.ssfusd.k12.ca.us. Superintendent: Barbara Olds. Gr.K to 12. 9,238 students. Avg. class size: 28.

Ten elem. schools (K-5). Avg. enrollment: 400. 1:21 teacher to student ratio. 5 students per computer. Three mid. schools (6-8). Avg. enrollment: 750. 1:24 teacher to student ratio. 6 students per computer. Uniforms at some schools. Extended care at all elem. sites from 7 AM - 6 PM, open during school holidays. Tutorial centers at elem. and mid. schools. Business partnerships. GATE. classroom enrichment. ESL programs at all schools. Parent literacy program at Spruce, Martin, and Parkway Heights Middle School; Newcomers program at Parkway Heights. 94% of teachers credentialed. Avg. yrs. teaching exp: 12. Summer programs.

Two high schools (9-12). Avg. enrollment: 1,450. 1:22 teacher to student ratio. 5 students per computer. Six period day. Closed campuses. Spanish, French, and Italian. AP classes. One counselor/550 students. Special programs include Capitol Focus, Project Close-Up, Partnerships in Education, Baile Folklorico, History Day, Mock Trial, large well-equipped Business Department, ESL program. 36% students fulfill UC req. 20% of grads attend 4 yr. colleges; 50% attend 2 yr. colleges. Scholarships available for good athletes with good grades who will attend college.

WOODSIDE ELEMENTARY

3195 Woodside Road, Woodside, CA 94062. Phone: 650-851-1571. Fax: 650-851-5577. www.woodside.k12.ca.us. Superintendent: Dr. Daniel Vinson. Gr.K to 8. 426 students. Avg. class size: 21.

One elem. school (K-8). Enrollment: 425. 1:12 teacher to student ratio. 3 students per computer. Full day K, 8:30 AM - 2:30 PM. K-gr.4 classroom music; gr.4-8, instrumental and strings. Extensive art program. Computers in all classrooms. Spanish instruction in gr.1-8. Art and P.E. for all grades. Two computer labs. GATE program integrated into the classroom. 94% of teachers credentialed. Avg. yrs. teaching exp: 14. District foundation raises over $1 million/yr.

PUBLIC SCHOOL DISTRICTS IN SANTA CLARA COUNTY

Santa Clara County Office of Education
(408) 453-6500
www.sccoe.org

ALUM ROCK UNION ELEMENTARY

2930 Gay Avenue, San Jose, CA 95127. Phone: 408-928-6800. Fax: 408-928-6416. www.arusd.org. Superintendent: Alfonso R. Anaya. Gr.K to 8. 13,782 students. Avg. class size: 28.

Twenty elem. schools (K-5). Avg. enrollment: 500. 1:21 teacher to student ratio. Aides in K-5. 1 student per computer. Six mid. schools (6-8). Avg. enrollment: 550. 1:22 teacher to student ratio. 5 students per computer. Extended care available through Kidango at Arbuckle, Cureton, Linda Vista, and Presley, 7 AM - 6 PM. Transportation for K-gr.5 students who live more than 1.5 miles from school; for gr.6-8, more than 2 miles away. GATE students' needs addressed through differentiation, pullout, and afterschool programs. Choir, instrumental music, and jazz band. Spanish. Many business partnerships. Sixteen schools have been modernized. Sheppard Mid. School has school-age mothers' program. 83% of teachers credentialed. Avg. yrs. teaching exp: 10. Alum Rock Foundation raises additional funding for the district. Summer programs for at-risk students, special education, elementary enrichment, GATE enrichment, middle school math.

KIPP Heartwood Academy is a public, college-preparatory middle school committed to providing students with the knowledge, skills, character, and intellectual habits needed to excel in college. Each year, the school will grow by one grade level until reaching 320 students in grades 5-8 in 2007. 99% percent of students are of color; over 78% qualify for the National Free/Reduced Lunch program; over 60% designated as English Language Learners. The school is based upon the founding principles of the Knowledge is Power Program (KIPP). KIPP schools have achieved success by focusing upon five principles: 1) High Expectations; 2) Choice and Commitment; 3) More Time on Task; 7:15am – 5pm daily, 9am – 1pm two Saturdays a month, and three weeks during the summer 4) Power to Lead; and 5) Focus on Results. To learn more about KIPP Heartwood Academy, please contact Sehba Zhumkhawala, Founder and Principal, at szhumkhawala@kippheartwood.org.

Renaissance Academy of Arts, Science, and Social Justice is the flagship middle school of the new small autonomous schools movement in Alum Rock Union School District. Renaissance Academy is focused on high achievement and student leadership through project-based research, public exhibitions of student work, learner-led conferences, and small group advisory sessions. Extensive instruction-focused faculty collaboration. As a catalyst for social consciousness, Renaissance utilizes visual and performing arts in the teaching and learning process and nurtures the development of respectful, trustworthy, and meaningful relationships between students, parents, and teachers for a strong learning community. The school provides an academically rigorous curriculum and fosters a culture in which the entire school community is constantly learning and exploring how to create a more just world.

Learning in an Urban Community with High Achievement (LUCHA) offers an innovative K-5 learning environment with family and community involvement at the foundation. The community focuses on high achievement, academic success and the deep involvement of parents in all aspects of the school. Project-based learning, community activities, trips, and a longer day allow students to learn reading, writing, math, science, art, and much more. Students and families participate in monthly trips to exciting places like the Tech Museum, the Children's Discovery Museum, and professional performances, like the Nutcracker. L.U.C.H.A. will grow into a K-5 school of approximately 240 students- small enough so that all children and parents will be well-known.

Adelante is a dual language immersion academy, located on the campus of Cesar Chavez Elementary School in San Jose. The school serves kindergarten - 2nd grades, and will add a grade each year until the campus houses grades K-8, with approximately 380 students. It is a learning community where each child and family is well known and an active participant. All members of the school family are held to a high standard of academic achievement, work ethic, and accountability. Each student will exit 8th grade bilingual and bi-literate in English and Spanish; well prepared to participate fully in the global economy of the 21st century.

BERRYESSA UNION ELEMENTARY

1376 Piedmont Road, San Jose, CA 95132. Phone: 408-923-1800. Fax: 408-259-3869. www.berryessa.k12.ca.us. Superintendent: Marc B. Liebman, Ph.D. Gr.K to 8. 8,471 students. Avg. class size: 28.

Ten elem. schools (K-5). Avg. enrollment: 550. 1:21 teacher to student ratio. 8 students per computer. Three mid. schools (6-8). Avg. enrollment: 1,000. 1:24 teacher to student ratio. 5 students per computer. Uniforms at Morrill Mid. School. Extended care avail. at Toyon, Northwood, Brooktree. Afterschool sports, HW club, youth center co-sponsored by city of San Jose. Business partnerships at all schools. Spanish offered at middle school level. Instrumental music in elem. schools; band and orchestra in mid. schools. GATE programs at all school sites. Computer in every class, every school has a computer lab, science labs available. Parent participation alternative programs for 10 elem. classrooms located at 3 sites (Northwood, Toyon and Noble). Home School study offered as an alternative education program. English Language Development (ELD) at all schools. 93% of teachers credentialed. Avg. yrs. teaching exp: 14. District foundation raises approx $100,000/yr. Summer remedial programs.

CAMBRIAN ELEMENTARY

4115 Jacksol Drive, San Jose, CA 95124. Phone: 408-377-2103. Fax: 408-559-3122. www.cambrian.k12.ca.us. Superintendent: Dr. Barry Groves. Gr.K to 8. 2,788 students. Avg. class size: 26.

Four elem. schools (K-5). Avg. enrollment: 450. 1:20 teacher to student ratio. 3 students per computer. One mid. school (6-8). Enrollment: 950. 1:23 teacher to student ratio. 8 students per computer. All elem. sites have extended care, open during school holidays. Music program in all grades. IBM National Demonstration District. Chorus, band, Price News Network (in-school T.V. program). Spanish. GATE: in-class enrichment in K-5; special honors classes at mid. school. New science and music classrooms and $7 million community center/gymnasium. 96% of teachers credentialed. Avg. yrs. teaching exp: 11. District foundation operates at five sites. Four wk. summer academic and recreational programs.

All schools, except for Bagby Elementary, are charter schools; out of district students are accepted at these schools on a space available basis.

Fammatre Elementary Charter School (K-5), 460 students. In addition to the core curriculum, Fammatre offers enrichment opportunities in art, music, PE, and science. Parent participation is very high, providing a valuable cadre of classroom volunteers while also supporting fund raising opportunities for extra programs such as reading intervention, assemblies, field trips, and after school enrichment.

Farnham Elementary Charter School (K-5), 415 students. Full-day K. School emphasizes academics and incorporates developmental activities. Wide variety of activities promote a well-rounded educational experience including Student Council, assemblies, field trips, Art Vistas, P.E. program, Lifeskills, instrumental music program, homework center, enrichment programs, vocal music, and extended care coordinated by the YMCA.

Sartorette Elementary Charter School (K-5), 500 students. Solid parental and community support. Variety of student experiences such as library activities, motor skills program, instrumental and vocal music, technology support, and school garden.

Price Charter Middle School (6-8), 920+ students, emphasis on standards-based instruction. Flexible scheduling and a challenging curriculum with choices. Extensive after school activities; sports-basketball, soccer, volleyball, track and cross-country; clubs-computer, homework, art/ceramics, chess, community service, Roots & Shoots; music-color-guard, percussion ensemble, symphonic & concerts bands, marching band, and choir. Award-winning student activities program promotes leadership development and a sense of pride. Numerous opportunities for parent involvement. Acceptance from surrounding areas based on lottery. School hours: 7:30 AM - 4:00 PM.

CAMPBELL UNION ELEMENTARY

155 N. 3rd Street, Campbell, CA 95008. Phone: 408-364-4200. Fax: 408-341-7280. www.campbellusd.k12.ca.us. Superintendent: Johanna VanderMolen. Gr.K to 8. 7,462 students. Avg. class size: 27.

Nine elem. schools (eight K-5, one K-4). Avg. enrollment: 525. 1:20 teacher to student ratio. Aides available. 4 students per computer. Three mid. schools (5-8). Avg. enroll- ment: 925. 1:22 teacher to student ratio. 5 students per computer. Extended care avail. at all elems. GATE integrated into classroom. Intro. to French and Spanish and instrumental music in gr.5-8. Afterschool programs: Odyssey of the Mind; performing arts. Alterna- tive middle school program for students experiencing social, emotional, behavioral and school adjustment problems. 97% of teachers credentialed. Avg. yrs. teaching exp: 12. District foundation. All schools have business partnerships. Schools awarded numerous grants. Summer recreation and enrichment, summer music camp.

Village School uses a holistic approach to primary education. Using district and state guidelines to shape the school's philosophy and curriculum, parents, students and teachers collaborate to create a strong school community in which parents are involved in governance, in the classrooms, and in program/curriculum support. Parents provide a wealth of resources to enrich the child-centered, developmental, hands-on educational experience. The increased adult to student ratio (1 to 6 for grades K-3: 1 to 8 for grades 4 and 5) allows for small groups of students to successfully work as a team, as well as for each student to be given individual attention in the classroom.

Sherman Oaks Charter Community School "provides a quality learning environment and strong academics with relevant, real-life applications." The school features clusters of large classrooms with kitchens in each cluster, outdoor science lab stations, garden areas. Dual immersion program in Spanish and English; project-based learning; state-of- the-art technology; full day K. Member of the GAT Small School Network and Bay Area School Reform Collaborative. For more information, phone 408-795-1140 or look on district's website.

CAMPBELL UNION HIGH

3235 Union Avenue, San Jose, CA 95124. Phone: 408-371-0960. Fax: 408-558-3006. www.cuhsd.org. Superintendent: Rhonda E. Farber, Ph.D. Gr.9 to 12. 7,209 students. Avg. class size: 28.

Five high schools (9-12). Avg. enrollment: 1,450. 1:26 teacher to student ratio. 9th grade English classes have no more than 20 students. 5 students per computer. Closed cam- puses. Block scheduling- 4 class periods/day. Spanish, Latin, and French. 10-17 AP classes offered at each site, with 50 offered in district. All schools on-line. Computer Academy; School to Work Program; multiple business partnerships. Peer assistance program to assist new teachers. Two counselors at each school. On-going articulation with district's 5 elementary partner districts. 35% students fulfill UC req. 30% of grads attend 4 yr. colleges, 58% to 2 yr. 87% of teachers credentialed. Avg. yrs. teaching exp: 13.

In 2006, **Leadership Public Schools**, a non-profit organization that operates charter college preparatory high schools serving economically and ethnically diverse students, will open a campus serving students in the Campbell High School District. The first year the school will be open to 9th graders, and each year the school will add a grade. For description of Leadership schools, go to the website www.leadps.org.

CUPERTINO UNION ELEMENTARY

10301 Vista Drive, Cupertino, CA 95014. Phone: 408-252-3000. Fax: 408-255-4450. www.cupertino.k12.ca.us. Superintendent: William E. Bragg, Ph.D. Gr.K to 8. 16,500 students. Avg. class size: 29.

Twenty elem. schools (nineteen K-5, one K-8). Avg. enrollment: 550. 1:22 teacher to student ratio. Max class size: K, 33; gr.1-3, 20, gr.4-6, 33. 4 students per computer. 5 mid. schools (6-8). Avg. enrollment: 1,200. 1:25 teacher to student ratio. 8 students per computer. Extended care at all elem. sites, open school holidays, hours vary by site. Extracurricular GATE programs avail. throughout the district. 100% of teachers credentialed. Avg. yrs. teaching exp: 11. Remedial summer program along with enrichment summer programs at De Anza.

The following alternative schools are open to any student living in the district. Students are selected from a lottery that is held each spring:

Cupertino Language Immersion Program (CLIP) at Meyerholz. The goal of this K-gr.8 program is to produce fully bi-literate children who can speak, read, write, and think in both English and Mandarin. Children acquire both languages naturally in the classroom setting as they participate in hands-on learning experiences that are directly related to the Cupertino Union School district standards. The Mandarin language arts curriculum starts with BoPoMoFo, traditional, then simplified characters, and then transitions to Pin-Ying. Chinese cultural and enrichment activities, such as calligraphy courses and Chinese folk dance assemblies. Children enrolled in CLIP participate in activities with the larger Meyerholz community.

Faria Academics Plus Program emphasizes development, mastery, and application of the basic skills in a traditionally-structured classroom, characterized by whole-group, teacher-directed instruction in single grade-level classrooms with one teacher per classroom. Emphasis on reading, mathematics, English (including grammar, spelling, penmanship) and composition skills, with a solid curriculum in science, history, and geography. Other areas in the curriculum (e.g. music, art, P.E.) are included, but basics receive priority. Parents receive weekly graded work. Through repetition, review and drill, students master basic skills. Whole group instruction is the usual teaching method. Parents sign a contract agreeing to support the school's philosophy and must participate in school fund raising programs.

Christa McAuliffe Alternative is a parent-participation, experiential K-gr.8 program based on a developmental education philosophy that emphasizes the needs of the total child. The school encourages children to develop lifelong learning skills by promoting critical thinking and problem-solving skills and stressing the interrelationship and equal importance of all the disciplines, including the arts and physical education. Each family assists in the classroom on a weekly basis and monthly meetings are required. Parents serve as aides to lead small groups. Children have frequent opportunities to exercise choice within planned learning activities. All subject areas are integrated around selected themes or units. Children set and monitor their own rules of behavior with guidance from the teacher and learn to work cooperatively. For more information, go to mcauliffeweb@pacbell.net.

Murdock-Portal Elementary is a K-gr.5 school, on a modified year-round calendar, in which staff members combine direct instruction and project-based strategies and emphasize group learning and real world experiences. Students work as self-directed learners in open, multi-age villages in which they remain with one teacher for two years. Students practice critical thinking, problem solving, and communication skills. Learning plans developed collaboratively between students, parents, and teachers. Technology integrated into all areas of the curriculum.

EAST SIDE UNION HIGH

830 North Capitol Avenue, San Jose, CA 95133. Phone: 408-347-5000. Fax: 408-347-5045. www.esuhsd.org. Interim Superintendent: Bob Nunez. Gr.9 to 12. 24,728 students. Avg. class size: 27.

Eleven high schools (9-12). Avg. enrollment: 1,675. 1:22 teacher to student ratio. Many 9th grade core classes have 20-25 students. 3 students per computer. Avg. enrollment 160. 1 to 9 teacher student ratio. Several schools on block schedules. Closed campuses. Common dress required at Andrew Hill, Yerba Buena, Santa Teresa, and Foothill. AP courses offered at every school; 6 foreign languages. Tutorial assistance available. One counselor/800 students. 83% of teachers credentialed. Avg. yrs. teaching exp: 15. 25% students fulfill UC req. 30% attend 4 yr. colleges; 50% attend 2 yr. colleges.

East Side Magnets: Medical Health Professions, Space Science and Technology, Teaching Academy, Animation Studio, Manufacturing Industrial Technology, Aerospace Science (JROTC), Academy of Travel and Tourism, Entrepreneurship and Applications, Business Careers, Legal Studies, Pacific Rim International Studies, Forensic Science, Telecommunications, and Pre-Engineering. Priority sign-ups in April of 8th grade year. Placement depends on space and ethnic and racial balance. Other academy programs are biotechnology, multimedia, finance, electronics, and construction technology.

Accel Middle College at Evergreen Valley College is a cooperative program between ESUHSD and the College. The program allows high school juniors and seniors residing in the district to complete their high school education while getting a head start on earning a college degree. The program is designed for students who are capable of handling a rigorous academic program and will thrive at a small, supportive school in an enriched and flexible educational setting. Students must have a good attendance record and at least a 2.0 G.P.A. Informational meetings are held in March at each campus in the district and a placement test is given at the end of March. For more information. phone (408) 274-7900 x6881.

Charter schools operating in the ESUHSD:

MACSA Academia Calmecac (9-10): primarily English Language Learners (ELL).

Latino College Preparatory Academy (9-10): primarily English Language Learners.

San Jose Conservation Corp: former dropouts between 17 and 28 years of age.

Escuela Popular (K-12): primarily English Language Learners.

California Youth Outreach Academy: Vocational charter.

In 2004, **Leadership Public Schools**, a not-for-profit organization that operates charter college preparatory high schools serving economically and ethnically diverse students, opened a campus located until 2006 at Piedmont Hills High School. In 2006, it will move to a permanent spot at Overfelt H.S. Leadership schools focus on producing strong academic performance and student leadership development. For more information, phone 408-937-2709 or go to the website www.leadps.org/san_jose.html.

EVERGREEN ELEMENTARY

3188 Quimby Road, San Jose, CA 95148. Phone: 408-270-6800. Fax: 408-274-3894. www.eesd.org. Superintendent: Clif Black. Gr.K to 8. 13,111 students. Avg. class size: 28.

Fourteen elem. schools (two K-5, twelve K-6). Avg. enrollment: 700. 1:22 teacher to student ratio. Max class size: K, 20; gr.1-3, 20. 13 students per computer. Three mid. schools (two 6-8, one 7-8). Avg. enrollment: 1,100. 1:25 teacher to student ratio. Max class size: 29. 7 students per computer. GATE students in elem. schools receive approx. 180 minutes of qualitatively different education. Honors and music programs in middle schools. 100% of teachers credentialed. Avg. yrs teaching exp: 12. Academic summer school.

FRANKLIN - MCKINLEY ELEMENTARY

645 Wool Creek Drive, San Jose, CA 95112. Phone: 408-283-6000. Fax: 408-283-6022. www.fmsd.k12.ca.us. Superintendent: Larry Aceves. Gr.K to 8. 10,100 students. Avg. class size: 26.

Fifteen elem. schools (thirteen K-6, two K-8). Avg. enrollment: 550. 1:20 teacher to student ratio. 7 students per computer. Two mid. schools (7-8). Avg. enrollment: 900. 1:19 teacher to student ratio. 7 students per computer. Santee and Stonegate have extended care. Uniforms at all schools but Stonegate and Windmill Springs. GATE program varies according to school. Slingerland program at Franklin and Stonegate. Services avail. through district include health care, probation officer, Project Crackdown, family counseling, and child care. 97% of teachers credentialed. Avg. yrs. teaching exp: 14. Summer school.

FREMONT UNION HIGH

589 W. Fremont Avenue, Sunnyvale, CA 94087. Phone: 408-522-2200. Fax: 408-245-5325. www.fuhsd.org. Superintendent: Steve Rowley. Gr.9 to 12. 9,305 students. Avg. class size: 30.

Five high schools (9-12). Avg. enrollment: 1,850. 1:24 teacher to student ratio. Max class size in 9th grade English: 21. 5 students per computer. Seven period day. Open campus. Modernized facilities. Courses in music, theater, dance and visual arts. Community service encouraged Seniors who have completed 80 hrs. of service to a non-profit organization are recognized with a "Community Service Award." Many AP classes; Spanish, French, German, Japanese, Mandarin Chinese. Numerous business and community partnerships. Tutorial centers. 71% students fulfill UC req. 78% take SAT. 90% go on to college. 90% of teachers credentialed. Avg. yrs. teaching exp: 13. All schools have garnered awards and recognition for both student achievement and programs. District foundation.

Middle College program at De Anza Community College is designed for juniors and seniors who are academically very capable but for a variety of reasons are not performing up to their potential. By interacting with a more mature role group and taking advantage of advanced course work, students develop responsibility and a sense of self-direction. **New Start**, an independent study program, is designed for students 16 yrs. or older (including adults) who are working full or part-time and need flexibility in their instructional time. Through weekly tutorial study groups and course work based on individual plans, students earn a high school diploma.

GILROY UNIFIED

7810 Arroyo Circle, Gilroy, CA 95020. Phone: 408-847-2700. Fax: 408-842-1158. www.gusd.k12.ca.us. Superintendent: Edwin Diaz. Gr.K to 12. 9,485 students. Avg. class size: 28.

Eight elem. schools (K-5). Avg. enrollment: 600. 1:20 teacher to student ratio. 5 students per computer. Three mid. schools (6-8). Avg. enrollment: 750. 1:23 teacher to student ratio. 5 students per computer. All K-8 schools require uniforms. Extended care at some sites; 6 AM - 6 PM. Music specialists, band, choir for gr.4-6. All schools have computer labs. Business partnerships in most schools. GATE: pull-out programs at all sites; self-contained program for gr.3-6 at Rucker. 100% of teachers credentialed. Avg. yrs. teaching exp: 15. Remedial summer programs.

Two high schools (9-12). Avg. enrollment: 1,250. 1:23 teacher to student ratio. 4 students per computer. 31% students fulfill UC req.

El Portal Leadership Academy is a charter high school in Gilroy, chartered by the Gilroy Unified School District and operated by The Mexican-American Community Services Agency. Offering a small (320 students), supportive learning environment with rigorous standards, the Academy aims to serve academically under-achieving students who might "fall through the cracks" in a large high school but are willing to work hard to prepare to attend a four-year college or university. The Academy features a 22:1 student teacher ratio, personalized learning plans, daily tutoring sessions, an extended school day, a summer bridge program, a strict code of conduct and uniforms, and requires family participation. Each teacher is advisor to 20 students for their entire 4 years of high school. For more information, call (408) 846-1715 or consult the website www.macsa.org.

LAKESIDE JOINT ELEMENTARY

19621 Black Road, Los Gatos, CA 95033. Phone: 408-354-2372. www.lakesidesd.k12.ca.us. Superintendent: Joyce Salisbury. Gr.K to 6. 81 students. Avg. class size: 18.

One elem. school (K-6). Enrollment: 80. 1:17 teacher to student ratio. 3 students per computer. Extended care 7 AM - 6:30 PM, open during school holidays. Computer lab, Art Scope, life science gardening program in school garden. Pull-out GATE program. 100% of teachers credentialed. Avg. yrs. teaching exp: 13. District foundation raises about $40,000/yr. Summer programs.

LOMA PRIETA UNION ELEMENTARY

23800 Summit Road, Los Gatos, CA 95033. Phone: 408-353-1101. Fax: 408-353-8051. www.loma.k12.ca.us. Superintendent: Henry Castaniada. Gr.K to 8. 659 students. Avg. class size: 23.

One elem. school (K-5). Enrollment: 400. 1:18 teacher to student ratio. Max class size: K, 20; gr.1-3, 20. 3 students per computer. One mid. school (6-8). Enrollment: 250. 1:22 teacher to student ratio. Max class size: 26. 3 students per computer. Extended care 6:30 AM - 6 PM for K-gr.8, open all weekdays during the year. High academic expectations, teacher leadership in curriculum and staff development; emphasizes parent involvement. New elementary school facilities; technology program at both schools. Music, GATE pull-out, and resource programs offered. Spanish in mid. school. 150 service hrs. req'd. 100% of teachers credentialed. Avg. yrs. teaching exp: 16.

LOS ALTOS ELEMENTARY

201 Covington Road, Los Altos, CA 94024. Phone: 650-947-1150. Fax: 650-947-0118. www.losaltos.k12.ca.us. Superintendent: Tim Justice. Gr.K to 8. 4,000 students. Avg. class size: 24.

Six (K-6) elem. schools. Avg. enrollment: 500. Max class size in K-3: 20. Avg. class size in gr.4-6: 27. 1:21 teacher to student ratio. Aides used in all classes. 5 students per computer. Two mid. schools (7-8). Avg. enrollment: 500. 1:19 teacher to student ratio.

4 students per computer. Extended care at all elementaries. GATE: advanced math, afterschool classes. Elementary schools have science labs, computer programs. Spanish and French at jr. high level. 98% of teachers credentialed. Avg. yrs. teaching exp: 10. District foundation raised over $1.3 million in 2004-2005 to pay for class size reduction and curriculum specialists. Summer enrichment and remedial programs.

Bullis Charter School is a tuition free, public school, sponsored by the Santa Clara County Office of Education. A small school with small class sizes, a challenging, enriched core academic program; many electives during school and optional electives afterschool. All children have individual learning plans designed to help them reach their potential using their unique strengths. Project based learning. Emphasis on visual and performing arts, environmental studies and service learning. The school uses a global perspective to teach about the interconnectedness of communities and their environments. For further information, go to www.bullischarterschool.com or phone 650-947-4939.

LOS GATOS - SARATOGA UNION HIGH

17421 Farley Road West, Los Gatos, CA 95030. Phone: 408-354-2520. Fax: 408-354-3375. www.lgsuhsd.org. Superintendent: Dr. Cynthia Hall Ranii. Gr.9 to 12. 2,948 students. Avg. class size: 28.

Two high schools (9-12). Avg. enrollment: 1,475. 1:23 teacher to student ratio. 5 students per computer. Science labs, Olympic size pools, theater on Saratoga campus. French, Spanish, Italian, German, Japanese, Chinese. Many AP courses at both campuses. Open campus at Los Gatos H.S.; open for upper grades at Saratoga. 76% students fulfill UC req. Saratoga: 72% of grads attend 4 yr college, 27% attend a 2 yr college. Los Gatos: 65% attend a 4 yr college, 32% attend a 2 yr college. 94% of teachers credentialed. Avg. yrs. teaching exp: 17. In recent years, the district foundations have raised about $4 - $6 million per year.

Nova is an alternative transition program with no more than 15 students per teacher that offers a core class with an interdisciplinary approach to instruction. The program helps students develop a love of learning while helping them improve attendance and study skills, manage anger, and learn behavioral responsibility. Students must make a commitment to the program and adhere to its rules. Students typically stay in the program for one or two semesters.

Middle College Program at West Valley College is a cooperative program between Los Gatos-Saratoga High School District and the college. The program allows high school juniors and seniors residing in the district to complete their high school education while getting a head start on earning a college degree. The program is designed for students who are capable of handling a rigorous academic program and will thrive at a supportive school in an enriched and flexible educational setting. Students must have a good attendance record and at least a 2.5. GPA Informational meetings are held in October and at the college. An extensive application package must be completed by the due date. For more information, phone 408-741-4038.

LOS GATOS UNION ELEMENTARY

15766 Poppy Lane, Los Gatos, CA 95030. Phone: 408-335-2000. Fax: 408-395-6481. www.lgusd.k12.ca.us. Superintendent: Mary Ann Park. Gr.K to 8. 2,597 students. Avg. class size: 25.

Four elem. schools (K-5). Avg. enrollment: 400. 1:20 teacher to student ratio. Aides in K-5. 3 students per computer. One mid. school (6-8). Enrollment: 1,000. 1:21 teacher to student ratio. 6 students per computer. Extended care at all elem. campuses, operated by Rec. Dept. Day care at one campus during spring and winter breaks. Computer labs, French and Spanish. District-wide character education program, inquiry-based science program which gives students hands-on experiences in life, earth, and physical sciences. Instrumental music, art docent program, substance abuse education. 99% of teachers credentialed. Avg. yrs. teaching exp: 17. District foundation raises over $1 million/yr. Summer recreation program through the Parks and Recreation Department and remedial programs.

LUTHER BURBANK ELEMENTARY

4 Wabash Avenue, San Jose, CA 95128. Phone: 408-295-2450. Fax: 408-295-3168. www.lbsd.k12.ca.us. Superintendent: Richard Rodriguez. Gr.K to 8. 440 students. Avg. class size: 22.

One elem. school (K-8). Enrollment: 450. 1:20 teacher to student ratio. 5 students per computer. Single track, year round school, 3 months on, 1 month off. Intersessions in December, April, July. One wk. intersession enrichment program at the beginning of each break. Uniforms. Homework club, Spanish. Afterschool activities program. GATE: enrichment in classroom setting. Computer lab. Fitness Center. District works closely with the Sheriff's Dept. and participates in the DARE program. 100% of teachers credentialed. 23% of teachers have adv. degrees. Avg. yrs. teaching exp: 6.

MILPITAS UNIFIED

1331 E. Calaveras Boulevard, Milpitas, CA 95035. Phone: 408-945-2300. Fax: 408-945-2421. www.musd.org. Superintendent: Dr. Karl Black. Gr.K to 12. 9,303 students. Avg. class size: 29.

Nine elem. schools (K-6). Avg. enrollment: 550. 1:22 teacher to student ratio. 6 students per computer. Most elem. sites have extended care. Two mid. schools (7-8). Avg. enrollment: 750. 1:23 teacher to student ratio. 6 students per computer. One of the most diverse school communities in the US; 50 languages, 20 dialects. Numerous business partnerships. Uniforms required at all schools, waiver avail. Open enrollment district. (Sinnott currently closed to open enrollment requests.) Applications for residents wishing to enroll in a school other than the "school of record" accepted in March for April lottery. Sheltered English Language Development Program at Rancho Middle School, gr.7-8, for students who need intense English language instruction. 100% of teachers credentialed. Avg. yrs. teaching exp: 12. Summer academic program for students who need additional credits to graduate.

Milpitas High School (9-12). Avg. enrollment: 2,700. 1:24 teacher to student ratio. 5 students per computer. Closed campus. Honors and AP classes. Spanish and French. One counselor/550 students. 35% students fulfill UC req.

Digital Business, Travel and Tourism, and Engineering and Technology Academy Programs, funded by local businesses and grants, are 3 yr. programs offered to sophomores who wish a technical or career focus. Academies include industry and college opportunities, fieldtrips, speakers, mentors, integrated curriculum and summer internship opportunities. Academic classes meet CSU and UC requirements.

MONTEBELLO ELEMENTARY

15101 Montebello Road, Cupertino, CA 95014. Phone: 408-867-3618. Fax: 408-867-8627. www.montebelloschool.org. Superintendent: Dr. Rodney Gabrielson. Gr.K to 6. 44 students. Avg. class size: 9.

One elem. school (K-6). Enrollment: 50. 1:14 teacher to student ratio. 2 students per computer. Bus transportation. Pullout help for LD students; those who need more help granted interdistrict transfers. Music, school play, field trips, Spanish available. Students are given individual attention within small group setting. 75% of teachers credentialed. Avg. yrs. teaching exp: 10. District foundation.

MORELAND ELEMENTARY

4835 Doyle Road, San Jose, CA 95129. Phone: 408-874-2900. Fax: 408-996-2370. www.moreland.k12.ca.us. Superintendent: Leslie Adelson. Gr.K to 8. 4,013 students. Avg. class size: 27.

Six elem. schools (K-5). Avg. enrollment: 425. 1:20 teacher to student ratio. 4 students per computer. Two mid. schools (6-8). Avg. enrollment: 725. 1:25 teacher to student ratio. 6 students per computer. Uniforms at Rogers Middle School, Latimer, Easterbrook and Country Lane. Extended care at all elem. sites, closed on school holidays. Choral music for gr.4-5; instrumental music gr.4-8. Computer labs and business partnerships at all schools. New multimedia centers at elem. sites. GATE programs incorporated in curriculum and offered afterschool at some sites. Will consider interdistrict transfers if space available. 99% of teachers credentialed. Avg. yrs. teaching exp: 13. District foundation raises $100,000/yr. Summer camp, enrichment, remedial.

Easterbrook Discovery School embraces a developmental philosophy towards education and requires parent participation. Emphasis on small groups, hands-on activity based learning, differentiated instruction. Priority given to students residing within the Easterbrook boundary area and siblings of current students. If space available, other students within the Moreland district welcome.

MORGAN HILL UNIFIED

15600 Concord Circle, Morgan Hill, CA 95037. Phone: 408-201-6023. Fax: 408-779-2124. www.mhu.k12.ca.us. Superintendent: Carolyn McKennan. Gr.K to 12. 8,797 students. Avg. class size: 28.

Ten elem. schools (K-6). Avg. enrollment: 500. 1:21 teacher to student ratio. Max class size: K, 20; gr.1-3, 20; upper grades, 29. 8 students per computer. Two mid. schools (7-8). Avg. enrollment: 1,000. 1:25 teacher to student ratio. 5 students per computer. Extended care available at most sites. Uniforms at some elem. sites. Extensive technology labs. GATE integrated into classroom. 87% of teachers credentialed. Avg. yrs. teaching exp: 14. Summer programs for at-risk students.

Two high schools (9-12). Avg. enrollment: 900. 1:23 teacher to student ratio. 4 students per computer. Award-winning journalism, drama, dance & art programs; extensive electives include clothing design, welding & woodworking. One counselor/530 students. 15 AP classes offered. German, French, Spanish. 37% students fulfill UC req.

Morgan Hill Charter School is a K-gr.8 school which "through strong family involvement, community interaction, and project-based learning develops lifelong learners prepared to be innovative participants in the global community." Priority to siblings and to Morgan Hill Unified residents during open enrollment period, but anyone from California may attend. www.csmh.org; 408-463-0618.

MOUNT PLEASANT ELEMENTARY

3434 Marten Avenue, San Jose, CA 95148. Phone: 408-223-3700. Fax: 408-223-3799. www.mountpleasant.k12.ca.us. Superintendent: George Perez. Gr.K to 8. 2,906 students. Avg. class size: 26.

Four elem. schools (two K-3, one K-4, one 4-6). Avg. enrollment: 575. 1:20 teacher to student ratio. Max class size: K, 20; gr.1-3, 20; upper grades, 33. 5 students per computer. One mid. school (7-8). Enrollment: 625. 1:22 teacher to student ratio. 5 students per computer. All schools require uniforms. Extended care at Valle Vista from 6:30 AM - 6:30 PM, open during school holidays. Computer labs and homework center at each school. Afterschool mentoring program. GATE: pull-out and interest groups. Dual immersion at Robert Saunders and Ida Jew. Migrant education program. 90% of teachers credentialed. Avg. yrs. teaching exp: 12. Summer school.

MOUNTAIN VIEW - LOS ALTOS UNION HIGH

1299 Bryant Avenue, Mountain View, CA 94040. Phone: 650-940-4650. Fax: 408-961-1346. www.mvla.net. Superintendent: Richard Fischer. Gr.9 to 12. 3,271 students. Avg. class size: 29.

Two high schools (9-12). Avg. enrollment: 1,625. 1:21 teacher to student ratio. 5 students per computer. 7+ periods/day. Tutorial and career centers staffed with paid paraprofessionals. Open campus. Community service integrated into the curriculum. One counselor/400 students; freshmen guidance monitoring program. Honors and AP classes. 18 AP courses; Spanish, Japanese, French, Latin. 54% students fulfill UC req. 96% of teachers credentialed. Avg. yrs. teaching exp: 12. District foundation raises $500,000/yr.

Middle College Program at Foothill College is designed for 90 juniors and seniors who are interested in learning but have been turned off in the large comprehensive high school environment. Students complete requirements for high school graduation while having the opportunity to enroll in up to nine units of college classes per quarter and have access to Foothill's facilities and services. Students must be enrolled or eligible to enroll in the Mountain View-Los Altos Union High School District or the Palo Alto Unified School District. Recruitment meetings at high school campuses in March. 650-949-7168. www.middlecollege@hotmail.com.

MOUNTAIN VIEW - WHISMAN ELEMENTARY

750-A San Pierre Way, Mountain View, CA 94043. Phone: 650-526-3500. Fax: 650-964-8907. www.mvwsd.k12.ca.us. Superintendent: Dr. Maurice Ghysels. Gr.K to 8. 4,440 students. Avg. class size: 26.

Seven elem. schools (K-5). Avg. enrollment: 450. 1:20 teacher to student ratio. 5 students per computer. Two mid. school (6-8). Avg. enrollment: 675. 1:22 teacher to student ratio. 5 students per computer. Extended care at all schools through YMCA. Parents are encouraged to visit and volunteer in classrooms. GATE integrated into classroom. Special programs: shadowing (students spend day at work sites), peer counseling and tutoring, migrant education programs, ELD. CHAC counselors. Project Cause, a partnership between the district and the community, implements programs to motivate students to stay in school. Interdistrict transfers granted when space available. 96% of teachers credentialed. Avg. yrs. teaching exp: 12. District Foundation raises over $250,000/yr. Summer school includes remedial classes and programs through YMCA and Mtn. View Rec. Dept.

Two-Way Language Immersion Program at Castro School unites native English-speaking and native Spanish-speaking students in the same classroom. In K-gr.2, most instruction in Spanish with increased English instruction each year. By gr.5, instruction is evenly split between the two languages and children are fluent in both. Monthly parent meetings. Lottery held in March to determine enrollment.

Parent Child Teacher (PACT) at Slater School is a parent participation program that is child-centered, develops critical thinking skills, actively teaches interpersonal skills, and includes experiential and hands-on learning. The classroom environment encourages children to be self-reliant and promotes growth, initiative, self-respect, and a desire to learn. Parent participation required. If Slater closes as scheduled in June 2006, PACT will move to Castro School.

OAK GROVE ELEMENTARY

6578 Santa Teresa Boulevard, San Jose, CA 95119. Phone: 408-227-8300. Fax: 408-227-2719. www.ogsd.k12.ca.us. Superintendent: Manny Barbara. Gr.K to 8. 11,614 students. Avg. class size: 26.

Sixteen elem. schools (K-6). Avg. enrollment: 575. 1:21 teacher to student ratio. 7 students per computer. Three mid. schools (7-8). Avg. enrollment: 850. 1:22 teacher to student ratio. Max class size: K, 20; gr.1-3, 20; upper grades, 30. 4 students per computer. 94% of teachers credentialed. Avg. yrs. teaching exp: 15.

ORCHARD ELEMENTARY

921 Fox Lane, San Jose, CA 95131. Phone: 408-944-0397. Fax: 408-944-0394. www.nosd.org. Superintendent: Dr. Lorna Horton. Gr.K to 8. 817 students. Avg. class size: 25.

One elem. school. Enrollment: 825. 1:21 teacher to student ratio. 7 students per computer. Onsite extended care, open on school holidays. Computer lab, art program, sports programs. 97% of teachers credentialed. Avg. yrs. teaching exp: 12. Partnership w/ Phillips.

PALO ALTO UNIFIED

25 Churchill Avenue, Palo Alto, CA 94306. Phone: 650-329-3700. Fax: 650-326-7463. www.pausd.org. Superintendent: Dr. Mary Frances Callan. Gr.K to 12. 10,648 students. Avg. class size: 20.

Twelve elem. schools (K-5). Avg. enrollment: 400. 1:18 teacher to student ratio. Aides in most K-gr.5 classes. 4 students per computer. Three mid. schools (6-8). Avg. enrollment: 775. 1:16 teacher to student ratio. 4 students per computer. Extended care at all elem. sites; open during some school holidays. Needs of GATE students met through classroom enrichment. Complete scope of special education programs. Technology integrated into classroom curriculum. Classroom visits encouraged. Register for schools under open enrollment in Feb-March. 100% of teachers credentialed. Avg. yrs. teaching exp: 12. District foundation raised $1.8 million for '05-'06 school year. Enrichment summer program.

Palo Alto and Gunn High Schools (9-12): Avg. enrollment: 1,500-1,600. Avg. class size 28.5. 1:19 teacher to student ratio. 4 students per computer. Seven period day. Gunn has 3 counselors; Palo Alto has teacher-advisors and 1 counselor. Both schools have a college advisor. Tutorial and academic centers. Many multicultural events and human relations activities. Spectra Art (identified by Carnegie Foundation as one of seven quality art programs in the nation), traveling music, and sports teams. 73% students fulfill UC req. 76% of grads attend 4 yr. colleges; 16% attend 2 yr. colleges. District offers Spanish, French, German, and Japanese; honors classes; many AP classes, ROP classes; music, drama, myriad of electives and a variety of options for completing high school. Both schools named 2 of top 5 high schools in Calif. by "College Prep," a publication of the College Board.

The following alternative schools are open to all students in the district; students selected by lottery in Feb.

Escondido's Spanish Immersion Program is designed to develop full bilingualism. English-speaking students and native Spanish speakers are taught together using Spanish and English instruction to develop bilingual academic fluency. The program begins in kindergarten and continues through fifth grade or middle school. The program aims to:

- Develop bilingual proficiency and literacy in Spanish and English
- Promote academic achievement at or above grade level in both languages
- Foster positive cross-cultural attitudes

Hoover offers a more structured learning environment than other PAUSD elementary schools. Teachers emphasize core curriculum, basic academic skills, and good study habits. The school is characterized by a quiet, orderly environment; self-contained, single-grade classrooms; teacher-initiated and directed activities; regular measurement of student progress through testing and grades.

Ohlone Alternative School's open school philosophy focuses on developmental education. Classrooms emphasize open-ended activities, personalized instruction, and peer tutoring. Teachers facilitate academic, social, and emotional learning. Classes are organized into two or three year cross-age groupings, and students progress at their own rate. The school emphasizes human relations and a problem-solving approach to arguments. Competition is de-emphasized. Grades are not given. Parent participation is integral.

Young Fives program is for children who are age eligible but not ready for kindergarten because they exhibit signs of immaturity. Parents participate once a week in the classroom and in monthly evening discussion sessions.

Middle School Programs
PAUSD offers several choice programs for grades 6-8. Admission is granted through a lottery system. Information packets are mailed to parents of 5th grade students in January. Applications are due in early April.

Direct Instruction (6th grade offered at all schools; 6-8th grade offered only at Terman). This program emphasizes basic academic skills and student acquisition of knowledge and skills. Focus is on core academic subjects in discrete, single-subject areas (rather than an interdisciplinary approach) of English, mathematics, social studies, and science. Emphasis is placed on the accountability of individual students, rather than on groups of students. Explicit teaching pedagogy is used in which teachers guide lessons and students respond, rather than teacher "coaching" or "facilitating".

The Connections program is a 3-year program offered at JLS which takes an interdisciplinary approach to teaching core subjects. A "village" of teachers, students, and parents within the larger school community focuses on interactive, project-based, experiential learning through hands-on experiences and field trips. The program emphasizes:

- Connections among various disciplines—teachers have a block of three to five periods to focus on an interdisciplinary approach to topics

- Connections among students and student-centered learning—students are responsible for their own progress by setting goals and assessing their progress while teachers serve mainly as guides and mentors

- Connections between curriculum and students' lives—core curriculum and student interests are enhanced with examples from current events and field trips

- Connections between curriculum and community—community and environmental service projects are part of the curriculum

Spanish Immersion (3-year program offered at Jordan) The middle school Spanish Immersion program is a continuation of the bilingual curriculum of elementary Spanish Immersion. For students who have been promoted from the elementary bilingual program at Escondido as well as other students who demonstrate grade-level bilingual fluency in Spanish and English.

Middle College Program at Foothill College. See description under Mountain View-Los Altos Union High School District.

SAN JOSE UNIFIED

855 Lenzen Avenue, San Jose, CA 95126. Phone: 408-535-6000. Fax: 408-535-2362. www.sjusd.org. Superintendent: Don Iglesias. Gr.K to 12. 26,850 students. Avg. class size: 30.

Twenty-six elem. schools (mostly K-5, one K-2, one K-3, one K-8, one gr.3-5). Avg. enrollment: 500. 1:19 teacher to student ratio. 3 students per computer. Six mid. schools (6-8). Avg. enrollment: 1,025. 1:21 teacher to student ratio. 3 students per computer. Uniforms at all elem. schools except Reed and all mid. schools except Bret Harte. On-site extended care at 19 elem. sites. Transportation provided for K-5 students who live 1.5 miles or more from their school, gr.6-12 students who live 3.5 miles or more from their school, or students for whom walking would be hazardous. 11 schools participates in robotics program. GATE programs offered at each elem. site according to the school's resources and environment. All elementary schools have classroom mini-labs, computer labs in the media center or classroom computer labs. Many programs incorporate technology, science, fine arts, and the development of leadership skills. "Break Through" college prep for middle school students, Spanish, French, ASL. Extensive business partnerships through the Adopt-a-School Program. 94% of teachers credentialed. 9 Avg. yrs. teaching exp: District foundation. Summer school at all levels.

Seven high schools (9-12). Avg. enrollment: 1,100. 1:22 teacher to student ratio. 2 students per computer. Closed campuses. Tutorial centers. Honors and advanced placement classes at all high schools. 65% students fulfill UC req. Visual arts are emphasized at Castillero and Hoover middle schools and at Lincoln High School. Preparation for the International Baccalaureate is offered at Burnett Middle and San Jose High Academy.

To learn more about the enrollment process and the focus of individual neighborhood schools and the special programs they offer, parents can go the district's website or obtain the Parents' Guides to Elementary (K-5) and Secondary Schools (6-12) from the Burnett Information and Enrollment Center at 408-535-6412 or Erickson Center at 408-535-6436.

Elementary magnet schools:

Hacienda Environmental Science Magnet is dedicated to teaching students to explore the natural world around them. One-acre outdoor classroom site features California native plants and pond communities. All students study science with a resource teacher as well as with the classroom teachers. Specialized instruction in science, including scheduled indoor and outdoor laboratory lessons and a computer-training center. The school also has a balanced music program, an Accelerated Reading Program for gr.1-5, and a cross-age tutoring program to help struggling readers in K-2. Accelerated math in grades three and five.

Hammer Montessori, K-5 at Galarza. The Montessori classroom is divided into special learning areas that include practical life, sensorial, language arts, mathematics, geography, history, science, and the arts. Individual and small group instruction. Uniquely designed and sequenced "hands-on" materials help isolate skills and lead the child through the curriculum. Teachers help children choose challenging materials to discover underlying concepts that lead to mastery of skills. Additional Hammer programs include PeaceBuilders, Cornerstone, SPARK PE, and Accelerated Reader.

River Glen Two-Way Spanish Language Immersion Magnet offers K-8 students the opportunity to learn to communicate naturally in Spanish and English. Our goal is to educate students who are bilingual and biliterate and enable them to meet the challenges of a global society. Within a nine-year time frame, students acquire the skills to read, write, speak, listen, and think in two languages. Every student, staff member, and parent is involved in the immersion program and its philosophy. Enrollment occurs primarily at the kindergarten level. Parents are required to attend an orientation meeting prior to choosing River Glen on the selection form.

Downtown College Prep (DCP) is a charter high school designed to provide a college prep program to students who underachieve in core academic subjects and will be the first college graduates in their family. The school's culture of achievement is fueled by high expectations and personalized attention. DCP has a singular goal for every student: graduates of DCP are able to matriculate at four-year colleges and succeed while there. College readiness classes, tutorials, and a focus on literacy and numeracy help students to achieve this goal. DCP performance outcomes are designed to promote academic resilience and independence among students and families. For more information, call 408-271-1730 or view the school's website www.downtowncollegeprep.org

SANTA CLARA UNIFIED

1889 Lawrence Road, Santa Clara, CA 95051. Phone: 408-423-2000. Fax: 408-423-2283. www.scu.k12.ca.us. Superintendent: Paul Perotti. Gr.K to 12. 13,499 students. Avg. class size: 29.

Sixteen elem. schools (K-5). Avg. enrollment: 425. 1:19 teacher to student ratio. 4 students per computer. Three mid. schools (6-8). Avg. enrollment: 1,050. 1:23 teacher to student ratio. 5 students per computer. Extended care at some elem. sites. GATE: pull-out for gr.4-5. State-of-the-art technology. Very active partnership program with over 100 private sector partners. 95% of teachers credentialed. Avg. yrs. teaching exp: 12.

Two high schools (9-12). Avg. enrollment: 1,800. 1:25 teacher to student ratio. 4 students per computer. Tutorial centers, 1 counselor/600 students. Six period day. Wilson High School offers an independent study program. 36% students fulfill UC req.

District has open enrollment policy; families interested in attending schools outside their attendance area should sign up in Jan. for district lottery. Acceptance into the following alternative programs, open to all families in the district, is determined by an annual lottery.

Millikin School's Basics + Formal Education Program open to any youngster in the Santa Clara Unified School District whose parents desire a more structured method of teaching. The program places high value on teaching academic skills in a self-contained setting. Emphasis is placed on a phonetic approach to reading, and all subjects are taught in a traditional manner.

Open Classroom Alternative at Washington School provides a loving and enriching environment where children can learn in their own way, at their own pace. The program emphasizes involvement of parents in the classroom so that learning can be an on-going process at home and school. Parent participation is required. Children receive individualized instruction and many choices of learning experiences. The primary objectives of this program are to develop in students a positive self-image, social responsibility, competence in the basic skills, aesthetic judgment, and creativity.

SARATOGA UNION ELEMENTARY

20460 Forrest Hills, Saratoga, CA 95070. Phone: 408-867-3424. Fax: 408-868-1539. www.saratogausd.org. Superintendent: Lane Weiss. Gr.K to 8. 2,413 students. Avg. class size: 27.

Three elem. schools (K-5). Avg. enrollment: 500. 1:21 teacher to student ratio. Aides used in K-gr.5. 3 students per computer. One mid. school (6-8). Enrollment: 950. 1:22 teacher to student ratio. 4 students per computer. Extended care at all elem. sites, 7:30 AM - 6 PM, open on school holidays. Vocal music for K-gr.5; instrumental gr.5-8. Business partnerships, computer labs, mentorships for highly gifted (e.g., NASA mentorship in science), accelerated math and science programs, French Connection (5th grade exchange program). GATE coordinator and classroom teachers present GATE programs to all students. Vertical acceleration for students who master subject material. 97% of teachers credentialed. Avg. yrs. teaching exp: 10. District foundation raised over $1.1 million for 2005-2006.

SUNNYVALE ELEMENTARY

819 W. Iowa Avenue, Sunnyvale, CA 94086. Phone: 408-522-8200. Fax: 408-522-8338. www.sesd.org. Superintendent: Dr. Joseph Rudnicki. Gr.K to 8. 5,967 students. Avg. class size: 27.

Eight elem. schools (K-5). Avg. enrollment: 500. 1:20 teacher to student ratio. 6 students per computer. Two mid. schools (6-8). Avg. enrollment: 950. 1:20 teacher to student ratio. 5 students per computer. All elem. sites have extended care 6:30 AM - 6:30 PM, open on school holidays. All schools have at least one business partner. All schools have computer labs; GATE at all sites, afterschool activities. Uniforms at Bishop, San Miguel, Vargas, and Lakewood. Sites modernized. 94% of teachers credentialed. Avg. yrs. teaching exp: 11. District foundation raises about $1 million/yr. Summer programs for students needing assistance.

UNION ELEMENTARY

5175 Union Avenue, San Jose, CA 95124. Phone: 408-377-8010. Fax: 408-377-7182. www.unionsd.org. Superintendent: Phil J. Quon. Gr.K to 8. 3,876 students. Avg. class size: 27.

Six elem. schools (K-5). Avg. enrollment: 375. 1:21 teacher to student ratio. 4 students per computer. Two mid. schools (6-8). Avg. enrollment: 825. 1:22 teacher to student ratio. 6 students per computer. Extended care at all elem. sites, 6 AM - 6 PM. GATE integrated into classroom. Each school has business partnership, computer lab, homework centers. Afterschool fee-based music program at elem. sites; mid. schools have music programs. Strong staff development program. 98% of teachers credentialed. Avg. yrs. teaching exp: 14. Summer school programs for special ed. and remedial.

DIRECTORY OF
PRIVATE SCHOOLS

Grade one, Our Lady of Mt. Carmel School, Redwood City, 1946

EXPLANATORY NOTES
FOR PRIVATE SCHOOL LISTINGS

In the summer of 2005, we contacted nearly every private school in Santa Clara and San Mateo Counties and every San Francisco private high school. No established private school has been intentionally omitted from this book. Every reasonable effort has been made to see that the listings in the directory are accurate. The authors assume no responsibility for inadvertent errors.

All information in the directory portion of this book was provided by the schools themselves. The authors cannot guarantee that the information provided is accurate. Parents should use the directory as a tool to identify which schools might meet their needs. They then should evaluate the schools for themselves by using the guidelines provided in the first section of this book.

Schools are divided by into three sections—elementary, high, and special education. Within each section, they are listed alphabetically by city. Schools that serve only grades six through eight are listed under high schools. If a school fits into more than one category, it may be cross-referenced.

Schools were asked to indicate the number of school days per year and how many instructional periods constituted a school day. (By law, public schools must have at least 175 instructional days a year.)

Kindergarten is noted with K.

Most, but not all, private schools that have extended day care charge extra for this service. Schools were asked if childcare is available during school vacations that are not legal holidays. If you need extended day care but are interested in a school that does not offer it, ask whether local day care centers or licensed homes serve children from the school.

High Schools were asked to indicate whether they have a closed or open campus (see explanation on page 64).

Class size: Average and maximum class size can vary from year to year and by grade and course offering. Many schools use aides and/or specialists in areas like physical education and music, so the student/staff ratio is smaller than the average class size. If schools indicated that this ratio is substantially smaller than the class size, the ratio is also given.

Tuition: Schools were asked to list their tuition and incidental fees for the 2005-06 school year. Many schools offer sibling discounts. Preschool fees are not listed. Most schools raise tuition at least every two or three years; many raise it annually. Unless otherwise noted, the tuition listed is per year. Parochial Catholic schools usually have a range of tuition, with the lowest rate for parishioners, a slightly higher rate for Catholics who are not part of the parish, and a higher rate for non-Catholics. Some schools reported the range; others just gave the basic rate.

Financial aid: Schools were asked to approximate the percentage of students receiving financial aid. Because the amount of financial aid available varies year-to-year, many schools just indicated fin. aid avail. to show that tuition reductions are granted to needy students when possible. Some schools reserve scholarship money for students who are already in the school but whose families can no longer afford tuition. Most, but not all, schools reserve financial aid for families that demonstrate financial need. A few schools give merit scholarships.

Middle Schools: If a private middle school is part of a K-8 school, it will be described in the elementary school section of the book. If it is a stand alone grade 6-8 school or part of a grade 6-12 high school, it will be described in the high school section.

Teacher information: Schools were asked the average years of teaching experience of their faculty and the percentage of teachers who have teaching credentials or advanced degrees.

Curriculum specialists: Private schools often hire specialists to teach different aspects of the curriculum, e.g., science, art, drama. Physical Education is noted with PE.

Special Education: Many private schools will take students with learning differences if they feel the student can benefit from their program; schools were asked to indicate whether they have on-site learning (LD) specialists (sometimes referred to as resource specialists) to help those students.

Special programs and facilities: Schools were asked to list special facilities and programs beyond basic academic instruction. Some did this in great detail; others did not. Therefore, some schools may have state-of-the-art libraries and after-school sports even though they did not list them.

Application procedures: Many schools list an application deadline but also state that they have rolling admissions. This indicates that, if classes do not fill up after the published deadline, they will continue to consider applications until the school is full. Almost all schools give priority to siblings of students currently enrolled in the school as long as the sibling is academically qualified. Schools with religious affiliations usually give priority to members of the sponsoring church.

Parent Participation: Many private schools require parent participation. There are many ways parents can fill these obligations: working in classrooms or in the school office, fundraising, and driving for field trips. Schools were asked to indicate how many hours of such help is required per year.

Accreditation: See explanation on page 30.

College preparatory: High schools were asked what percentage of their graduates attend four and two year colleges. They were also asked for most recent SAT scores (see explanation in appendix) and the percentage of students who usually take the test. Some schools provided this information but many did not. In addition, they were asked what percentage of their graduates fulfill the course requirements for the University of California.

Philosophy: The last paragraph of each listing includes the school's stated philosophy; it does not convey the authors' own evaluation of the extent to which that philosophy is carried out.

To the best of our knowledge, no school listed in this directory discriminates on the basis of race or national origin.

PRIVATE ELEMENTARY SCHOOLS
IN SAN MATEO AND SANTA CLARA COUNTIES

SAINT JOSEPH'S SCHOOL OF THE SACRED HEART   Atherton

50 Emilie Avenue, Atherton, CA 94027. Phone: 650-322-9931. www.shschools.org. Head: Dr. Joseph Ciancaglini. Admissions: Wendy Quattlebaum. Est. 1906. Nonprofit. Catholic. Uniforms.

Gr. Pre-K to 8. 500 students. 1 to 18 teacher to student ratio. Max class size: 24. K Hrs: full day program. Elementary: 8 AM - 3 PM. Extended care hrs: 7:30 AM - 6 PM. Tuition: $15,000 - $21,760. Other fees: $100 - $400. 17% receive fin. aid. Specialists: drama, band, math, science, art, music, PE. French, Latin, Spanish. Library, networked computers. Flag football, basketball, soccer, baseball, softball, volleyball, tennis, track and field, swimming. App. deadline: January. 95% of teachers credentialed. Avg. yrs. teaching exp: 15. Accreditation: WASC, CAIS, Network of Sacred Heart Schools.

Sacred Heart Schools, Atherton, are part of a national and international Network of Sacred Heart Schools which offers an education that is marked by a distinctive spirit. An education at Sacred Heart Schools is strong in studies, serious in principles and rich in the spirit of life and love. It is the essence of a Sacred Heart School that it be deeply concerned for each student's total development: spiritual, intellectual, emotional and physical.

BELMONT OAKS ACADEMY   Belmont

2200 Carlmont Drive, Belmont, CA 94002. Phone: 650-593-6175. belmont.ca.schoolwebpages.com. Head: Pamela Clarke. Admissions: Christine Shales. Est. 1948. Uniforms.

Gr. K to 5. 215 students. 1 to 14 teacher to student ratio. Max class size: K, 14; gr. 1-3, 28; upper grades, 28. Classes with more students have 2 teachers. K Hrs: 8:30 AM - 2 PM. Elementary: 8:30 AM - 3 PM. Extended care hrs: 7 AM - 6 PM, $100/mo. Tuition: $7,400 - $7,550. Specialists: computers, music, art. Spanish. Swimming pool, computer lab. Physical education, afterschool sports, swimming lessons. App. deadline: March. Summer day camp.

Belmont Oaks Academy's philosophy of education begins with your child. We feel that it is the school's responsibility to challenge each student to work to the best of their ability, while meeting their individual needs. The school's proven curriculum is built on a strong foundation of reading, writing, math, science, and social studies.

GLORIA DEI LUTHERAN SCHOOL   Belmont
2600 Ralston Avenue, Belmont, CA 94002. Phone: 650-593-3361. www.gdluth.org. Head: Adam R Mateske. Est. 1970. Nonprofit. Lutheran. Dress code.

Gr. Pre-K to 8. 20 students. 1 to 9 teacher to student ratio. Avg. class size: 5. Aides in K. K Hrs: 8:30 AM - 3:30 PM, 8:30 AM - 12 PM. School hrs: 8:30 AM - 3:30 PM. Extended care hrs: 7:15 AM - 6 PM, $3/hr. Tuition: $4,295. Other fees: $175. 25% receive fin. aid. Specialists: music, technology. French. Volleyball, basketball, track. 3 students per computer. 4,000 books in library. Rolling admissions. Parent participation encouraged. 50% of teachers credentialed. Avg. yrs. teaching exp: 5. 50% of teachers post HW online. Standardized tests administered. Accreditation: Wisconsin Evangelical Lutheran Synod.

Since 1970, Gloria Dei Lutheran School has been preparing students for a lifetime of service to their Lord, families, and community. At Gloria Dei, we offer a caring and Christian environment that is dedicated to proclaiming the glory of God through excellence in education.

IMMACULATE HEART OF MARY SCHOOL   Belmont
1000 Alameda de las Pulgas, Belmont, CA 94002. Phone: 650-593-4265. Fax: 650-593-4342. www.ihmschoolbelmont.com. Head: Dr. Margaret C. Purcell. Est. 1952. Nonprofit. Catholic. Dress code.

Gr. K to 8. 306 students. Max class size: K, 18; gr. 1-3, 35; upper grades, 35. Aides in grades 1-5. Elementary: 8 AM - 3 PM. Extended care hrs: 7:30 AM - 6 PM. Specialists: math, science, computer, music, art, PE. Spanish. Afterschool sports and cheerleading. 1 student per computer. Safety Patrol, touring theater groups, field trips. Waiting list. Standardized tests administered. Accreditation: WASC.

We, the community of Immaculate Heart of Mary School, believe in the four-fold purpose of Catholic education: to teach Catholic doctrine and to proclaim Gospel values, to build a community, to worship, and to foster service. We value the uniqueness of each child and strive to develop the total person spiritually, morally, intellectually, culturally, socially, physically, and psychologically.

NOTRE DAME ELEMENTARY SCHOOL   Belmont
1200 Notre Dame Avenue, Belmont, CA 94002. Phone: 650-591-2209. Fax: 650-591-4798. www.nde.org. Head: Sister Dolores Quigg. Est. 1851. Nonprofit. Catholic. Uniforms.

Gr. 1 to 8. 260 students. Max class size: 35. Aides in grades K-5. School hrs: 8 AM - 2:45 PM. Monday dismissals at 12:30 PM. Tuition: $3,650. Other fees: $425. Specialists: music, computers. Spanish. Library, studio. Basketball, baseball, volleyball, tennis, track. Strong technology program, peer counseling, numerous community service programs. App. deadline: March. 100% of teachers credentialed. Avg. yrs. teaching exp: 7. Accreditation: WASC, WCEA.

Notre Dame Elementary, an independent Catholic school, is committed to developing the whole child in the tradition of the Sisters of Notre Dame de Namur. NDE is a caring, compassionate community, striving to provide a quality Catholic education by imparting Christian values and promoting community service as well as an awareness of the needs of others. At NDE, we seek to help our students master skills needed to succeed and discover within themselves a love of learning and a love for the spiritual life.

OUR LADY OF ANGELS SCHOOL   Burlingame

1328 Cabrillo Avenue, Burlingame, CA 94010. Phone: 650-343-9200. www.olaschoolk8.org. Head: Carol Bender. Est. 1928. Nonprofit. Catholic. Uniforms.

Gr. K to 8. 316 students. Avg. class size: 35. Max class size: 36. K Hrs: 8 AM - 12 PM. Elementary: 8 AM - 3 PM. Tuition: $3,400 for in-parish students, fin. aid avail. Other fees: $225. Specialists: writing, computer, science. Spanish. Computer and science labs. App. deadline: February. 100% of teachers credentialed. Avg. yrs. teaching exp: 20. Accreditation: WASC, WCEA.

Our Lady of Angels School is committed to providing a quality education emphasizing the spiritual, intellectual, social, cultural, psychological, and physical growth of each child. We believe that, to be a faith community, we must have as our model the gospel of Jesus Christ. As facilitators, the teachers work in partnership with the parents, the primary educators of the student. Together, we guide the students to an understanding of the dignity and worth of each person. We teach and model Christian values and offer educational programs that identify the needs and learning styles of all students.

SAINT CATHERINE OF SIENA SCHOOL   Burlingame

1300 Bayswater Avenue, Burlingame, CA 94010. Phone: 650-344-7176. Fax: 650-344-7426. www.stcatherineofsiena.net. Head: Penny Donovan. Admissions: Adrian Peterson. Est. 1938. Nonprofit. Catholic. Uniforms.

Gr. K to 8. 292 students. 1 to 30 teacher to student ratio. Max class size: K, 18; gr. 1-3, 35; upper grades, 35. Aides in grades K-5. K Hrs: 8 AM -11:15 AM, 11:45 AM - 3 PM. Elementary: 8 AM - 3 PM. Extended care hrs: 7 AM - 6 PM, $4/hr. Tuition: $3,910. Other fees: $275 registration. 16% receive fin. aid. Specialists: music, PE, computer technology. Spanish, Italian. Library, computer labs, science lab. PPSL sports for grades four through eight: baseball, volleyball, basketball, track. 5 students per computer. Full time reading specialist. Parent participation encouraged. 85% of teachers credentialed. 27% of teachers have adv. degrees. Standardized tests administered. Accreditation: WASC, WCEA.

St. Catherine of Siena Parochial School is committed to a Catholic education in which the faith experience and academic excellence empower the student to live out the Gospel message.

CAMPBELL CHRISTIAN SCHOOL　　　　　　　　　　Campbell

1075 West Campbell Avenue, Campbell, CA 95008. Phone: 408-370-4900. Fax: 408-370-4907. www.campbellchristian.org. Head: Shawn Stuart. Est. 1967. Nonprofit. Christian. Uniforms.

Gr. Pre-K to 5. 325 students. Avg. class size: 20. Max class size: 25. Elementary: 8 AM - 2:30 PM. Extended care hrs: 7 AM - 6 PM. Care open some holidays. Tuition: $4,084 - $5,388, with additional child discounts. Other fees: school supplies, field trips, extended care. Specialists: computers (new notebooks), music, art, drama, dance. Library with extensive volumes and periodicals. Physical education. App. deadline: February. Admissions test. Avg. yrs. teaching exp: 8. Ten-week summer program. Accreditation: ACSI.

Campbell Christian School commits to educational excellence in conjunction with biblical values. In the spiritual area, we desire that each child develop a Christian worldview, a love for God and a greater understanding of His attributes as God develops faith in them. In the socio-emotional area, it is the goal of the school to develop a child who realizes who he is and how he relates to authority, family, and peers. In the intellectual area, our philosophy emphasizes an active learning environment where each child is challenged and an enthusiasm for learning is developed. In the physical area, we are committed to teaching skills and teamwork as well as healthy care and appreciation of their bodies.

CANYON HEIGHTS ACADEMY　　　　　　　　　　　Campbell

775 Waldo Road, Campbell, CA 95008. Phone: 408-984-2600. Fax: 408-985-7904. www.canyonheightsacademy.com. Head: Paul Parker. Admissions: Kasia Ostrowski. Est. 2000. Nonprofit. Uniforms.

Gr. K to 8. Avg. class size: 12. Max class size: 20. K Hrs: 8:30 AM - 3:15 PM. Elementary: 8:30 AM - 3:15 PM. Extended care hrs: 7:30 AM - 6 PM. Tuition: $7,500. Specialists: religion, fine arts, health. Latin, Spanish. Computers in classrooms and lab. Physical education, gymnastics, soccer. Music, art, retreats, drawing, ceramics, chess club, science club. App. deadline: February. Parent participation encouraged. 75% of teachers credentialed. Avg. yrs. teaching exp: 9. Summer camp.

The mission of Canyon Heights Academy is to provide the highest quality education which addresses all aspects of the human person; not only the child's mind, but the character and soul as well. Our school is committed to fostering Christian maturity in the fullness of the Catholic faith and developing the characteristics of true leadership so that each student can live out to the fullest the will of God for his or her life.

CASA DI MIR MONTESSORI SCHOOL　　　　　　　Campbell

90 East Latimer Avenue, Campbell, CA 95008. Phone: 408-370-3073. Fax: 408-370-3153. www.casadimir.org. Head: Wanda Whitehead. Admissions: Elanah Kutik. Est. 1989. Nonprofit. Dress code.

Gr. Pre-K to 6. 100 students. 1 to 15 teacher to student ratio. Max class size: K, 15; gr. 1-3, 15; upper grades, 30. Lower elementary runs 8:30 AM - 3:15 PM, Upper elementary runs 8 AM - 2:45 PM. Extended care hrs: 7 AM - 6 PM, $7/hr. Tuition: $8,800 Elementary, $7,250 Preschool. Other fees: $420 Elementary, $320 Preschool. 10% receive fin. aid. Specialists: art, music (Orff), aikido. Spanish. Computer lab, after school care, after school tutoring. 6 students per computer. Emphasis on cultural diversity, study of other cultures, peace education. App. deadline: March. Parent participation encouraged. 80% of teachers credentialed. 50% of teachers have adv. degrees. Avg. yrs. teaching exp: 15. Standardized tests administered. Accreditation: American Montessori Society.

Our core philososphy is to encourage and nurture the whole child, true to Dr. Maria Montessori's educational vision. Within each child is the innate joy in learning and the tremendous desire to grow healthy and strong - intellectually, emotionally, physically. Our Montessori learning environment enables the child to master academic skills, entices curiosity, creativity, and love of learning. It also encourages positive social skills such as effective communication, problem solving and acknowledges the uniqueness of each child.

OLD ORCHARD SCHOOL   Campbell
400 West Campbell, Campbell, CA 95008. Phone: 408-378-5935. Fax: 408-341-0782. www.oldorchardschool.com. Head: Bonnie Weston. Admissions: Bonnie Weston. Est. 1973. Uniforms.

Gr. Pre-K to 8. 150 students. 1 to 6 teacher to student ratio. Max class size: K-3, 24; upper grades, 30. Upper grades' academic classes limited to 15. Aides in grades K-5. K Hrs: 8:30 AM - 3 PM. School hrs: gr. K-5: 8:30 AM - 3 PM, gr. 6-8: 8 - 3:30 PM. Extended care hrs: 7:30 AM - 6 PM, $5.50/hr. Tuition: $11,000 - $12,500. Other fees: supplies, field trips expenses. Specialists: art, music, performing arts, computer arts, PE. Latin, Spanish. Computer labs. School divided into two campuses. Afterschool sports league: football, volleyball, basketball. 1 student per computer. Active visual and performing arts programs. Each grade prepares/performs a play/musical each year. Formal character Ed program in middle school. Advisory program. Reasonable classroom accomodations for mild LD students. 2 applicants per space. Rolling admissions. Waiting list. 90% of teachers credentialed. 85% of teachers have adv. degrees. Avg. yrs. teaching exp: 10. 40% of teachers post HW online. Standardized tests administered.

Students are taught to read with insight, write with clarity, speak effectively, and listen with curiosity and concern. Because education includes the development of character, creativity and confidence, Old Orchard School supplements the academics with a program of fine arts to help shape well-rounded individuals.

SAINT LUCY SCHOOL   Campbell

76 East Kennedy Avenue, Campbell, CA 95008. Phone: 408-871-8023. Fax: 408-378-4945. www.stlucyschool.org. Head: Jolene Schmitz. Est. 1953. Nonprofit. Catholic. Uniforms.

Gr. K to 8. 321 students. Max class size: 36. Aides in grades K-5. K Hrs: 8:13 AM - 11:20 AM, 11:50 AM - 3 PM. Elementary: 8 AM - 3 PM. Minimum day hours: 8 AM - 12:30 PM. Extended care hrs: 6:30 AM - 6 PM. Tuition: $5,950, fin. aid avail. Other fees: $350. Specialists: art, computer, PE. Spanish. Multimedia center, computer lab, gymnasium. Football, volleyball, basketball, softball, track. App. deadline: February. Admissions test. Waiting list. Parent participation required. 90% of teachers credentialed. Standardized tests administered. Academic summer program. Accreditation: WASC, WCEA.

Together teachers, parents and students pursue the educational mission of the Church in proclaiming the message of the Gospels, fostering the development of community, serving the community in need and coming together in celebration and worship. St. Lucy Parish School guides its students to develop an appreciation for learning and offers an education of academic excellence. We recognize our responsibility to create an atmosphere that will maximize each child's potential spiritually, morally, intellectually, physically, psychologically and socially.

SAN JOSE CHRISTIAN SCHOOL   Campbell

1300 Sheffield Avenue, Campbell, CA 95008. Phone: 408-371-7741. Fax: 408-371-5596. www.sjchristian.org. Head: Al Kosters. Admissions: Reba Ezell. Est. 1959. Nonprofit. Christian. Dress code.

Gr. Pre-K to 8. 311 students. 1 to 14 teacher to student ratio. Avg. class size: 18. Max class size: K, 26; gr. 1-3, 28; upper grades, 28. Aides in grades K-5. K Hrs: 8:30 AM - 11:45 PM, 8:30 AM - 3 PM. Elementary: 8:30 AM - 3 PM. Extended care hrs: 7 AM - 6 PM, $3.75/hr. Care open some holidays. Tuition: $4,675 - $8,030. Other fees: $100 enrollment. 10% receive fin. aid. Specialists: art, vocal music, instrumental music, PE, computers. Spanish. Mobile computer lab, a wireless laptop for each student. Softball, basketball, volleyball, soccer, track. 4 students per computer. 3,000 books in library. Bible classes, field trips, computer courses, band, and choir. Learning assistance for students in reading and math. Rolling admissions. Admissions test. Parent participation encouraged. 100% of teachers credentialed. 20% of teachers have adv. degrees. Avg. yrs. teaching exp: 12. 100% of teachers post HW online. Standardized tests administered. Summer day camp for enrolled families. Accreditation: Christian Schools International and National Council for Private School Accreditation.

San Jose Christian School supports and strengthens the spiritual priorities of your home and church. We offer a challenging curriculum which seeks development of each child's unique God-given gifts in mind, spirit, and body.

WEST VALLEY CHRISTIAN SCHOOL   Campbell

95 Dot Avenue, Campbell, CA 95008. Phone: 408-378-4327. Fax: 408-378-4371. www.wvcs.org. Head: Dr. Herbert Shand. Est. 1948. Nonprofit. Seventh Day Adventist. Uniforms.

Gr. 1 to 8. 100 students. Avg. class size: 20. Max class size: 25. Aides in grades 1-2. K Hrs: 8:30 AM - 2:45 PM. Elementary: 8 AM - 3:15 PM. Friday dismissals 2PM. Extended care hrs: 7 AM - 6 PM, $182/mo. Tuition: $4,088, discount for families in an SDA church. Other fees: $250. 30% receive fin. aid. Specialists: band, choir, piano, math, reading. Computer lab, Internet access in each classroom. Soccer, basketball. Rolling admissions. Admissions test. Parent participation encouraged. 100% of teachers credentialed. Avg. yrs. teaching exp: 8. Standardized tests administered. Accreditation: Council for Private School Accreditation, Pacific Union Conference of Seventh-day Adventists.

The ultimate goal of West Valley Christian School is the restoration of the character of God in our students. Working in partnership with the church and the family, we are dedicated to providing a caring environment where students are encouraged to: develop a personal relationship with Jesus, strive for academic excellence, grow spiritually, mentally, physically, and socially, and prepare for a life of service to God, family, and the community.

HOLY ANGELS ELEMENTARY SCHOOL   Colma

20 Reiner Street, Colma, CA 94014. Phone: 650-755-0220. Fax: 650-755-0258. www.holyangelscolma.com. Head: Sister Leonarda Montealto, O.P. Est. 1952. Nonprofit. Catholic. Uniforms.

Gr. K to 8. 320 students. Avg. class size: 36. Max class size: 40. K Hrs: 8:15 AM - 12:15 PM. School hrs: 8:15 AM - 2:15 PM. Extended care hrs: 7 AM - 6 PM, $6/hr. Tuition: $3,000, discounts earned by points. Other fees: $100 registration, $125 for books. Specialists: science, music, speech, drama, dance. Computer lab, library, science building. PE and an athletic program. Support for gifted and talented students. Learning disabilities testing and tutorial using Slingerland method. LD specialist on staff. App. deadline: January. Admissions test. Waiting list. Parent participation encouraged. 100% of teachers credentialed. Avg. yrs. teaching exp: 10. Standardized tests administered. Accreditation: WASC, WCEA.

A comprehensive and sequential course of study is offered. Development of each student's abilities extend beyond the attainment of basic skills through an appreciation of the arts and sciences. Skills are developed to analyze and evaluate so that our students may become responsible individuals.

BETHEL LUTHERAN SCHOOL   Cupertino

10181 Finch Avenue, Cupertino, CA 95014. Phone: 408-252-8512. Fax: 408-252-8465. www.bethells.org. Head: Yvonne Waters. Est. 1964. Lutheran. Uniforms.

Gr. Pre-K to 6. 200 students. 1 to 8 teacher to student ratio. Max class size: K-3, 18. K Hrs: 9 AM - 3 PM. Elementary: 9 AM - 3 PM. Extended care hrs: 7 AM - 6 PM, cost: morning, $1,700; PM, $2,240. Care open holidays. Tuition: $6,800. Other fees: $190 registration, $20 yearbook. 2% receive fin. aid. Specialists: PE, art, computers, resource teacher. Spanish. Computer lab, homework room, afterschool care, summer program. Annual track meet. 1 student per computer. Students with dyslexia and other learning disabilities served. Rolling admissions. Parent participation encouraged. 100% of teachers credentialed. Avg. yrs. teaching exp: 10. Standardized tests administered. Ten-week summer camp. Accreditation: WASC (in process), CSA.

Our role is to provide children with the tools they need to access their own possibilities, to guide the natural curiosity and joy of learning, and to help them become lifelong learners, problem solvers and thinkers in a loving Christian environment.

SAINT JOSEPH OF CUPERTINO SCHOOL   Cupertino

10120 North De Anza Boulevard, Cupertino, CA 95014. Phone: 408-252-6441. Fax: 408-252-9771. www.sjcschool.org. Head: Mary Lyons. Est. 1956. Nonprofit. Catholic. Uniforms.

Gr. K to 8. 303 students. 1 to 17 teacher to student ratio. Avg. class size: 35. Max class size: K-3, 36; upper grades, 35. Teacher and aide in each class. K Hrs: 8:20 AM - 3 PM. Elementary: 8:15 AM - 3 PM. Extended care hrs: 7 AM - 6 PM, $3.50/hr. Tuition: $5,080 - $6,980. Other fees: $125 registration; $250 for books. 8% receive fin. aid. Specialists: science, art, music, physical education, technology, library. Spanish. Networked Internet, library, computer lab, science lab. Flag football, soccer, basketball, baseball, softball, volleyball, track, swimming. 2 students per computer. Band, creative dance, choir, foreign language, technology, scouts. Tutoring for students with learning disabilities and special needs. App. deadline: February. Waiting list. Parent participation required. 100% of teachers credentialed. 50% of teachers have adv. degrees. Avg. yrs. teaching exp: 15. Standardized tests administered. Accreditation: WASC, WCEA, NCEA.

St. Joseph of Cupertino School, with the support of our families, is committed to educating the whole child. We place importance on the spiritual, intellectual, emotional, social and physical development of each unique child. We base our education upon the teachings of Jesus - teachings which foster respect, responsibility, justice, gratitude, and peacefulness.

HILLDALE SCHOOL   Daly City

79 Florence Street, Daly City, CA 94014. Phone: 650-756-4737. Fax: 650-756-3162. hilldale.pinnacleschools.net. Head: Dr. Robert Baker. Admissions: Dr. Robert Baker. Est. 1948. Uniforms.

Gr. Pre-K to 8. 80 students. 1 to 16 teacher to student ratio. Max class size: 16; upper grades, 16. Aides in K. K Hrs: 8:30 AM - 3:30 PM. School hrs: 8:30 AM - 3:30 PM. Extended care hrs: 7:30 AM - 6 PM, no charge except for optional workshops. Tuition: $8,100. Other fees: $200 for books. 5% receive fin. aid. Specialists: art, music, P.E. Spanish. Pool, computer lab, library, before and after school care including homework center and workshops. Swimming lessons and weekly afterschool free swim. 1 student per computer. 3,000 books in library. 2 applicants per space. Rolling admissions. Admissions test. 90% of teachers credentialed. 50% of teachers have adv. degrees. Avg. yrs. teaching exp: 6. Standardized tests administered. Four-week academic summer camp including Club Invention, Rising Stars, and our own Camp Quest programs, as well as daily swimming and fun camp activities.

Our goal is to provide a world-class education which challenges the intellect and prepares bright students to succeed in a competitive world. We also aim to guide our students to become responsible, positive, self-disciplined people who are life-long learners and leaders.

HOPE LUTHERAN ELEMENTARY SCHOOL   Daly City

55 San Fernando Way, Daly City, CA 94105. Phone: 650-991-HOPE. Fax: 650-991-9723. www.hopedalycity.org. Head: Rev. Jeff Schufreider. Est. 1951. Lutheran. Uniforms.

Gr. K to 6. Elementary: 8:30 AM - 3 PM. Extended care hrs: 7 AM - 6 PM, $2.50/day for before, $5.50/day for after. Afterschool sports. 100% of teachers credentialed. Standardized tests administered.

Our school seeks close cooperation of home, school and church with the goal of guiding young people to fulfill their purpose in life as educated, dedicated Christian citizens.

OUR LADY OF MERCY SCHOOL   Daly City

7 Elmwood Drive, Daly City, CA 94015. Phone: 650-756-3395. Fax: 650-756-5872. www.olmbulldogs.com. Head: Ms. Arlene Fife. Est. 1955. Nonprofit. Catholic. Uniforms.

Gr. K to 8. 625 students. Max class size: 35. K Hrs: 8:10 AM - 12:30 PM. Elementary: 8 AM - 3 PM. Extended care hrs: 7 AM - 6 PM, $10/stay. Tuition: $4,950, fin. aid avail. Specialists: dance, art, drama, band, chorus. Wireless high speed Internet throughout the school, library-media center, computer lab. Basketball, soccer, baseball, volleyball. 7,000 books in library. Parent participation required. Accreditation: WASC, WCEA.

Our Lady of Mercy School is a community of faith which provides for the growth of the whole person based on Christian values. This community is permeated with the Gospel spirit of freedom and love. The students are helped to develop their unique abilities and are prepared to live effectively in the Church, civic and cultural communities.

OUR LADY OF PERPETUAL HELP SCHOOL   Daly City

80 Wellington Avenue, Daly City, CA 94014. Phone: 650-755-4438. Head: James Costello. Est. 1933. Nonprofit. Catholic.

Gr. K to 8. 625 students. 1 to 30 teacher to student ratio. Max class size: 35; upper grades, 35. School hrs: 8:25 AM - 3 PM. Tuition: $2,475. Other fees: $250. Specialists: computers, PE, music. App. deadline: February. Admissions test. Waiting list. Parent participation required. 90% of teachers credentialed. Avg. yrs. teaching exp: 14. Accreditation: WASC, WCEA.

We believe education is a partnership of parents and teachers and dedicated to the creation of a Christian environment of care, encouragement, and love; the pursuit of academic excellence; and the joy of learning.

WILKINSON SCHOOL   El Granada

750 Avenue Alhambra, El Granada, CA 94018. Phone: 650-726-4582. www.wilkinsonschool.com. Head: Ms. Alibhai. Est. 1977.

Small class sizes. Extended care hrs: 7 AM - 6 PM. Specialists: music, dance. Spanish. Annual extended family field trip, annual egg drop, science fair. Standardized tests administered. Summer academic program and day camp.

A cutting edge school in a cottage? The pursuit of an innovative education in an old-fashioned country schoolhouse has made the Wilkinson School and Early Childhood Center exceptional from the start. A quarter of a century later, the school's founder, Linda Wilkinson and her husband, Ed Wilkinson, remain true to their original vision — integrating academics, the arts and empathy in a school without walls.

KIDS CONNECTION   Foster City

1998 Beach Park Boulevard, Foster City, CA 94404. Phone: 650-578-6690. www.kidsconn.com. Head: Diane Marcum. Est. 1928. Uniforms.

Gr. Pre-K to 5. Avg. class size: 15. Max class size: 20. K Hrs: 8:20 AM - 1 PM. Elementary: 8:15 AM - 2:45 PM. Extended care hrs: 7 AM - 6 PM. Tuition: $4,600 - $5,750. Specialists: music, PE. Spanish. Computers. Science fair, author visits, afterschool recreational programs. App. deadline: March. Admissions test. Parent participation encouraged. 100% of teachers credentialed. 20% of teachers have adv. degrees. Avg. yrs. teaching exp: 20. Standardized tests administered. Summer academic and recreational camps.

Kids Connection School provides a personalized, affordable approach to education for high achieving students. Four themes accurately describe Kids Connection Elementary School: A safe, secure, loving environment provided. A strong academic program that encourages lifelong learning. The emphasis on character development that helps children learn to be quality individuals and ethical leaders. The importance of partnership between parents and teachers in these endeavors.

RONALD C. WORNICK JEWISH DAY SCHOOL Foster City

800 Foster City Boulevard, Foster City, CA 94404. Phone: 650-378-2600. Fax: 650-378-2669. www.wornickjds.org. Head: Mervyn K. Danker. Admissions: Erika Schuetze. Est. 1986. Nonprofit. Jewish.

Gr. K to 8. 206 students. 1 to 8 teacher to student ratio. Avg. class size: 15. Max class size: 18. Aides in K. K Hrs: 8:30 AM - 1:30 PM. School hrs: 8 AM - 3:30 PM. Extended care hrs: 7:30 AM - 6 PM. Tuition: $12,100 - $14,700. Other fees: $75. Specialists: art, music, PE, health, Jewish studies. Hebrew, Spanish. Science lab, library, performance hall, indoor pool, gym. League sports teams: volleyball, flag football, basketball, soccer. 10,000 books in library. Onsite learning specialist. App. deadline: January. Rolling admissions. Waiting list. Parent participation required. 100% of teachers credentialed. Avg. yrs. teaching exp: 12. Standardized tests administered. Accreditation: WASC, CAIS, member of the RAVSAK Jewish Community Day School Network.

Our program places a high value on personal qualities and abilities. These include intellectual, social, emotional, physical as well as spiritual growth. We strive to weave into the curriculum an understanding and appreciation of the world's cultural diversity, the importance of integrity, problem-solving, patience, curiosity, and using good judgment.

PACIFIC WEST CHRISTIAN ACADEMY Gilroy

1575A Mantelli Drive, Gilroy, CA 95020. Phone: 408-847-7922. Head: Donna Garcia. Est. 1995. Nonprofit. Christian. Uniforms.

Gr. K to 8. 370 students. Max class size: K, 24; gr. 1-8, 25. Aides in grades K-1. K Hrs: 8:15 AM - 3 PM. Elementary: 8:15 AM - 3 PM. Extended care hrs: 7:30 AM - 6 PM, $4/hr pre-pay and $5/hr if billed. Care open some holidays. Tuition: $4,600 - $4,800. Other fees: $320 enrollment/testing fee; $270 re-enrollment annually. 10% receive fin. aid. Afterschool sports, cheerleading. App. deadline: February. Waiting list. Parent participation required. Standardized tests administered.

Pacific West Christian Academy seeks to provide quality education in a Christ-centered, nurturing and disciplined environment.

SAINT MARY SCHOOL Gilroy

7900 Church Street, Gilroy, CA 95020. Phone: 408-842-2827. www.stmarygilroy.org. Head: Christa Hanson. Admissions: Mollie Botill. Est. 1871. Nonprofit. Catholic. Uniforms.

Gr. K to 8. 310 students. Max class size: 35. Aides in grades K-3. K Hrs: 8:15 AM - 11:30 AM, 10:30 AM - 1:30 PM. Elementary: 8:15 AM - 3 PM. Extended care hrs: 7:30 AM - 6 PM, $4/hr. Care open some holidays. Tuition: $5,728. Other fees: $400. 5% receive fin. aid. Specialists: art, music, PE. Spanish. Computer lab, gym, library. Enrichment programs in math and science. App. deadline: February. Parent participation required. Summer program. Accreditation: WASC, WCEA.

St. Mary Parish School shares in the educational mission of the Catholic Church, striving to develop a personal and communal commitment to a life of faith. Together with families, we instill Christian principles in a caring and active Catholic community. Through a loving and nurturing environment, we affirm that all persons are created in God's image; therefore, students are challenged to fulfill their unique potential. We provide a quality education emphasizing spiritual development, social responsibility, physical well being, psychological health, and academic accomplishment.

SEA CREST SCHOOL   Half Moon Bay

901 Arnold Way, Half Moon Bay, CA 94019. Phone: 650-712-9892. Fax: 650-712-9892. www.seacrestschool.org. Head: John Wilson. Admissions: Sue Reyneri. Est. 1996. Nonprofit. Dress code.

Gr. K to 8. 250 students. 1 to 12 teacher to student ratio. Max class size: K-3, 16; upper grades, 20. Aides in grades K-2. K Hrs: 8:30 AM - 2:30 PM. Elementary: 8:30 AM - 3 PM. Extended care hrs: 7:45 AM - 6 PM, $5/hr, additional fees may be charged for classes. Tuition: $10,820. Other fees: $200 - $700 program fees, depending on grade level. 10% receive fin. aid. Specialists: art, music, technology, drama, P.E. Spanish. Technology lab, art room, music room, drama room, full gymnasium. Cross country, volleyball, flag football, basketball, soccer, golf, swimming, tennis. 1 student per computer. 2 applicants per space. App. deadline: January. Rolling admissions. Admissions test. Waiting list. Parent participation encouraged. 98% of teachers credentialed. 35% of teachers have adv. degrees. Avg. yrs. teaching exp: 6. Standardized tests administered. Kindergarten introduction program. Science adventure and sports summer camp. Accreditation: WASC, CAIS.

At Sea Crest, the curriculum presents students with a challenging, relevant, and varied array of activities that meet individual needs and personal interests. Sea Crest's mission is to provide a superior education in a nurturing environment which cultivates strong academic skills, promotes good character and develops a love for learning which extends beyond the classroom.

NUEVA SCHOOL   Hillsborough

6565 Skyline Boulevard, Hillsborough, CA 94010. Phone: 650-348-2272. Fax: 650-348-3642. www.nuevaschool.org. Head: Diane Rosenberg. Admissions: Beth Noonan. Est. 1967. Nonprofit. No dress code.

Gr. Pre-K to 8. 352 students. 1 to 7 teacher to student ratio. Max class size: K, 18; gr. 1-8, 19. Aides in grades K-5. K Hrs: 8:30 AM - 3:30 PM, with the option of picking up child as early as 1:30 PM daily. School hrs: 8:30 AM - 3:30 PM. Extended care hrs: 7:30 AM - 6 PM, $3,000. Tuition: $21,000. Other fees: $40 - $3,310. 20% receive fin. aid. Specialists: art, music, PE, science, math, computers, social-emotional learning. Japanese, Spanish. 33 acre campus, climbing wall, state-of-the-art gym, sports field. PE program includes basketball, volleyball, badmitten, yoga, track, flag football, dance, soccer. 1 student per computer. 20,000 books in library. Social-emotional learning, Oberlin

Dance Company works with Pre-K to gr.1 , trips outside of CA (5th-7th) and continent (8th grade), literature club. Lower school reading specialist. App. deadline: January. Admissions test. Waiting list. Parent participation encouraged. 56% of teachers have adv. degrees. Avg. yrs. teaching exp: 14. Standardized tests administered. Nueva Summer Challenge for kids 5 and up. Accreditation: WASC, CAIS.

Nueva is a child-centered, progressive school for gifted and talented children. The program emphasizes integrated studies, creative arts, and social-emotional learning.

CANTERBURY CHRISTIAN SCHOOL   Los Altos

101 North El Monte Avenue, Los Altos, CA 94022. Phone: 650-949-0909. Fax: 650-949-0909. Head: Rev. Normand Milbank. Nonprofit. Christian. Uniforms.

Gr. K to 6. 112 students. 1 to 16 teacher to student ratio. Max class size: K, 16; gr. 1-3, 16. K Hrs: 8:20 AM - 11:45 PM. Elementary: 8:15 AM - 3 PM. Extended care hrs: 7:30 AM - 5:30 PM. Tuition: K $4,588, gr. 1-6 $5,187. Other fees: book fees. Specialists: art, music, PE. Latin. PE program. App. deadline: March. Rolling admissions. Admissions test. One parent must be Christian. Waiting list. Avg. yrs. teaching exp: 8. Standardized tests administered.

The school is designed as a missionary outreach to prepare children spiritually, mentally, and physically to be able to live effective, productive lives based upon the Bible.

LOS ALTOS CHRISTIAN SCHOOL   Los Altos

625 Magdalena Avenue, Los Altos, CA 94024. Phone: 650-948-3738. Fax: 650-949-6092. www.lacs.com. Head: Susan N. Torode. Admissions: Bev Peterson. Est. 1981. Nonprofit. Christian. Uniforms.

Gr. Pre-K to 6. 240 students. Max class size: K, 26; gr. 1-6, 25. Aides in grades K-5. School hrs: Pre-K 8:30 AM - 12:45 PM, K 8:30 AM - 2:05 PM. Elementary: 8:30 AM - 3 PM. Extended care hrs: 7:30 AM - 6 PM, $7.70/hr or $2,376/yr. Tuition: $6,100-$11,700. Other fees: $525 - $825. 2% receive fin. aid. Specialists: art, music, PE, computer, library. Spanish. Computer lab, gym, library. Afterschool sports, volleyball, flag football, basketball. 8,000 books in library. For gifted students, we have Math ExL and Writing ExL pull out classes. Tutoring services available. Academics Plus program for mild to moderate specific language learning disablity, such as dyslexia and auditory processing difficulty. Self-contained small classes for each grade level with teachers trained in the Slingerland/Orton-Gillingham multisensory instructional approach. Admissions test: for LAD classes, a complete psychological/educational evaluation is required. For mainstream classes, an achievement test (SAT or STAR) is required. Waiting list. Parent participation encouraged. 90% of teachers credentialed. 10% of teachers have adv. degrees. Avg. yrs. teaching exp: 12. 100% of teachers post HW online. Standardized tests administered. Summer academic program. Accreditation: WASC, ACSI.

It is our purpose to provide a quality education in a warm Christian atmosphere for all our students. We feel that Christian schools reflect a return to the Biblical principles of our national heritage: American patriotism, Christian morals, a conservative philosophy, and personal integrity. Clear behavioral expectations and individual accountability are emphasized.

MIRAMONTE SCHOOL   Los Altos

1175 Altamead Drive, Los Altos, CA 94024. Phone: 650-967-2783. Fax: 650-967-0833. www.miramonteschool.org. Head: Shelley Hulin. Est. 1906. Nonprofit. Seventh-Day Adventist. Dress code.

Gr. Pre-K to 8. 177 students. 1 to 17 teacher to student ratio. Max class size: 25. Aides in grades K-5. Elementary: 8 AM - 3 PM. School hrs: 8 AM - 3 PM. K,1,2 dismissal at 2:30 PM; Friday dismissals at 1:30 PM. Extended care hrs: 7 AM - 6 PM. Tuition: $4,779. Other fees: $75 waiting list, $275 registration, $150 for books. Specialists: music, P.E. Computer lab. Intramural basketball, flag football, softball, soccer, volleyball. 1 student per computer. 3,700 books in library. Admissions test. Waiting list. Parent participation encouraged. 29% of teachers credentialed. 22% of teachers have adv. degrees. Avg. yrs. teaching exp: 12.7. 22% of teachers post HW online. Standardized tests administered. Accreditation: WASC (in process), North American Division Commission on Accreditation - SDA.

Miramonte School is a learning-centered environment that reflects active partnership of students, staff, parents and community, openness to seeking and evaluating new ideas, and an atmosphere conducive to developing responsible Christian learners.

PINEWOOD ELEMENTARY SCHOOL   Los Altos

327 Fremont Avenue, Los Altos, CA 94024. Phone: 650-949-5775 (Gr. K-2 Campus), 650-941-2828 (Gr. 3-6 Campus). Fax: 650-941-2459. www.pinewood.edu. Head: Scott Riches. Admissions: Barbara Hantke (K-6). Nonprofit.

Gr. K to 12. 300 students. 1 to 7 teacher to student ratio. Max class size: K, 16; gr. 1-3, 20; upper grades, 20. K Hrs: 8:25 AM - 11:55 AM. School hrs: (Gr. 1-2) 8:25 AM - 3 PM, (Gr. 3-6) 8:25 AM - 3:10 PM. Extended care hrs: 8 AM - 5:30 PM. Specialists: art, music, drama, PE, computer. Basketball, soccer, flag football, baseball, softball. Part-time learning specialist available. Accreditation: WASC.

We create a learning climate wherein students may acquire academic stamina, intellectual vitality, and a high standard of behavior in order that they may live a life of purpose, dignity and concern for others.

SAINT NICHOLAS SCHOOL   Los Altos

12816 South El Monte Avenue, Los Altos, CA 94022. Phone: 650-941-4056. Fax: 650-917-9872. www.stnicholaslah.com. Head: Matt Komar. Est. 1960. Nonprofit. Catholic. Uniforms.

Gr. K to 8. 270 students. 1 to 20 teacher to student ratio. Avg. class size: 30. Max class size: 35. Aides in grades K-4. K Hrs: 8 AM - 2 PM. Elementary: 8 AM - 3 PM. Extended care available. Tuition: $4,950 - $7,245. Other fees: $315. 5% receive fin. aid. Specialists: literature, PE, religion. Spanish. Library, gymnasium, technology center, science labs, multi-use room. Flag football, basketball, soccer, baseball, softball, volleyball. No Bully Program, community outreach, field trips. On-site LD specialist. App. deadline: January. Admissions test. Waiting list. Accreditation: WASC, WCEA.

St. Nicholas School is dedicated to providing a values-centered learning environment that shows children the way to witness the reality of the Risen Christ. The Gospel message is the core of our educational process. It guides our students to develop into articulate, participatory members of their community.

SAINT SIMON SCHOOL   Los Altos

1840 Grant Road, Los Altos, CA 94024. Phone: 650-968-9952. Fax: 650-988-9308. www.stsimon.com. Head: Mrs. Mary Johnson. Est. 1961. Nonprofit. Catholic. Uniforms.

Gr. K to 8. 600 students. Max class size: K, 22; gr. 1-8, 35. Aides in grades K-5. K Hrs: 7:55 AM - 10:55 AM or 11:45 AM - 2:45 PM. Elementary: 8 AM - 3 PM. Early dismissal on first and third Wednesdays. Extended care hrs: 7 AM - 6 PM, $5 - $7/hr. Care open some holidays. Tuition: $3,975 (K), $4,975 (Grades 1-8), sibling discounts. Other fees: $350. Specialists: computer, music, PE, art, band. Spanish. Gym, multi-purpose room, computer lab, library, music room, science room, turf area. Flag football, baseball, basketball, softball, volleyball, soccer, swim meet, track meet, cheerleading. Student council, choir, band, chess club, altar servers. Educational therapist, speech and language therapist. Rolling admissions. Admissions test. Parent participation encouraged. Standardized tests administered. Accreditation: WASC, WCEA, nationally recognized as a Blue Ribbon School of Excellence.

St. Simon School strives to form a Community of Faith dedicated to living and teaching the message and mission that Jesus Christ entrusted to His Church. In this school, Jesus is the Center, and Mary is the Model. We recognize that parents are the primary educators of their children. Teachers facilitate the learning process. Together, we are committed to educating the whole child in a student-centered atmosphere, which reflects the Gospel message and fosters each student's spiritual, intellectual, emotional, social, aesthetic, and physical growth. In accordance with each child's gifts and abilities, we strive to provide the students with the environment needed to become children of faith, character, compassion, justice, honor, and knowledge.

WALDORF SCHOOL OF THE PENINSULA   Los Altos

11311 Mora Drive, Los Altos, CA 94024. Phone: 650-948-8433. Fax: 650-949-2494. www.waldorfpeninsula.org. Head: Stephanie Rynas. Est. 1984. Nonprofit. Dress code.

Gr. Pre-K to 8. 245 students. Max class size: K, 18; gr. 1-8, 28. K Hrs: 8:30 AM - 12:30 PM. Elementary: 8:30 AM - 3 PM. Extended care available afterschool until 5:45 PM, $7/hr. Care open some holidays. Tuition: $11,880, sibling discount avail. Other fees: $100. Specialists: eurythmy (movement), art, hand work, gardening, orchestra. Spanish. Biodynamic garden, spacious classrooms, woodworking studio, handwork room, gift store, newly expanded play area. 5-day classroom visit required. "Summer Days in the Waldorf Kindergarten" program for 2 weeks. Accreditation: WASC, Association of Waldorf Schools of North America.

Waldorf students are educated in recognition of their own spirits and in rhythm with their own physical, mental, and emotional development. Their lessons, which are alive and interesting, challenge and stimulate their imaginations, for the children are not addressed as beings of head alone, but of hands and heart as well. A Waldorf education prepares the student to enter adulthood with the gifts of self-discipline, independence, mastery of ana-lytical and critical faculties, and reverence for the beauty and wonder of the world.

HILLBROOK SCHOOL   Los Gatos

300 Marchmont Drive, Los Gatos, CA 95032. Phone: 408-356-6116. Fax: 408-356-1286. www.hillbrook.org. Head: Sarah Bayne. Est. 1936. Nonprofit. Uniforms.

Gr. Pre-K to 8. 315 students. 1 to 9 teacher to student ratio. Max class size: K, 12; gr. 1-8, 18. K Hrs: 8 AM - 2:45 PM. Elementary: 7:45 AM - 3:15 PM. Extended care available afterschool until 6 PM. Care open some holidays. Tuition: $17,400. 10% re-ceive fin. aid. Specialists: art, music, outdoor education. Chinese, Spanish. Outdoor The-atre Under the Oaks, gymnasium, 3 outdoor play areas, community garden, pool, com-puter lab, photography/digital imaging lab, library, woodshop, ceramics studio. Football, basketball, soccer, volleyball, softball. 3 students per computer. 15,000 books in library. Drama, chorus, buddy program, art show. 5 applicants per space. App. deadline: January. Parent participation encouraged. Avg. yrs. teaching exp: 12. 100% of teachers post HW online. Standardized tests administered. Summer sports camp. Accreditation: CAIS, NAIS.

Hillbrook educates, nurtures and inspires students to achieve their highest academic po-tential and to become socially responsible, ethical leaders.

LOS GATOS CHRISTIAN SCHOOL   Los Gatos

16845 Hicks Road, Los Gatos, CA 95032. Phone: 408-997-4681. Fax: 408-268-4107. www.losgatoschristian.org. Head: Treva Black. Admissions: Linda Rosenberry. Est. 1977. Nonprofit. Christian. Uniforms.

Gr. Pre-K to 8. 524 students. Max class size: K-3, 20; upper grades, 25. Aides in grades K-1. K Hrs: 8:15 AM - 3 PM. Elementary: 8:15 AM - 3 PM. Extended care hrs: 7 AM - 6 PM, $4.75/hr. Tuition: $6,225 - $6,975. Other fees: $470. Specialists: choir, computer, drama, piano, art. Spanish. Competitive sports. Science camp, speech meets, spelling bee, authors' fair, science fair. Educational therapy for LD students, Barton reading/spelling program for struggling students. App. deadline: October. Waiting list. Parent participation required. 90% of teachers credentialed. Avg. yrs. teaching exp: 12. Standardized tests administered. Accreditation: WASC (in process), ACSI.

Los Gatos Christian School does four things as it prepares students for life. The staff will proclaim the Gospel, offer strong academics, teach character development, and include a comprehensive enrichment program all within a nurturing family environment.

MULBERRY SCHOOL   Los Gatos

220 Bel Gatos Road, Los Gatos, CA 95032. Phone: 408-358-9080. www.mulberry.org. Head: January Handl and Sharon Hiller. Est. 1963. Nonprofit. No dress code.

Gr. Pre-K to 5. 200 students. 1 to 20 teacher to student ratio. Max class size: 20. K Hrs: 9 AM - 1 PM. Elementary: 9 AM - 3 PM. Extended care hrs: 7:30 AM - 6 PM, $5/hr for contract, $7/hr for drop in. Tuition: $5,625 - $7,920. Other fees: $75. 3% receive fin. aid. Specialists: PE, music and movement. 18 students per computer. We address emotional/social skill building. Our resource specialist works with children who have mild to moderate difficulty and need additional support. App. deadline: March. Admissions test: 2 hour play-based assessment for Pre-K, K; upper grades: shadow for 2 days. Waiting list. Parent participation required. 98% of teachers credentialed. 2% of teachers have adv. degrees. Avg. yrs. teaching exp: 8. 8 weeks of summer school camps. Accreditation: WASC, NAEYC for preschool.

At Mulberry School, the teachers, staff, and parents provide a nurturing learning environment that develops the whole child academically, socially, emotionally, and physically. The curriculum responds to the individual student's learning needs by offering a variety of educational approaches. Mulberry provides an environment where students are encouraged to question, to explore, and to follow logical paths to their own understandings. The partnership between home and school produces a stimulating, challenging environment in which each child has the freedom to grow and learn at his or her own pace.

SAINT MARY'S SCHOOL   LOS GATOS

30 Lyndon Avenue, Los Gatos, CA 95030. Phone: 408-354-3944. Fax: 408-395-9151. www.stmaryslg.org. Head: Sister Nicki Thomas. Est. 1954. Nonprofit. Catholic. Uniforms.

Gr. K to 8. 315 students. 1 to 12 teacher to student ratio. Max class size: 35. Aides in grades K-5. K Hrs: 8:15 AM - 2 PM, 8:15 AM - 12:30 PM on Wednesdays. Elementary: 8:15 AM - 3 PM. Extended care available afterschool until 6 PM., $4/hr - $6/hr. Tuition: $4,720 - $7,100. Other fees: $275. 5% receive fin. aid. Specialists: art, music, PE, computer, science. Spanish. Individual laptops for each student in grades 5-8, mobile class cart for K-4, wireless access to the Internet for all. Touch football, basketball, track and field, volleyball, softball. Lower grade reading specialists. App. deadline: February. Waiting list. Parent participation encouraged. 100% of teachers credentialed. 50% of teachers have adv. degrees. 50% of teachers post HW online. Standardized tests administered. Accreditation: WASC, WCEA.

We believe and honor that every child is created in the image and likeness of God. We believe in and honor the importance of the faith community in living and modeling Gospel values. We believe and honor that parents and/or guardians are the primary educators of their children while teachers facilitate and complement the learning process. We believe and strive to create an environment which allows a child to learn and grow while developing a social sense of responsibility for self and others.

STRATFORD SCHOOL   Los Gatos

220 Kensington Way, Los Gatos, CA 95032. Phone: 408-371-3020. Fax: 408-371-3250. www.stratfordschools.com. Head: Sherry Adams. Est. 1999. Uniforms.

Gr. Pre-K to 5. 325 students. 1 to 22 teacher to student ratio. Max class size: K, 28; gr. 1-5, 22. K Hrs: full day 8 AM - 3:30 PM, morning 8 AM - 11:30 AM, afternoon 12 PM - 3:30 PM. School hrs: 8 AM - 3:30 PM. Extended care hrs: 7 AM - 6 PM, $215/month. Care open some holidays. Tuition: $10,000. Specialists: music, and computer. Spanish. 1 student per computer. Standardized tests administered. Academic summer program.

Our mission is to inspire students to achieve an excellent academic education by offering a challenging curriculum focused on core subjects, creating a safe and disciplined school environment conducive to learning, and motivating students through high expectations.

YAVNEH DAY SCHOOL   Los Gatos

14855 Oka Road #100, Los Gatos, CA 95032. Phone: 408-984-6700. Fax: 408-984-3696. www.yavnehdayschool.org. Head: Lori L. Abramson, MAJE. Admissions: Shelley Leveson. Est. 1981. Nonprofit. Jewish. Dress code.

Gr. K to 8. 130 students. 1 to 12 teacher to student ratio. Max class size: 24. Aides in grades K-5. K Hrs: 8:30 AM - 3:30 PM. School hrs: 8:30 AM - 3:30 PM. Extended care hrs: 8 AM - 6 PM. Care open some holidays. Tuition: $11,900. Other fees: $100. 40% receive fin. aid. Specialists: PE, music, art, computers. Hebrew. Pool, tennis courts, mobile technology unit. League sports: basketball, volleyball, flag football, wide range of on site after school athletics programs. Onsite LD specialist. Parent participation encouraged. Avg. yrs. teaching exp: 10. 7% of teachers post HW online. Standardized tests administered. Accreditation: CAIS, Solomon Schechter Day School Association.

We provide excellent general academics, meaningful Judaics and modern Hebrew in a warm, nurturing environment.

BEECHWOOD SCHOOL   Menlo Park

50 Terminal Avenue, Menlo Park, CA 94025. Phone: 650-327-5052. Fax: 650-327-5066. www.beechwoodschool.org. Head: Priscilla Hamilton-Taylor. Admissions: Isabel Jimenez. Est. 1984. Nonprofit.

Gr. Pre-K to 8. 160 students. 1 to 8 teacher to student ratio. Avg. class size: 16. Max class size: 18. School hrs: 8:30 AM - 3 PM. Tuition: $1,500. Specialists: music, drama, art. Spanish. Computer and science labs. Physical education. Special needs teacher on staff. App. deadline: March. Admissions test. Parent participation required.

Beechwood focuses on developing self-confident, academically competent students with the skills to be successful personally and professionally. The teachers and staff work hard to instill the principles of self-reliance, self-control, personal responsibility, hard work, honesty, integrity, kindness, unselfishness, reverence for life and love of God and country- leaving students better prepared to make their own meaningful contributions to their communities.

GERMAN-AMERICAN INTERNATIONAL SCHOOL   Menlo Park

275 Elliott Drive, Menlo Park, CA 94025. Phone: 650-324-8617. Fax: 650-324-9548. www.germanamericanschool.org. Head: Hans Peter Metzger. Est. 1988. Nonprofit. No dress code.

Gr. Pre-K to 8. 185 students. 1 to 7 teacher to student ratio. Max class size: 15. Aides in K. K Hrs: 8:30 AM - 1:45 AM. School hrs: 8:30 AM - 1:55 PM. Extended care hrs: 7 AM - 6 PM. Care open some holidays. Tuition: $12,600 - $16,000. Other fees: $500 annual fee. French, German, Spanish. Extracurricular programs are offered. App. deadline: March. Rolling admissions. Knowledge of German language required to enter first grade. Waiting list. Accreditation: WASC.

Our Mission is to develop inquiring, knowledgeable and caring young people who help to create a better and more peaceful world through intercultural understanding and respect. The German-American International School inspires the students of today to become tomorrow's global thinkers. The school's philosophy is exemplified by its international program, which integrates the best teaching methodologies of the world. It develops the imaginative mind, fosters creative, experimental learning, and encourages hands-on discovery in a nurturing environment.

NATIVITY SCHOOL   Menlo Park

1250 Laurel Street, Menlo Park, CA 94025. Phone: 650-325-7304. Fax: 650-325-3841. www.nativityschool.com. Head: Mrs. Carol Trelut. Est. 1956. Catholic. Uniforms.

Gr. K to 8. 290 students. Max class size: 35. Aides in grades K-2. K Hrs: 8 AM - 3 PM. Elementary: 8 AM - 3 PM. Extended care hrs: 7 AM - 5:45 PM, $4.25/hr. Tuition: $4,350 - $6,050, prices lowered for parent participation (40 hrs and $3,000 in Scrip). Other fees: $350. 12% receive fin. aid. Specialists: computers, PE, music. Spanish. Computer lab, library (accessible online). Basketball, volleyball. Choir, chess. App. deadline: May. Waiting list. Parent participation encouraged. 100% of teachers credentialed. Nine-week summer program. Accreditation: WASC, WCEA.

The school's mission is to educate and prepare the whole child in a nurturing environment based on Catholic values and beliefs in order that the child may become a responsible and active member of the Church and society.

PENINSULA SCHOOL   Menlo Park

920 Penisula Way, Menlo Park, CA 94025. Phone: 650-325-1584. Fax: 650-325-1313. www.peninsulaschool.org. Head: Katy Dalgleish. Admissions: Mary Lou Lacina. Est. 1925. Nonprofit. No dress code.

Gr. Pre-K to 8. 250 students. 1 to 5 teacher to student ratio. Max class size: K-3, 18; upper grades, 21. Aides in grades K-5. K Hrs: 9 AM - 12:30 PM or 9 AM - 3 PM. Elementary: 9 AM - 3 PM. Extended care hrs: 7:45 AM - 5:30 PM, $80/week. Care open some holidays. Tuition: $8,875 - $11,600. Other fees: $175. 22% receive fin. aid. Specialists: art, clay, dance, drama, library, math, music, P.E., science, weaving, woodshop. Ceramics studio, weaving room, woodshop, science room, music room, art room, library, math room, gym. Basketball team, ultimate frisbee. Annual drama productions, annual Rock Concert. Learning specialist on staff. App. deadline: February. Rolling admissions. Waiting list. Parent participation encouraged. 90% of teachers credentialed. 50% of teachers have adv. degrees. Avg. yrs. teaching exp: 15.

Since its founding, Peninsula's mission has been to foster the development of the whole child by promoting creativity, respect, independence, joy of learning, personal responsibility, and self esteem as well as academic excellence. The success of the mission has depended upon the creation of an extended family of children, staff and parents. Teachers and parents provide the guidance, trust and unconditional support necessary for children to experiment and learn about themselves and their world.

PHILLIPS BROOKS SCHOOL   Menlo Park

2245 Avy Avenue, Menlo Park, CA 94025. Phone: 650-854-4545. Fax: 650-854-6532. www.phillipsbrooks.org. Head: Kristi Kerins. Admissions: John Kulhanek. Est. 1978. Nonprofit. Uniforms.

Gr. Pre-K to 5. 270 students. 1 to 8 teacher to student ratio. Max class size: K, 18; gr. 1-5, 16. Aides in grades K-5. K Hrs: 8:20 AM - 2:10 PM. Elementary: 8:15 AM - 3:15 PM. Extended care hrs: 7:30 AM - 6 PM, $2,500 (5 days), $500 (1 day), no charge for morning care. Tuition: $10,500 - $18,900. Other fees: $500. 17% receive fin. aid. Specialists: art, communication, library, music, physical education, science, technology. French, Spanish. Computer lab, outdoor amphitheatre. Basketball, volleyball. Afterschool sports, chess program, computer program. App. deadline: January. Rolling admissions. Waiting list. Parent participation encouraged. Standardized tests administered. Summer enrichment program. Accreditation: WASC (in process), CAIS.

The Phillips Brooks School prepares each student to live a creative, humane, and compassionate life and to be a contributing member of society. The school believes in blend-

ing the academic, physical and social aspects of its program with spiritual awareness and understanding. This balance provides an environment that celebrates individuality, promotes problem solving through critical thinking, and encourages students to fulfill their potential.

SAINT RAYMOND'S SCHOOL   Menlo Park

1211 Arbor Road, Menlo Park, CA 94025. Phone: 650-322-2312. Fax: 650-322-2910. www.straymond.org. Head: Sister Ann Bernard O'Shea, CSJ. Nonprofit. Catholic. Uniforms.

Gr. K to 8. 275 students. Max class size: 33. Aides in grades K-4. School hrs: 8 AM - 3 PM. Extended care hrs: 7 AM - 6 PM, $4/hr. Tuition: $4,250. Other fees: $275. Specialists: art, computer, PE, math, science, music. Computer lab. Track and field, basketball, volleyball, baseball. Large afterschool sports program. App. deadline: March. Admissions test. Waiting list. Parent participation required. 100% of teachers credentialed. Accreditation: WASC, CAIS.

St. Raymond Parish School is a Christian Community united in the Catholic Faith. The faculty holds to teaching the values, heritage, and traditions of the Catholic Church and provides opportunities to participate in prayer and charitable works. Our curriculum offers students the opportunity to develop self-esteem, mutual respect, and an appreciation for diversity. We encourage academic excellence and offer our students a positive and caring environment. Our goal is for our students to function effectively and responsibly so that they may be prepared to live productively in our Church, society and culture.

TRINITY SCHOOL   Menlo Park

2650 Sand Hill Road, Menlo Park, CA 94025. Phone: 650-854-0288. Fax: 650-854-1374. www.trinity-mp.org. Head: Mary Menacho. Admissions: Sarah Ross. Est. 1961. Nonprofit. Episcopal. Uniforms.

Gr. Pre-K to 5. 160 students. 1 to 9 teacher to student ratio. Max class size: K-3, 20; upper grades, 18. Each class has a lead teacher and an assistant teacher. K Hrs: 8 AM - 3 PM. Elementary: 8 AM - 3 PM. Extended care hrs: 7:30 AM - 6 PM. Tuition: Pre-K $11,000, elementary $17,100. 20% receive fin. aid. Specialists: science/garden, library, advanced math, music, art, physical education, religious studies. Spanish. On-site Chapel, Great Hall, state-of-the- art library. Computers in every classroom with Internet access; 80 computers campus-wide. Greenhouse and garden, indigenous planting, an outdoor stage, a lunch terrace. Physical education, basketball league. 8 students per computer. 13,000 books in library. Instrumental music. 5 applicants per space. App. deadline: January. Rolling admissions. Waiting list. 90% of teachers credentialed. 70% of teachers have adv. degrees. Avg. yrs. teaching exp: 7. Accreditation: WASC, CAIS, NAEYC.

Trinity School gives each child a voice. We guide children to self-discovery. We celebrate the child's growth in critical thinking, character development, and social responsibility. Trinity School encourages children from all backgrounds to love learning. We foster rigorous academics grounded in child-centered content. Trinity upholds the values and traditions of the Episcopal Church and honors the role of the family in educating children. The legacy of a Trinity education is a curious mind and a discerning heart.

MILLS MONTESSORI SCHOOL   Millbrae

One Alp Way, Millbrae, CA 94030. Phone: 650-697-5561. www.millsmontessori.com. Head: Dr. Fallah. Admissions: Mrs. Simin Fallah. Est. 1988. Nonprofit. No dress code.

Gr. Pre-K to 5. 120 students. 1 to 12 teacher to student ratio. Max class size: K, 24; gr. 1-3, 17. Aides in grades K-5. K Hrs: 9 AM - 2:30 PM. Elementary: 8:45 AM - 2:30 PM. Extended care hrs: 7 AM - 6 PM, $1,044. Care open some holidays. Tuition: $5,760 - $10,440. Other fees: $400. 2% receive fin. aid. Specialists: computers, art, music, ceramic. Chinese, French, Spanish. 7 students per computer. Ballet, martial arts, foreign language, music, ceramics. App. deadline: February. Waiting list. 100% of teachers credentialed. 80% of teachers have adv. degrees. Avg. yrs. teaching exp: 10. Standardized tests administered. Extracuricular afterschool programs are year round. Accreditation: AMI Montessori.

Mills School is dedicated to providing a warm and accepting environment which promotes the physical, emotional and cognitive development of each child.

SAINT DUNSTAN'S SCHOOL   Millbrae

1150 Magnolia Avenue, Millbrae, CA 94030. Phone: 650-697-8119. Fax: 650-697-9295. www.st-dunstan.org. Head: Bill Hambleton. Est. 1953. Nonprofit. Catholic. Uniforms.

Gr. K to 8. 315 students. 1 to 17 teacher to student ratio. Max class size: 35. K Hrs: 8:20 AM - 12:20 PM. Elementary: 8:15 AM - 3 PM. Extended care hrs: 7 AM - 6 PM. Tuition: $3,830 - $5,280. Other fees: $3,500 worth of Scrip. 5% receive fin. aid. Specialists: science, math, PE, reading, music, computer. Spanish. Science lab, computer lab, library, auditorium. Volleyball, track, baseball, basketball. App. deadline: January. Parent participation required. 95% of teachers credentialed. Avg. yrs. teaching exp: 25. Accreditation: WASC, WCEA.

St. Dunstan Parish School is a Catholic School committed to carrying out the ministry of Jesus Christ in the education of youth. In our educational program, we emphasize the development of the whole person: spiritual, moral, social, intellectual, artistic, physical, and emotional. We are a partnership with parish, school and family.

FOOTHILL SEVENTH DAY ADVENTIST SCHOOL   Milpitas

1991 Landess Avenue, Milpitas, CA 95035. Phone: 408-263-2568. Fax: 408-263-1994. www.foothilladventistschool.org. Head: Coreen Hicks. Est. 1979. Nonprofit. Seventh-Day Adventist. Uniforms.

Gr. K to 8. 90 students. 1 to 2 teacher to student ratio. Avg. class size: 20. Max class size: 24. Aides in grades K-5. K Hrs: 8 AM - 3 PM. Elementary: 8 AM - 3 PM. Extended care hrs: 6:30 AM - 6 PM, $208/mo. Tuition: $4,600 - $7,000. Other fees: $230. Specialists: choir, art, keyboarding. Computer lab and computers in every room. Basketball, volleyball. Waiting list. Parent participation required. 100% of teachers credentialed. Avg. yrs. teaching exp: 10. Standardized tests administered. Summer camp. Accreditation: National Council of Private Schools.

To Seventh-Day Adventists, true education goes far beyond the confines of the classroom. It involves a cooperative effort between the home, the church, and the school. It integrates a balanced development of four primary aspects of a child's life: mental, physical, spiritual, and social. It is our purpose at Foothill to provide a sound, Christ-centered, uniquely Seventh-Day Adventist education. Each student is taught to cherish the practical teachings of the Bible and the Spirit of Prophecy, maintaining at the same time a high degree of academic excellence.

MILPITAS MONTESSORI   Milpitas

1500 Yosemite Drive, Rm. 12, Milpitas, CA 95035. Phone: 408-263-0991. Fax: 408-263-0991. Head: Lois Evans. Admissions: Lois Evans. Est. 1975. Dress code.

Gr. Pre-K to 3. 110 students. 1 to 13 teacher to student ratio. Max class size: K, 26; gr. 1-3, 26. Aides in grades K-3. K Hrs: 8:30 AM - 3 PM. Elementary: 8:30 AM - 3 PM. Extended care hrs: 7 AM - 6 PM. Tuition: $4,500 - $10,044. Other fees: $100 registration, $55 - $100 material fee, $65 summer activity fee. 2% receive fin. aid. Specialists: ballet/tap dance, martial arts, fine arts, tumbling, music/keyboarding. Chinese, some basic conversation in other languages. Waiting list. 100% of teachers credentialed. 75% of teachers have adv. degrees. Avg. yrs. teaching exp: 9. Standardized tests administered. Hands-on summer day camp and academic program. Accreditation: AMS.

We follow the Montessori philosophy of learning, emphasizing hands-on experience.

RAINBOW BRIDGE MERRYHILL SCHOOL   Milpitas

1500 Yosemite Drive, Milpitas, CA 95035. Phone: 408-945-9090. Fax: 408-262-1141. www.rainbowbridgeacademy.com. Head: Vickie Burns. Est. 1983. Uniforms.

Gr. Pre-K to 8. 440 students. Max class size: 29. Aides in grades K-5. K Hrs: 8:30 AM - 2:30 PM. Elementary: 8 AM - 3 PM. Extended care hrs: 6:30 AM - 6 PM, cost included in tuition. Tuition: $6,500. Specialists: music, fine arts, drama, technology. Second location in San Jose. Gymsters, karate. App. deadline: February. Rolling admissions. Admissions test. Standardized tests administered. Summer camp program with academics, athletics, and field trips.

Nobel Learning Communities offer children an opportunity to learn and develop in a secure, creative, and stimulating environment. We focus on activity-based, high quality academic programs, planned around a child's developmental needs. It is important to us that every child receives the best education, care, and attention possible. Our philosophy is based on personalized instruction that offers developmentally appropriate, challenging learning activities, which encourage positive self-esteem and emotional well being. Nobel Learning Communities seek to relate a child's learning at school to dynamic problems in the larger world.

SAINT JOHN THE BAPTIST SCHOOL   Milpitas

360 South Abel Street, Milpitas, CA 95035. Phone: 408-262-8110. Fax: 408-262-0814. www.sjbs.org. Head: Judith Perkowski. Admissions: Karen Campbell and Peggy Horyza. Est. 1987. Nonprofit. Catholic. Uniforms.

Gr. Pre-K to 8. 275 students. 1 to 15 teacher to student ratio. Max class size: 35. Teachers' aides in K-5 provide one-on-one instruction. K Hrs: K Early Birds: 8:10 AM-11:45 AM, K Late Birds: 10:15 AM-2 PM. Elementary: 8:15 AM - 3 PM. School hrs: 8:10 AM - 3 PM. Extended care hrs: 6:30 AM - 6 PM, $15/day. Tuition: $4,400, for Catholics. Other fees: $320. Computer/science lab, full court basketball gym. Afterschool sports: basketball, volleyball, track & field, flag football. 2 students per computer. 12,000 books in library. Music, physical education. App. deadline: March. 100% of teachers credentialed. 10% of teachers have adv. degrees. Avg. yrs. teaching exp: 15. 50% of teachers post HW online. Standardized tests administered. Accreditation: WASC, WCEA.

Our aim is to provide an educational environment that includes all dimensions of human life — spiritual, moral, intellectual and social.

CARDEN ACADEMY MORGAN HILL   Morgan Hill

410 Llagas Road, Morgan Hill, CA 95037. Phone: 408-776-8801. Fax: 408-776-8804. www.cardenacademymh.com. Head: Geralyn Vasquez. Admissions: Brigitte Heiser. Est. 1994. Uniforms.

Gr. Pre-K to 8. 100 students. 1 to 12 teacher to student ratio. Max class size: 22. Aides in K-5. K Hrs: 8:30 AM - 3:30 PM. School hrs: 8:30 AM - 3:30 PM. Extended care hrs: 7 AM - 6:30 PM, $5/hr. Tuition: $10,400. Other fees: $500 registration fee. 5% receive fin. aid. Specialists: art, music, PE, computers. French, Latin, Spanish. Computer lab, study hall, art room. Daily PE. 1 student per computer. 5,000 books in library. Afterschool art, gymnastics, chess. Admissions test. Parent participation encouraged. 25% of teachers credentialed. 50% of teachers have adv. degrees. Avg. yrs. teaching exp: 10. Standardized tests administered. Summer school and camp. Accreditation: WASC (in process), CAIS (in process).

Carden Academy Morgan Hill is a remarkable place – a place where children experience the beauty of art and music, the satisfaction gained from doing for others, and the joy of learning. Carden students learn more than the basics of reading, writing, and arithmetic. They learn to believe in themselves and their abilities, to find peace and pleasure in giving and sharing, and to explore the world around them with open eyes and open minds.

CROSSROADS CHRISTIAN   Morgan Hill

145 Wright Avenue, Morgan Hill, CA 95037. Phone: 408-779-8850. Fax: 408-779-0444. www.crossroadschristianschool.org. Head: Mr. Jim Wallace, M.Ed. Est. 1975. Nonprofit. Assemblies of God. Uniforms.

Gr. Pre-K to 8. 250 students. 1 to 20 teacher to student ratio. Avg. class size: 16. Max class size: 24. Aides in K. K Hrs: Full Day Only 8:30 AM - 2:50 PM. Elementary: 8:30 AM - 3 PM. Extended care hrs: 7 AM - 6:30 PM. Tuition: $5,475. Other fees: $300 Registration. Specialists: music and band, technology, PE. French, Spanish. Up-to-date computer lab, modern gymnasium. Intramural sports and competitive league sports: basketball, soccer, volleyball, flag football, volleyball. Tutoring programs, Powerline Reading Program. Parent participation encouraged. Summer care, music camp, science camps. Accreditation: ACSI.

Education is complete when knowing Christ is the ultimate goal of that process. The Creator and His creation are inseparable subjects at our school, and together provide a foundation for successful living as they are understood by our students.

OAKWOOD COUNTRY SCHOOL   Morgan Hill

105 John Wilson Way, Morgan Hill, CA 95037. Phone: 408-782-7177. Fax: 408-782-7138. www.oakwoodmh.org. Head: Ted Helvey. Admissions: Jackie Matthews. Est. 1998. Nonprofit. Dress code.

Gr. Pre-K to 9. 425 students. Max class size: K, 12; gr. 1-3, 20; upper grades, 24. K Hrs: 8 AM - 11 AM or 12 PM - 3 PM. Elementary: 8 AM - 3 PM. Tuition: $2,950 - $6,950 (Pre-K - K), $10,200 (1 - 9). Other fees: $500 (Pre-K) and $1,000 (K-9) enrollment/re-enrollment fee. Specialists: art, music, drama, PE, computers, library, science. French, Spanish. Spacious classrooms, classroom gardens, two science labs, a star lab, a computer lab, a gymnasium, a stage, state of the art buildings, beautiful landscaping. PE, afterschool sports: flag football, volleyball, basketball, soccer, track and field, cross-country. 11,000 books in library. Waiting list. Parent participation encouraged. Standardized tests administered. Accreditation: WASC.

At Oakwood, we value learning in an atmosphere of respect through courtesy, cooperation, patriotism, honesty, good citizenship and appreciation of diversity. With these values at the helm of our school, we believe that faculty, students and parents will contribute to the well-being and stability of our community and our society. Our purpose as a school is clear: we want children to succeed in their educational, social and personal endeavors. In the process, our students become concerned, kind, committed members of society, ready to make significant contributions to our world.

SAINT CATHERINE SCHOOL   Morgan Hill

17500 Peak Avenue, Morgan Hill, CA 95037. Phone: 408-779-9950. Fax: 408-779-9928. www.stcaschool.org. Head: Suzanne Rich. Est. 1963. Nonprofit. Catholic. Uniforms.

Gr. K to 8. 300 students. 1 to 18 teacher to student ratio. Max class size: K-3, 20; upper grades, 36. K Hrs: Minimum day 8 AM - 12:30 PM, Full day 8 AM - 2 PM. Elementary: 8 AM - 3 PM. Extended care hrs: 7 AM - 6 PM, $25 registration plus hourly. Tuition: $3,840. Other fees: $300. 5% receive fin. aid. Specialists: computer, math, music, PE. Spanish. Computer lab. Afterschool sports. Reading specialist. App. deadline: February. Waiting list. Parent participation required. Accreditation: WASC, WCEA.

GERMAN INTERNATIONAL SCHOOL OF SILICON VALLEY   Mountain View

310 Easy Street, Mountain View, CA 94043. Phone: 650-254-0748. Fax: 650-254-0749. www.gissv.org. Head: Michael Spahn-Senge. Admissions: Office@gissv.org. Est. 1999. Nonprofit. No dress code.

Gr. Pre-K to 12. 100 students. 1 to 10 teacher to student ratio. Max class size: 20. Aides in grades K-1. K Hrs: 7:30 AM - 6 PM. School hrs: 8 AM - 1:30 PM., $1,000/semester. Tuition: $10,900 - $13,604, siblings and early payment discounts avail. Other fees: $550. 10% receive fin. aid. French, German, Spanish. Computer lab, homework club, pottery room. Swimming, tennis, track and field, basketball. 3 students per computer. 5,000 books in library. App. deadline: May. Rolling admissions. 85% of teachers credentialed. Avg. yrs. teaching exp: 10. Summer Camp for gr. 1-4. Accreditation: German Government.

The GISSV has committed itself to ensuring students reach their full academic potential in a nurturing environment that fosters critical and imaginative thinking, a passion for lifelong learning and an appreciation for cultural diversity.

SAINT JOSEPH SCHOOL   Mountain View

1120 Miramonte Avenue, Mountain View, CA 94040. Phone: 650-967-1839. www.sjmv.org. Head: Stephanie Mirenda Knight. Est. 1952. Nonprofit. Catholic. Uniforms.

Gr. K to 8. 300 students. Max class size: 32. K Hrs: 7:55 AM - 11:10 AM, 11:50 AM - 3 PM. Elementary: 8 AM - 3 PM. Extended care hrs: 7 AM - 6 PM, $3.50/hr or $100/wk. Tuition: $4,400 - $5,200. Science room, computer lab, learning assistance room (for one-on-one tutoring), library. Football, swimming basketball, soccer, track and field, volleyball, baseball. 4,000 books in library. Band, choir. 100% of teachers credentialed. Six week summer program and extended daycare. Accreditation: WASC, WCEA.

We, in partnership with the parents and as facilitators of learning, commit ourselves to educating the whole child in an environment where spiritual growth, academic excellence and an appreciation of multicultural values are fostered. Psychological, social, emotional and physical growth support and augment our commitment to educating the whole child. Teaching is based on the doctrine of the Roman Catholic Church that aims to instill respect, integrity, social justice and the acceptance of everyone in the community. To this end St. Joseph Catholic School seeks to foster and deepen relationships among families, the parish and the global community.

SAINT STEPHEN LUTHERAN SCHOOL   Mountain View

320 Moorpark Way, Mountain View, CA 94041. Phone: 650-961-2071. Fax: 650-961-2071. www.ssls.org. Head: Sara Pfeiffer. Admissions: Mary Ryan. Est. 1995. Nonprofit. Christian.

Gr. 1 to 8. 35 students. 1 to 5 teacher to student ratio. K Hrs: 8 AM - 3:15 PM. Elementary: 8 AM - 3:15 PM. K meets MWF. Extended care hrs: 7:30 AM - 6 PM. Tuition: $4,900. Other fees: $500. Specialists: drama, music, computer. German. Field trips, science camp.

For us, education takes its direction from the Holy Scriptures, which reveal God's eternal presence in all creation, man's sinful nature and need for redemption from sin, the grace God has shown to us in our Savior Jesus Christ, and the Holy Spirit's work of renewing and creating in us a new person in God's image. The school stresses academics, good discipline and character development, all within the framework of this philosophy. We endeavor to give your child a well-rounded education to prepare him or her for this life and eternity.

YEW CHUNG INTERNATIONAL SCHOOL   Mountain View

310 Easy Street, Mountain View, CA 94043. Phone: 650-903-0986. Fax: 650-903-0976. www.ycis-sv.com.

Gr. K to 5. Extended care available. Tuition: $9,850 - $11,280. Specialists: music, art, PE. Multi-purpose room, computer lab, library. English and Chinese dual language learning program for all grades. App. deadline: March. Rolling admissions. Bilingual summer program English and Mandarin Chinese with a strong academic program in the morning and a variety of musical and recreational activities in the afternoon. Accreditation: Council of International Schools.

At Yew Chung, we strive to unite the best elements of Eastern and Western traditions and practices, the growth of the individual and the inquiring mind as well as develop a sense of personal responsibility and social welfare of all. The Yew Chung international curriculum is designed to be developmentally appropriate for each age level, rooted in bilingual education in multicultural environments utilizing instructional and information technology, fusing both Western and Chinese philosophies for character formation. Our holistic approach to education involves cooperation with parents, family, community and the world around us.

ALMA HEIGHTS CHRISTIAN ACADEMY   Pacifica

1295 Seville Drive, Pacifica, CA 94044. Phone: 650-359-0555. Fax: 650-359-5020. www.almaheights.org. Head: David Welling. Admissions: Jackie Flynn. Est. 1955. Nonprofit. Christian. Uniforms.

Gr. K to 12. 300 students. 1 to 10 teacher to student ratio. Avg. class size: 20. Max class size: 27. K Hrs: 8:15 AM - 12 PM. School hrs: 8:15 PM - 3:15 AM. Extended care hrs: 7 AM - 6 PM, $3.50/hr. Care open some holidays. Tuition: $5,082 - $5,940. Other fees: $540 registration and student fees. Spanish. Gymnasium, library, media and science center. Bay Area Christian Athletic League (BACAL): baseball, basketball, soccer, softball, volleyball. Phonics, garden project, class plays. App. deadline: June. Rolling admissions. Admissions test. Waiting list. Parent participation required. 70% of teachers credentialed. Avg. yrs. teaching exp: 10. Standardized tests administered. Summer soccer, academic camps, and a reading program. Accreditation: WASC, ASCI, Western Association of Christian Schools.

Education is the search for truth and all truth ultimately derives from God, especially through the Bible. Our wish is to guide students in the pursuit of a sound traditional educational program, in an atmosphere of Christian love and care for the individual.

GOOD SHEPHERD ELEMENTARY SCHOOL   Pacifica

909 Oceana Boulevard, Pacifica, CA 94044. Phone: 650-359-4544. Fax: 650-359-4558. www.goodshepherd-school.org. Head: Patricia Volan. Est. 1968. Nonprofit. Catholic. Uniforms.

Gr. K to 8. 350 students. 1 to 25 teacher to student ratio. Max class size: 40. Aides in grades K-5. Elementary: 8 AM - 2:45 PM. School hrs: 8:10 AM - 2:45 PM. Extended care hrs: 7 AM - 6 PM, $4/hr or $150/mo. Tuition: $3,700 - $4,500, sibling discounts and financial aid avail. Other fees: $220 registration. Specialists: computer, music, choir. Computer lab, library, multi-purpose room. Specialist on staff. App. deadline: January. Waiting list. Parent participation required. Accreditation: WASC, WCEA.

The Good Shepherd School community, in partnership with parents as the primary educators of their children, believes in facilitating a comprehensive Catholic environment that reinforces Christian ethics and values, builds strong academic skills, and maximizes personal growth in each student.

BOWMAN INTERNATIONAL SCHOOL   Palo Alto

4000 Terman Drive, Palo Alto, CA 94306. Phone: 650-813-9131. Fax: 650-813 9132. www.bowmanschool.org. Head: Margaret Bowman Ricks. Est. 1995. Nonprofit. No dress code.

Gr. K to 8. 160 students. Max class size: 20. K Hrs: 8:30 AM - 3:30 AM. School hrs: 8:30 AM - 3:30 PM. Extended care hrs: 7:30 AM - 6 PM, cost included in tuition. Tuition: $14,850. Specialists: art, music, PE. Japanese, Latin, Spanish. App. deadline: March. 2 1/2 day visit to the school. Waiting list. Standardized tests administered.

At Bowman we offer a unique educational opportunity for elementary aged children, built on the principles of Maria Montessori. All classroom experiences are designed to help the children become life-long learners who take responsibility for their own education and who develop respect for themselves, others, and the environment.

CHALLENGER SCHOOL   Palo Alto

3880 Middlefield Road, Palo Alto, CA 94303. Phone: 650-213-8245. www.challengerschool.com. Head: Michelle Defaee. Est. 1963. Uniforms.

Gr. Pre-K to 8. 500 students. Max class size: 28. Average class size: 24. K Hrs: half days 8:45 AM - 11:40 AM, 12:50 PM - 3:40 PM, full day 8:45 AM - 3:20 PM. Elementary: 8:30 AM - 3:15 PM. Extended care hrs: 7 AM - 6 PM, $1,800/yr. Tuition: $8,983 - $10,381. Specialists: art, music, dance, karate. Karate, gymster. Advanced curriculum with a heavy emphasis on reading and writing. App. deadline: March. Admissions test. Standardized tests administered. Accreditation: NIPSA.

Challenger's mission is to prepare children to become self-reliant, productive individuals; to teach them to think, speak, and write with clarity, precision, and independence; and to inspire them to embrace challenge and find joy and self-worth through achievement.

EMERSON SCHOOL   Palo Alto

4251 El Camino Real, Palo Alto, CA 94306. Phone: 650-424-1267. Fax: 650-856-2778. www.headsup.org. Head: Peter Glassman, Ph.D.

Gr. 1 to 6. 1 to 12 teacher to student ratio. Max class size: 24. Classes with more than 12 students have multiple teachers. The school operates year-round. Extended care hrs: 7:30 AM - 6 PM. Care open some holidays. Tuition: $13,095 - $15,480. Specialists: music. Spanish. Computer for each child. Non-graded multi-age classrooms. App. deadline: March. 100% of teachers credentialed.

The goals of the school are to foster optimum development of the whole child, to promote academic excellence, to respond sensitively to each child's unique interests, talents and needs, and to involve the whole family in its mission. The school combines an innovative approach to learning with traditional values and the joy of discovery.

GIDEON HAUSNER JEWISH DAY SCHOOL   Palo Alto

450 San Antonio Road, Palo Alto, CA 94306. Phone: 650-494-8200. Fax: 650-424-0714. www.hausner.com. Head: Gerald H. Elgarten, Ph.D. Admissions: Audrey Fox. Est. 1989. Nonprofit. Jewish. Dress code.

Gr. K to 8. 372 students. Max class size: K, 24; gr. 1-3, 24; upper grades, 18. Aides in grades K-5. K Hrs: 8:30 AM - 3:15 PM. Elementary: 8:30 AM - 3:15 PM. Extended care hrs: 7:30 AM - 5:30 PM. Tuition: $12,960 - $14,244. Specialists: music, drama, poetry, Jewish studies. Hebrew. Library, science labs, two media centers, art room. Volleyball, soccer, basketball, flag football. Learning support specialist. App. deadline: January. Waiting list. Parent participation required. 20% of teachers post HW online. Standardized tests administered. One week summer camp for sports, arts and crafts. Accreditation: CAIS.

We are committed to providing an excellent general and Judaic education to our students. Our goal is to provide this in a nurturing environment, with emphasis placed on social/emotional learning along with rigorous academic goals.

INTERNATIONAL SCHOOL OF THE PENINSULA   Palo Alto

151 Laura Lane, Palo Alto, CA 94303. Phone: 650-251-8500. Fax: 650-251-8501. www.istp.org. Head: Philippe Dietz. Admissions: James Pao. Est. 1979. Nonprofit. No dress code.

Gr. Pre-K to 8. 500 students. 1 to 10 teacher to student ratio. Max class size: K, 25; gr. 1-3, 20; upper grades, 20. Aides in K. K Hrs: 8:30 AM - 3 PM. Elementary: 8:15 AM - 3:15 PM. Extended care hrs: 7:30 AM - 6 PM, $12/hr or $8/hr prepaid. Care open some holidays. Tuition: $13,610 - $16,500. Other fees: $950 one-time enrollment; annual fees of $500-750. 20% receive fin. aid. French/English or Chinese/English dual language immersion school. Music room, art room, computer lab, science lab, 2 libraries, multipurpose room. Afterschool sports available. 12 students per computer. Wide variety of afterschool programs: arts, dance, sports, martial arts, foreign languages. French-as-a-Second-Language specialist is available. 2 applicants per space. App. deadline: February. Admissions test. For students applying for either the French or Chinese dual immersion program, language proficiency required to enter 1st grade or above. Waiting list. 90% of teachers credentialed. Avg. yrs. teaching exp: 12. Standardized tests administered. Four 2-week themed summer sessions with language emphasis in French, Chinese, Spanish, or English-as-a-Second-Language. Accreditation: WASC, CAIS, French Ministry of Education.

The goal of the International School of the Peninsula is to provide a superior academic experience while developing students with a broader international awareness and an ability to speak two languages. We believe that through immersion, students not only learn to speak a second language, they are transformed in other ways-adaptability, confidence, expression, cultural awareness, and an ability to participate in international communities. Our objective is to develop whole individuals with a strong academic foundation and a lifelong passion for learning, and encourage the development of responsibility, integrity, and leadership.

KEYS SCHOOL Palo Alto

2890 Middlefield Road, Palo Alto, CA 94306. Phone: 650-328-1711. Fax: 650-328-4506. www.keysschool.com. Head: Jon Ninnemann. Admissions: Jan Bruzzese. Est. 1973. Nonprofit. Dress code.

Gr. K to 8. 176 students. 1 to 7 teacher to student ratio. Avg. class size: 18. Max class size: 21. K Hrs: 8:30 AM - 3 PM. Elementary: 8:30 AM - 3:15 PM. Extended care hrs: 7:30 AM - 6 PM, $10/day until 4:30 PM, $20/day until 6 PM or $250/mo. Tuition: $16,300 - $17,150. 5% receive fin. aid. Specialists: art, music, drama, PE, science, technology, dance, speech, self-science. Spanish. Technology lab with multimedia computers and Internet access, science lab. Afterschool sports, SJCAL League sports: soccer, baseball, flag football, basketball, soccer, softball, volleyball. App. deadline: January. Admissions test. Waiting list. Parent participation encouraged. Standardized tests administered. Accreditation: CAIS.

Keys School is an independent, K-8 school that offers a broad, hands-on curriculum. It fosters high academic achievement and emphasizes balanced growth - intellectually, physically, emotionally, and socially - for every student. Within a diverse and supportive community, Keys is committed to maintaining a caring and creative environment that encourages children to love learning, to take intellectual risks, and to treat others with respect and empathy.

LIVING WISDOM SCHOOL OF PALO ALTO Palo Alto

456 Colege Avenue, Palo Alto, CA 94306. Phone: 650-462-8150. Fax: 650-462-8152. www.livingwisdomschool.org. Head: Helen Purcell. Admissions: Helen Purcell. Est. 1992. Nonprofit.

Gr. Pre-K to 8. 50 students. 1 to 8 teacher to student ratio. Max class size: K, 12; gr. 1-3, 12; upper grades, 20. Aides in K. K Hrs: 8:45 AM - 3 PM. School hrs: 8:45 AM - 3 PM. Afterschool care until 6 PM., $6/hr. Care open some holidays. Tuition: $11,800 - $12,600. 14% receive fin. aid. French. Upper grade classrooms have wireless Internet and offer film making opportunities in the middle school. 2 students per computer. 3,000 books in library. Music, art, drama, dance, yoga. Math solvers league, computer programming, community service projects. Living Wisdom School treats each individual student as an individual, making whatever accommodations necessary. Specialists on staff for dyslexia remediation. Admissions test. Parent participation required. 60% of teachers credentialed. 60% of teachers have adv. degrees. Avg. yrs. teaching exp: 10.

Living Wisdom School offers academic excellence and the tools to become a successful, emotionally mature, and self-confident person. The school also nurtures spiritual development that is non-sectarian in nature, emphasizing the importance of each student's individual spiritual path.

SAINT ELIZABETH SETON SCHOOL   Palo Alto

1095 Channing Avenue, Palo Alto, CA 94301. Phone: 650-326-9004. Fax: 650-326-2949. seton.ca.campusgrid.net. Head: Sister Theresa Marie McDermott. Est. 1978. Uniforms.

Gr. K to 8. 250 students. Max class size: 26. K Hrs: AM and PM hours. Elementary: 8 AM - 3 PM. Tuition: $2,400. Other fees: $100. 100% receive fin. aid. Spanish. Library, gym. Basketball, soccer, volleyball. Challenge Math Program for grades 6-8, Computer Program K-8, afterschool sports. Early Intervention Literacy Program. Accreditation: WASC, WCEA.

Our intellectual and academic goals are to challenge students to achieve their intellectual and academic potential; we endeavor to recognize and address their individual needs, differences, and learning styles.

STRATFORD SCHOOL   Palo Alto

870 N. California Avenue, Palo Alto, CA 94303. Phone: 650-493-1151.

Please see complete listing under Los Gatos.

WOODLAND SCHOOL   Portola Valley

360 La Cuesta Drive, Portola Valley, CA 94028. Phone: 650-854-9065. Fax: 650-854-6006. www.woodland-school.org. Head: Mr. Scott Bell. Admissions: Mrs. Rosemary Malouf. Est. 1981. Nonprofit. Uniforms.

Gr. Pre-K to 8. 240 students. 1 to 14 teacher to student ratio. Max class size: 20. Aides in grades K-2. K Hrs: 8:20 AM - 3 PM. Elementary: 8:15 AM - 3 PM. Extended care hrs: 7:30 AM - 5:30 PM. Tuition: $14,250. Other fees: $900. 20% receive fin. aid. Specialists: art, music, computers, PE, gymnastics, upper grades (5-8) are departmentalized with specialists. French. Sports field, computer lab, science lab library, multi-use room. Basketball, volleyball, flag football, tennis. 1 student per computer. 1,200 books in library. App. deadline: March. Rolling admissions. Waiting list. 100% of teachers credentialed. 10% of teachers have adv. degrees. Avg. yrs. teaching exp: 12. Standardized tests administered. 5 week summer program. Academic AM; camp activies PM: arts & crafts, horseback riding, field trips, sports, overnight.

We offer a challenging academic program at all grade levels along with computer science, art, music, sports, gymnastics, French and etiquette. While students benefit intellectually from these enrichment programs, they also grow emotionally and socially. Our students are well-rounded students with interests and experiences in many areas.

OUR LADY OF MT. CARMEL SCHOOL   Redwood City

301 Grand Street, Redwood City, CA 94062. Phone: 650-366-6127. Fax: 650-366-0902. www.mountcarmel.org. Head: Teresa Anthony. Est. 1885. Nonprofit. Catholic. Uniforms.

Gr. K to 8. 300 students. 1 to 18 teacher to student ratio. Max class size: 35. K Hrs: 8 AM - 9:40 AM, 12:30 PM - 2:45 PM. Elementary: 8 AM - 2:45 PM. Extended care hrs: 7 AM - 6 PM, $4.50/hr or $250/mo. Tuition: $3,990 - $5,190. Other fees: $200. 16% receive fin. aid. Specialists: music, technology, physical education, drama, art. Baseball, volleyball, basketball, track and field. App. deadline: January. Parent participation required. 100% of teachers credentialed. Avg. yrs. teaching exp: 14. Standardized tests administered. Summer program. Accreditation: WASC, WCEA.

We, the faculty of Mt. Carmel School, strive as Catholic educators to inspire our students to share in the Life of Christ. We provide an educational environment, which will strengthen the spiritual and social values of the students and equip them with the necessary skills. Our Lady of Mt. Carmel School is a faith community rooted in the understanding that each child is created by God, our loving Father. In the light of Jesus' teachings, each student is challenged to grow spiritually, morally, socially, intellectually, physically and emotionally.

PENINSULA CHRISTIAN SCHOOL   Redwood City

1305 Middlefield Road, Redwood City, CA 94063. Phone: 650-366-3842. Head: Dr. Wilbur F. Martin. Est. 1971. Nonprofit. Christian. Dress code.

Gr. Pre-K to 8. 136 students. Avg. class size: 18. Max class size: 25. K Hrs: 8:45 AM - 3 PM. School hrs: 8:30 AM - 3 PM. Extended care hrs: 7 AM - 6 PM, $165/mo. Tuition: $3,650. Other fees: $225. 10% receive fin. aid. Specialists: music, art, computers, chapel. Rolling admissions. Parent participation required. Summer program. Accreditation: ACSI.

Peninsula Christian School provides a quality academic program and a structured setting in which students of diverse backgrounds are challenged to strive for excellence, to discover and develop their full potential, enabling each of them to serve as a productive member of Church and society. We uphold high spiritual, academic, and behavioral standards that openly integrate a Biblical lifestyle of discipleship and education. PCS has a curriculum that teaches our students to think critically and creatively, and to value the importance of their studies.

REDEEMER LUTHERAN SCHOOL   Redwood City

468 Grand Street, Redwood City, CA 94062. Phone: 650-366-3466. Fax: 650-366-5897. www.redeemer-school.org. Head: Mike Mancini. Admissions: Gale Olsen-Administrative Assistant. Est. 1957. Nonprofit. Christian. Uniforms.

Gr. K to 8. 152 students. 1 to 15 teacher to student ratio. Avg. class size: 16. Max class size: K, 20; gr. 1-3, 24; upper grades, 24. Aides in grades K-3. K Hrs: 8:30 AM - 3 PM. Elementary: 8:30 AM - 3 PM. Extended care hrs: 7 AM - 5:45 PM. Care open some holidays. Tuition: $5,900 1st Child, $5,310 2nd Child. Other fees: $350 registration. 10% receive fin. aid. Specialists: PE, Bell and Vocal Choir, technology, public speaking. New 11 classroom school building home to grades K-8; media center, homework center, and extended care facility. Lutheran Schools Athletic Association: volleyball, basketball, track. 2 students per computer. Educational specialist offers individual tutoring and testing for children with special needs. App. deadline: May. Admissions test. Waiting list. Parent participation encouraged. 90% of teachers credentialed. 20% of teachers have adv. degrees. Avg. yrs. teaching exp: 7. 100% of teachers post HW online. Standardized tests administered. Summer program. Accreditation: WASC, NLSA.

Our primary goal is to help children develop a positive view of the future and acquire the attitudes, knowledge and skills necessary to become successful, contributing Christians in a rapidly changing world. The teachers, parents and congregation members will inter- act so that students will be nurtured with God's love and grace. Students' attitudes and views of the future will be positively enhanced by the demonstration of spiritual values in the school community. All students will be actively and enthusiastically involved in the learning process. Classroom instruction will include contemporary technology and tools that encourage productive, effective and successful learning.

SAINT PIUS SCHOOL   Redwood City

1100 Woodside Road, Redwood City, CA 94061. Phone: 650-368-8327. Fax: 650-368-7031. www.stpiusschool. Head: Rita Carroll. Admissions: Rita Carroll. Est. 1954. Nonprofit. Catholic. Uniforms.

Gr. K to 8. 302 students. 1 to 21 teacher to student ratio. Max class size: 35. Aides in grades K-3. K Hrs: 8AM - 12 PM, 10:45 AM - 2:30 PM. School hrs: 8 AM - 3 PM. Extended care hrs: 7:30 AM - 6 PM, $4.20/hr. Tuition: $3,640. Other fees: $275. 3% receive fin. aid. Specialists: art, math, science, computer, music, PE. Computer lab, science room, art room. Baseball, basketball, volleyball, track. 3 students per computer. Resource teacher on staff to help students with learning differences. Rolling admissions. Admissions test. Waiting list. Parent participation encouraged. 100% of teachers credentialed. 30% of teachers have adv. degrees. Avg. yrs. teaching exp: 12. Standardized tests administered. Summer enrichment program, sports, and day care. Accreditation: WASC, WCEA.

Our primary aim is to be a community of faith and our goal is to nourish each child's spiritual, academic, physical, social and emotional growth. We feel that we can only achieve these goals with the full cooperation of the parents. We encourage our students to put forth their best effort at all times, and we daily provide an environment where students may feel comfortable and safe so that they may work to their fullest potential.

WHERRY ACADEMY ELEMENTARY SCHOOL   Redwood City

452 Fifth Avenue, Redwood City, CA 94063. Phone: 650-367-6791. Est. 1983. Dress code.

Gr. K to 8. 40 students. 1 to 10 teacher to student ratio. Avg. class size: 10. Max class size: 16. K Hrs: 8:30 AM - 11:30 AM. Elementary: 8 AM - 2 PM., $3.15/hr. Tuition: $5,900. Other fees: $100 registration, $20/mo for materials. 10% receive fin. aid. Specialists:

math, science, music. French. remedial program. Rolling admissions. Admissions test. 100% of teachers credentialed. Avg. yrs. teaching exp: 19. Summer enrichment and remedial programs.

Each student is an individual. With that in mind, Wherry Academy offers a full program and the student benefits in every area. We welcome all students with acceptable behavior. They will progress as far toward college preparation as possible.

HIGHLANDS CHRISTIAN SCHOOL   San Bruno

1900 Monterey Drive, San Bruno, CA 94066. Phone: 650-873-4090. www.churchofthehighlands.org/school. Head: Vernita Sheley. Est. 1966. Nonprofit. Christian. Uniforms.

Gr. Pre-K to 10. 1,050 students. Max class size: 29. K Hrs: 9 AM - 3 PM. Elementary: 8:15 AM - 3 PM. Extended care hrs: 7 AM - 6 PM. Tuition: $4,300 - $4,500, fin. aid avail. Other fees: $100 registration, $200 supplies. Specialists: computers. Spanish. PE and afterschool sports. Science fair, fine arts, speech meets, and other enrichment. Waiting list. 90% of teachers credentialed. Avg. yrs. teaching exp: 15. Summer programs available for current students. Accreditation: WASC, ACSI.

We are sponsored by Church of the Highlands, a non-denominational Protestant church. We believe each child is unique, endowed with special gifts, and has a God-ordained purpose in life. We endeavor to supplement the educational process in the home to train up a child in the way he should go (Proverbs 22:66) and to meet his/her needs in all areas: academically, physically, spiritually and socially.

SAINT ROBERT CATHOLIC SCHOOL   San Bruno

345 Oak Avenue, San Bruno, CA 94066. Phone: 650-583-5065. Fax: 650-583-1418. www.saintroberts.org. Head: Yvonne Olcomendy. Est. 1949. Nonprofit. Catholic. Uniforms.

Gr. K to 8. 315 students. 1 to 17 teacher to student ratio. Max class size: 36. Aides in grades K-4. K Hrs: 8 AM - 1 PM. Elementary: 8 AM - 3 PM. Extended care hrs: 7 AM - 6 PM, $200/mo with a $50 registration. Tuition: $4,224. Other fees: $238. 5% receive fin. aid. Specialists: computer, music, PE. Spanish. Computers in classrooms. Students may participate in organized sports on school-sponsored teams in the Peninsula Parish Schools League. Field trips, DARE, speech meets, spelling bee. App. deadline: January. Waiting list. Parent participation required. 100% of teachers credentialed. Avg. yrs. teaching exp: 18. Standardized tests administered. Academic summer program. Accreditation: WASC, WCEA.

Our education challenges our students to understand their roles as contributors to each community to which they belong. At St. Robert School, we teach community by experiencing it. We believe that the feeling of belonging to a community leads to a sense of service. Our education encourages our students to recognize their call to grow spiritually, intel-

lectually, physically, psychologically, and socially so that through their personal growth they may better serve the members of God's family.

SAINT CHARLES SCHOOL   San Carlos

850 Tamarack Avenue, San Carlos, CA 94070. Phone: 650-593-1629. www.stcharlesschoolsc.org. Head: Deborah Bell. Est. 1950. Nonprofit. Catholic. Uniforms.

Gr. K to 8. 310 students. 1 to 17 teacher to student ratio. Max class size: 35. Aides in grades K-5. Elementary: 8 AM - 3 PM. Extended care hrs: 7 AM - 6 PM, $4.25/hr, $25 registration. Tuition: $4,800. Other fees: $300. 5% receive fin. aid. Specialists: computer, music, art, PE. Spanish. Gymnasium, science lab, library, networked computer lab and classrooms. Baseball, basketball, volleyball, track, cheerleading. Accelerated reading program. App. deadline: January. Parents contribute 20hrs/yr. 95% of teachers credentialed. Avg. yrs. teaching exp: 8. Accreditation: WASC, WCEA.

St. Charles School is a Catholic parish school dedicated to providing a safe and nurturing environment for students. The faculty, in partnership with parents, promotes a community of faith and endeavors to challenge students to reach their fullest potential. Inspired by Jesus' life, students are encouraged to become participating members of the Church and world community in the twenty-first century.

ACHIEVER CHRISTIAN SCHOOL   San Jose

540 Sands Drive, San Jose, CA 95125. Phone: 408-264-6789. Fax: 408-264-6350. www.achieverchristian.com. Head: Dr. Jett Wideman. Admissions: Teresa Camp. Est. 1971. Nonprofit. Christian. Uniforms.

Gr. Pre-K to 8. 550 students. Max class size: 25. Aides in grades K-1. K Hrs: 8:30 AM - 2:45 PM. Elementary: 8:30 AM - 3:15 PM. Extended care hrs: 7:30 AM - 6 PM, $4.50/hr. Tuition: $6,000 - $8,000, sibling discount avail. Other fees: $150 tech fee per family. Specialists: art, PE, music, computers. Pool, computer lab. Softball, basketball, volleyball, soccer, flag football. 1 student per computer. 14,000 books in library. Educational intervention help. App. deadline: March. Waiting list. 90% of teachers credentialed. 20% of teachers have adv. degrees. Avg. yrs. teaching exp: 9. 25% of teachers post HW online. Standardized tests administered.

The school partners with parents to provide an outstanding Christian education to help students achieve their God-given potential.

ALMADEN COUNTRY SCHOOL   San Jose

6835 Trinidad Drive, San Jose, CA 95120. Phone: 408-997-0424. www.a-cs.org. Head: Jean Delwiche. Admissions: Patty Falk. Est. 1982. Uniforms.

Gr. Pre-K to 8. 425 students. Max class size: 20. K Hrs: 8 AM - 11 AM, 12 AM - 3 PM. Elementary: 8 AM - 3 PM. Extended care hrs: 8 AM - 6 PM. Tuition: $6,950 - $8,950, fin.

aid avail. Other fees: $1,000. Specialists: science, art, drama, music, PE. French, Spanish. Afterschool athletics and intramural sports. Block C service club, Big Buddy program. 5 applicants per space. App. deadline: September. 2 day in-class visit for student. Waiting list. Summer drama, crafts, science programs. Accreditation: WASC.

We want children to succeed in educational, social, and personal endeavors. We concentrate on developing each child's innate strengths and talents. We promote the basic human values of kindness, compassion, and concern for others. In the process, we hope to develop individuals with a high sense of self-worth who will make significant contributions to our world.

ALMADEN PREPARATORY SCHOOL   San Jose
5670 Camden Avenue, San Jose, CA 95124. Phone: 408-723-9017. Fax: 408-723-0230. www.almadenprep.com. Head: Nancy Cyester. Est. 1980. Dress code.

Gr. Pre-K to 8. 102 students. Max class size: 22. Elementary: 9 AM - 3 PM. Extended care hrs: 7 AM - 6 PM, $165/mo. Care open holidays. Tuition: $5,400 - $7,875. Specialists: music, art, aikido. Spanish. Athletic fields, blacktop areas. Extracurricular and summer sports programs. 80% of teachers credentialed. Avg. yrs. teaching exp: 5. Summer program includes two one-month sessions.

Almaden Preparatory strongly believes that a child's success in school is a result of shared responsibility between the parent and the school. Academics, personal development, study-skills, and self-esteem are fostered through the combined efforts of the student, teacher, and parent. Independence and self-reliance are a goal for all students at Almaden Preparatory. Cooperation and teamwork are imperative in order to produce excellent results.

APOSTLES LUTHERAN SCHOOL   San Jose
5828 Santa Teresa Boulevard, San Jose, CA 95123. Phone: 408-578-4800. Fax: 408-225-0720. www.apostlessj.org. Head: Shaun Luehring. Est. 1970. Nonprofit. Lutheran. Dress code.

Gr. Pre-K to 8. 190 students. Max class size: K, 24; gr. 1-3, 25; upper grades, 25. Aides in K. K Hrs: 8:30 AM - 12 PM. Elementary: 8:30 AM - 3 PM. Extended care hrs: 6:30 AM - 6 PM, $3.50/hr. Tuition: $5,400. Other fees: $200 Registration. Specialists: religion, arts, computer, choir, piano lessons, musicals. Flag football, volleyball, basketball, track. 3 students per computer. Remedial reading and speech/language services. App. deadline: May. 20% of teachers credentialed. Avg. yrs. teaching exp: 11. Standardized tests administered. Summer Bible camp.

Apostles Lutheran School works to provide an excellent, Christ-centered academic education so that children may be well-equipped for high school, college and beyond.

CALVARY CHAPEL CHRISTIAN SCHOOL   San Jose

1175 Hillsdale Avenue, San Jose, CA 95118. Phone: 408-269-2222. Fax: 408-269-8341. www.calvarysj.org. Head: Pat Thompson. Nonprofit. Christian. Uniforms.

Gr. K to 5. Aides in K. K Hrs: full-time or part-time. Elementary: 8:30 AM - 3 PM. Extended care hrs: 7 AM - 6 PM, $5/half hr or $200/mo. Tuition: $4,830. Specialists: art, PE, computers. Computer lab, library. 1 student per computer.

Our mission is to assist Christian parents in raising and educating their children in such a way that fosters a desire to grow close to God and to do all to glorify Him.

CARDEN DAY SCHOOL OF SAN JOSE   San Jose

890 Meridian Way, San Jose, CA 95126. Phone: 408-286-7323. Fax: 408-971-2081. www.cardendayschool.com. Head: Elizabeth Asadi.

Gr. K to 8. 85 students. 1 to 6 teacher to student ratio. School hrs: 8:30 AM - 4:30 PM. Extended care hrs: 7:30 AM - 6 PM, $7/hr. Specialists: computers, science, art, music, physical education. French, Latin. Study hall, science lab. Myriad of sports and physical activities. Admissions test. 100% of teachers credentialed. Summer school held each August for two weeks.

The goal of Carden Day School is to develop students who excel in academic areas, speak well, are poised and well-mannered, are cognizant of ethics, and appreciate and enjoy various cultural aspects of life. We strive to nurture and develop the whole child through classic academic structure, service opportunities, and an environment filled with respect and humor.

CHALLENGER SCHOOL   San Jose

19950 McKean Road, San Jose, CA 95120. Phone: 408-927-5771. Head: Judy Burbank. Grades Pre-K to 8.

711 East Gish Road, San Jose, CA 95112. Phone: 408-998-2860. Head: Joseph Morrison. Grades Pre-K to 8.

4977 Dent Avenue, San Jose, CA 95118. Phone: 408-266-7073. Head: Geeta Matani. Grades Pre-K to 8.

4949 Harwood Road, San Jose, CA 95124. Phone: 408-723-0111. Head: Christel Soriano. Grades Pre-K to 8.

500 Shawnee Lane, San Jose, CA 95123. Phone: 408-365-9298. Head: Gina Richter. Grades Pre-K to 8.

730 Camina Escuela, San Jose, CA 95129. Phone: 408-213-0083. Head: Molly Bauer. Grades Pre-K to 5.

Please see complete listing under Palo Alto.

CHRYSALLIS ELEMENTARY SCHOOL   San Jose

3001 Ross Avenue, San Jose, CA 95124. Phone: 408-445-8432. Fax: 408-445-8432. Head: Joyce Langley. Admissions: Joyce Langley. Est. 2001. Dress code.

Gr. K to 6. 24 students. 1 to 10 teacher to student ratio. Avg. class size: 8. Max class size: K, 8; gr. 1-3, 10; upper grades, 12. Each child is given individual attention and works at own pace. K Hrs: 9 AM - 1:30 PM. Elementary: 9 AM - 3:15 PM. Extended care hrs: 7 AM - 6 PM, $1,400. Tuition: $5,500 - $6,300. Other fees: $600 - $900. 3% receive fin. aid. Specialists: dance, music, foreign language. Spanish. Afterschool center: homework, arts & crafts, computers. Individual or group tutoring. 3.5 students per computer. 5 applicants per space. App. deadline: May. Parent participation encouraged. Avg. yrs. teaching exp: 15. Standardized tests administered. Summer program is composed of 10 weekly sessions, M-F. Academic review/grade readiness in mornings. Field trips or activities in the PM. Accreditation: In process.

Children should be provided an outstanding academic curriculum with many opportunities for real-life, "hands-on" experiences in a nurturing, supportive, and respectful environment. Lessons should be challenging, enriching, and fun. Yet, children should be given the time to develop at their own pace, with the goal of attaining a life time love of learning.

EAST VALLEY CHRISTIAN SCHOOL   San Jose

2715 South White Road, San Jose, CA 95148. Phone: 408-270-2500. www.evpc.org. Head: Steve Caballero. Est. 1988. Nonprofit. Christian. Uniforms.

Gr. K to 8. 1 to 18 teacher to student ratio. Max class size: gr. 1-3, 32; upper grades, 32. School hrs: 8:30 AM - 3 PM. Extended care hrs: 7:30 AM - 6 PM, $3.50/hr. Tuition: $3,000. Other fees: $100 for registration. Computer lab, new facilities. Parent participation encouraged. Accreditation: ACE.

The school's goal is to assist its members & other interested families of the community in training their children according to the biblical commandments found in Devotion 6:59, Prov. 22:6 & II Tim 2:15.

FIVE WOUNDS SCHOOL   San Jose

1390 Five Wounds Lane, San Jose, CA 95116. Phone: 408-293-0425. Fax: 408-971-7607. www.fivewounds.org. Head: Dr. S. Fulton. Est. 1960. Nonprofit. Catholic. Uniforms.

Gr. K to 8. 275 students. Max class size: 35. K Hrs: 8 AM - 11:15 PM, 11:45 AM - 3 PM. Elementary: 8 AM - 3 PM. Extended care hrs: 6:30 AM - 6 PM, $5/hr. Tuition: $4,390. Other fees: $370. Specialists: art, music. Dual platform computer lab. Afterschool sports are available in our Youth League. Student council focused on community service and leadership training, yearly diocesan-wide Academic Decathlon competition, chess club, after school lessons for both voice and instrumental music. Parent participation required. Accreditation: WASC, WCEA.

As Catholic educators, we seek to emulate the teachings of Jesus and will strive To Teach As Jesus Did. It is the joint responsibility of parents and teachers to develop a Gospel-centered and a holistic educational environment for each student in the school. As the primary educators of their children, parents must engage themselves fully in their child's educational process. In an atmosphere of best teaching practices and in a student-centered environment, academic growth and spiritual formation will be encouraged in each of our students. We must strive to promote academic achievement and to nurture the spiritual, intellectual, social, physical, and psychological potential of each member of our student community.

GRACE CHRISTIAN SCHOOL   San Jose

2350 Leigh Avenue, San Jose, CA 95124. Phone: 408-377-2387. www.covenantopc.org/gcschool. Est. 1988. Covenant Presbyterian Church.

Gr. K to 8. School hrs: 9 AM - 2:30 PM. Grace Christian School provides an alternative to conventional classroom experience. Our one-room schoolhouse-style classroom encompasses educational opportunities for grades K-8. The small class size affords individual attention to each student. The A Beka Book Christian Curriculum gives your child a solid, fact based, foundation of knowledge that is reinforced by an integrated and thorough review system, known as a spiraling curriculum. Parent participation encouraged.

The goal of Grace Christian School is to support parents in the educational process while providing a learning environment that exalts the Lordship of Jesus Christ in every area.

HARKER SCHOOL – LOWER SCHOOL   San Jose

4300 Bucknall Road, San Jose, CA 95131. Phone: 408-871-4600. Fax: 408-871-4320. www.harker.org. Head: Christopher Nikoloff. Admissions: Nan Nielsen. Est. 1893. Nonprofit. Uniforms.

Gr. K to 5. 576 students. 1 to 10 teacher to student ratio. Avg. class size: 17. Max class size: 22. K Hrs: 8:20 AM - 3:20 PM. School hrs: 8:20 AM - 3:20 PM. 8 period day. Extended care hrs: 7 AM - 6 PM, no additional charge. Tuition: $19,923 - $21,641. Other fees: $200 - $600. 10% receive fin. aid. Specialists: art, science, PE, computer, performing arts, music. French, Spanish. Computer labs, library, art center, gymnasium, pool, dance/music room. Flag football, volleyball, basketball, baseball, softball, soccer, swimming. 28,500 books in library. App. deadline: February. Admissions test. 100% of teachers credentialed. Standardized tests administered. Harker Summer Programs offer academic enrichment and sports and recreation activities. Accreditation: WASC, CAIS, ACA, WAIC.

The Harker School is a coeducational, non-sectarian, college preparatory day school serving grades Kindergarten through twelfth. Our goal is to develop well-rounded global citizens and lifelong learners. Through comprehensive programs of sound academics and character development, Harker provides a challenging and balanced education for college-bound students.

HOLY FAMILY SCHOOL   San Jose

4850 Pearl Avenue, San Jose, CA 95136. Phone: 498-978-1355. Fax: 408-978-0290. www.hfec.net. Head: Gail Harrell, Principal. Admissions: Sheryl Citta. Est. 1986. Nonprofit. Catholic. Dress code.

Gr. K to 8. 505 students. 1 to 17 teacher to student ratio. Max class size: K, 30; gr. 1-3, 35; upper grades, 35. Aides in grades K-5. K Hrs: 7:55 AM to 1:30 PM. Elementary: 7:45 AM - 3 PM. Extended care hrs: 7 AM - 6 PM, $60/mo - $220/mo. Tuition: $4,825 - $6,545. Other fees: $375. 10% receive fin. aid. Specialists: Art Vista Program, Rhythm & Moves, P.E., computer classes all grades. Spanish. State-of-the-Art science and computer labs, library, gym. Volleyball, basketball, flag football, softball. 1 student per computer. 7,300 books in library. Destination ImagiNation, Art Vista, Academic Decathlon, after school sports, monthly outreach. Learning Specialist onsite. 2 applicants per space. App. deadline: February. Parent participation encouraged. 100% of teachers credentialed. 17% of teachers have adv. degrees. Avg. yrs. teaching exp: 15. Standardized tests administered. Summer Camp Galileo on site. Accreditation: WASC, WCEA.

Holy Family School is a parish school rich in the tradition of Catholic education and committed to academic excellence. Our mission is to foster and to support the development of Catholic faith and identity while nurturing the whole child. In partnership with family, educators, and the whole parish community, we strive to promote the spiritual, intellectual, and social development of our students.

HOLY SPIRIT SCHOOL   San Jose

1198 Redmond Avenue, San Jose, CA 95120. Phone: 408-268-0794, Ext. 1115. Fax: 408-268-5281. www. holyspirit-school.org. Head: Eileen Beck. Admissions: Claudia Gilbert. Est. 2000. Nonprofit. Catholic. Uniforms.

Gr. Pre-K to 8. 500 students. Max class size: 30. Aides in grades K-3. K Hrs: 8 AM - 2:55 PM. Elementary: 8 AM - 3 PM. Extended care hrs: 7 AM - 6 PM, $6/hr. Tuition: $4,725 - $6,825. Other fees: $400. 6% receive fin. aid. Specialists: science, music, math, computer technology. Spanish. Computer and science labs, a multi-media library, and gymnasium. A separate kindergarten complex, Pre-K program, and on-site extended care program. School is fully computer networked. Afterschool sports: football, volleyball, basketball, softball, track. Computer technology, music, and art programs, advanced math. Learning resource teacher for language arts and math. App. deadline: February. Waiting list. Parent participation required. 100% of teachers credentialed. Avg. yrs. teaching exp: 16. 20% of teachers post HW online. Standardized tests administered. K-6 grade summer academic and enrichment. Accreditation: WASC, WCEA.

We endeavor to live according to the principles which are consistent with our Catholic Christian heritage. We believe that parents are the primary educators of their children and that teachers are to complement and continue what parents have begun. We believe that every child has a right to be led to an awareness of God within himself/herself and others and to appreciate and live out the Gospel values of human dignity, freedom, peace and justice. We believe that the school should provide an environment in which each child can develop a good self image and an awareness of his/her uniqueness. We believe that the school should provide an environment in which each child can develop to his/her potential.

LIBERTY BAPTIST ELEMENTARY SCHOOL San Jose

2790 South King Road, San Jose, CA 95122. Phone: 408-274-5613. www.libertybaptist.org. Head: Russel Barnes. Est. 1968. Nonprofit. Christian. Dress code.

Gr. Pre-K to 12. 350 students. 1 to 13 teacher to student ratio. Max class size: 25. Aides in K. Elementary: 8:30 AM - 3 PM. Extended care hrs: 7 AM - 6 PM. Tuition: $4,000 - $6,289, sibling discount avail. Other fees: $300. Specialists: band, choir, drama. Spanish. Christian/Private School Athletic League sports: soccer, basketball, softball, volleyball, baseball. We accept children with disabilities to the extent that we can meet their needs. Parent participation encouraged. 36% of teachers credentialed. Avg. yrs. teaching exp: 11. Standardized tests administered. Summer recreation program. Accreditation: WASC (in process).

The primary purpose of Liberty Baptist School is to assist parents who wish to provide their children a Christian education. Liberty Baptist School is an integral and inseparable ministry of Liberty Baptist Church. Accordingly, we will strive to train young people in the principles of Christian leadership, Godly character, self-discipline, individual responsibility, personal integrity, and good citizenship.

LITTLE SCHOLARS SCHOOL San Jose

3703 Silver Creek Road, San Jose, CA 95121. Phone: 408-238-2500. www.littlescholarsschool.org. Head: Anima Desai. Admissions: Arshia Ali. Est. 1984. Uniforms.

Gr. K to 6. 75 students. 1 to 18 teacher to student ratio. Max class size: 18. K Hrs: 9 AM - 2 PM. Elementary: 8 AM - 3 PM., $160/mo. Tuition: $5,600. Other fees: $500. Outsourced programs are Karate, gymnastics and soccer. App. deadline: July. Parent participation encouraged. 100% of teachers credentialed. Avg. yrs. teaching exp: 10. Standardized tests administered. Summer academic and social events.

The school offers a traditional back -to-basics approach, giving challenge to those students who are ready and providing as many enrichment opportunities as we can.

MILPITAS CHRISTIAN SCHOOL San Jose

3435 Birchwood Lane, San Jose, CA 95132. Phone: 408-945-6530. www.mcsi.org. Head: Judy Morasci. Admissions: Leta Leggitt. Est. 1974. Nonprofit. Christian. Uniforms.

Gr. K to 8. 700 students. Max class size: K, 25; gr. 1-3, 25; upper grades, 28. Aides in grades K-5. K Hrs: 8:25 AM - 2:30 PM. Elementary: 8:15 AM - 3 PM. Extended care hrs: 7 AM - 6:30 PM, $230/mo. Care open some holidays. Tuition: $6,650 - $8,110. Other fees: $300. Specialists: computer, PE, band, orchestra, jazz band, drama. Spanish. Computer lab. Softball, basketball, volleyball, soccer. FAME-fine arts program, chess, gymnastics, art. Parent participation required. 85% of teachers credentialed. Avg. yrs. teaching exp: 9.5. Standardized tests administered. Summer school and day camp. Accreditation: WASC, ACSI.

The academic program, while stressing basics, must provide a wide range of studies and use both traditional and modern methodology, with materials which are current and academically sound. Along with the acquisition of facts, stress will be placed on development of skill in logical, Biblical, and creative thinking and ability to share information with others clearly and concisely in both written and oral form.

MOST HOLY TRINITY SCHOOL — San Jose

1940 Cunningham Avenue, San Jose, CA 95122. Phone: 408-729-3431. Fax: 408-272-4945. www.mht-school.org. Head: Sandra Jewett-Silva. Est. 1965. Nonprofit. Catholic. Uniforms.

Gr. K to 8. 315 students. 1 to 17 teacher to student ratio. Max class size: 35. Aides in grades K-5. K Hrs: 8 AM - 3 PM. Elementary: 8 AM - 3 PM. Extended care hrs: 7 AM - 6 PM, $4/hr. Tuition: $4,390. 10% receive fin. aid. Specialists: art, music, computer. German, Spanish. Gym, science lab, computer lab, art room. Basketball, softball, volleyball, track, flag football. 1 student per computer. App. deadline: June. Rolling admissions. Admissions test. Waiting list. Parent participation required. 100% of teachers credentialed. 90% of teachers have adv. degrees. Avg. yrs. teaching exp: 10. Standardized tests administered. Summer academic, music camp, sports camp. Accreditation: WASC, WCEA.

In a student-centered environment, we use best teaching practices to foster well-rounded academic growth and spiritual formation. This promotes practice of lifelong learning and interpersonal skills for each of our students and nurtures the spiritual, intellectual, social, physical, and psychological potential of each member of our student community.

ONE WORLD MONTESSORI SCHOOL — San Jose

5331 Dent Avenue, San Jose, CA 95118. Phone: 408-723-5140. www.oneworldmontessori.org. Head: Rebecca Keith & Jeanette Montoto. Est. 1979. Nonprofit.

Gr. Pre-K to 8. 1 to 15 teacher to student ratio. Max class size: 33. K Hrs: 9 AM - 12 PM. School hrs: 8:30 AM - 3:30 PM. Extended care hrs: 7:30 AM - 6:30 PM, $3,000/yr. Tuition: $6,200 - $8,900. 5% receive fin. aid. Specialists: music, piano, aikido, drama, art. Spanish. Another location available in Santa Clara. Waiting list. Parent participation required. 100% of teachers credentialed. Eight-week summer program for relaxation, recreation, exploration, includes field trips, swimming, gymnastics, and arts and crafts.

147

Our objective is for children to become independent, self-reliant people, aware of what they want from life, with the tools necessary to achieve their goals, develop a sense of self, and make their unique contribution to society.

PRIMARY PLUS & WEST VALLEY MIDDLE SCHOOL   San Jose

3500 Amber Drive, San Jose, CA 95117. Phone: 408-244-1968. Fax: 408-248-7433. www.primaryplus.com. Head: Linda White. Admissions: Kathy McDermott. Est. 1969. No dress code.

Gr. Pre-K to 8. 400 students. 1 to 18 teacher to student ratio. Max class size: K, 18; gr. 1-3, 21; upper grades, 21. K Hrs: 8:30 AM - 2:30 PM. Elementary: 8:30 AM - 3 PM. Extended care hrs: 7:30 AM - 6 PM. Care open some holidays. Tuition: $7,800 - $9,400. Other fees: $150. Specialists: PE, music. Spanish. Computer/Homework Center. Soccer, basketball, soccer, flag football, volleyball. 5 students per computer. Waiting list. 100% of teachers credentialed. Avg. yrs. teaching exp: 10. Standardized tests administered. Summer program includes swimming, tennis, karate, dance.

The school encourages maximum educational, social, and personal growth in each student.

QUEEN OF APOSTLES ELEMENTARY SCHOOL   San Jose

4950 Mitty Way, San Jose, CA 95129. Phone: 408-252-3659. www.qofa-school.org. Head: Marty Chargin. Est. 1964. Nonprofit. Catholic. Uniforms.

Gr. K to 8. 307 students. 1 to 17 teacher to student ratio. Max class size: K, 35; gr. 1-3, 40; upper grades, 40. Aides in grades K-5. K Hrs: 8 AM - 2:40 PM. Elementary: 8 AM - 3 PM. Extended care hrs: 7:30 AM - 6 PM, $7/hr. Care open some holidays. Tuition: $5,500. 2% receive fin. aid. Specialists: reading. Spanish. Gym, computer lab. 2 students per computer. 5 applicants per space. Rolling admissions. Aptitude screening test. Waiting list. Parent participation encouraged. 100% of teachers credentialed. 30% of teachers have adv. degrees. Avg. yrs. teaching exp: 12. 12% of teachers post HW online. Standardized tests administered. Academic and recreational summer program. Accreditation: WASC, WCEA.

We emphasize basic skills in a warm, friendly atmosphere and seek to nurture Christian values by developing self-esteem, respect for others, and responsibility. Parents are encouraged to participae in school activities and help in fund-raising.

RAINBOW BRIDGE MERRYHILL SCHOOL   San Jose

750 N Capitol Ave, San Jose, CA 95133. Phone: (408) 254-1280. Head: Jennifer Okimura. Est. 1983. Uniforms.

Please see complete listing under Milpitas.

RAINBOW OF KNOWLEDGE SCHOOL — San Jose

1975 Cambrianna Drive, San Jose, CA 95124. Phone: 408-377-5730. Fax: 408-264-3166. www.rainbowofknowledge.org. Head: Lynne Lewin. Est. 1976. No dress code.

Gr. Pre-K to 5. 250 students. 1 to 10 teacher to student ratio. Max class size: 20. K Hrs: 8:30 AM - 12:30 PM. Elementary: 8:30 AM - 3 PM. Extended care hrs: 6:30 AM - 6:30 PM, $181/mo - $418/mo. Care open some holidays. Tuition: $5,300 - $8,100. Other fees: $250. 7% receive fin. aid. Specialists: music, PE, computer. Spanish, ASL. 5 students per computer. Centering, Friends of the Earth, Happy Thinking, Happy Faces. Afterschool soccer, dance, karate. Parent participation required. Avg. yrs. teaching exp: 15. Summer camps change every week.

At Rainbow of Knowledge we believe not only in teaching your child the fundamentals of education but also the philosophy of Happy Thinking and the importance of being a friend of the earth. We strive to teach a sense of values and ways to deal with stress. We also provide an open and caring atmosphere to encourage self-confidence and the importance of education.

SAINT CHRISTOPHER SCHOOL — San Jose

2278 Booksin Avenue, San Jose, CA 95125. Phone: 408-723-7223. Fax: 408-978-5458. www.stchris.us. Head: Mrs. Cathy Parent. Est. 1955. Nonprofit. Catholic. Uniforms.

Gr. K to 8. 620 students. 1 to 15 teacher to student ratio. Max class size: K, 15; gr. 1-3, 35; upper grades, 35. Elementary: 8:15 AM - 3 PM. Extended care hrs: 7 AM - 6 PM. Tuition: $4,450, fin. aid and sibling discount available. Specialists: computer, art, PE, reading, health, math, science, music. Spanish. Gymnasium, science building, computer lab, library. Volleyball, basketball, flag football, softball, track. Onsite LD specialist. App. deadline: February. Parent participation encouraged. Accreditation: WASC, WCEA.

The development of Catholic citizens is the joint responsibility of the parents, the school, and the Church. The fulfillment of developing the whole child — the ideas, the attitudes, the habits, the values, and the principles — can be achieved though a quality Catholic education which centers around the message of Jesus. Recognizing the potential of the students for leadership, they are encouraged to appreciate their own self worth, continue to develop their talents and become aware of their responsibilities to self, God, Church and society.

SAINT FRANCIS CABRINI SCHOOL — San Jose

15325 Woodard Road, San Jose, CA 95124. Phone: 408-377-6545. Fax: 408-377-8491. www.sfcschool.org. Head: Mrs. Gail Cirone. Est. 1963. Nonprofit. Catholic.

Gr. Pre-K to 8. 680 students. Max class size: K, 18; gr. 1-3, 35; upper grades, 35. Aides in grades K-5. K Hrs: 8 AM - 11 AM, 12 PM - 3 PM. Elementary: 8 AM - 3 PM. Extended care hrs: 6:30 AM - 6 PM, $6/hr. Care open some holidays. Tuition: $3,975 - $7,945.

Other fees: $360. Spanish. Computer and science labs, library/media center. Basketball, volleyball, football, softball, track. Field trips every year, accelerated reading program. App. deadline: October. Admissions test. Parent participation required. Accreditation: WASC, WCEA.

Saint Frances Cabrini is committed to developing the whole child by supporting the principles of the Catholic Faith and by providing a solid academic education. Our goal is to provide both the opportunity and the motivation for a child to develop spiritually, intellectually, physically and socially.

SAINT JOHN VIANNEY SCHOOL   San Jose
4601 Hyland Avenue, San Jose, CA 95127. Phone: 408-258-7677. Fax: 408-258-5997. www.sjvsj.org. Head: Sr. Michelle A. Murphy, Ms. Martha Wood. Catholic. Uniforms.

Gr. K to 8. 620 students. 1 to 27 teacher to student ratio. Max class size: K, 18; upper grades, 35. Aides in grades K-4. K Hrs: AM 8 AM - 11:50 PM, PM 11 AM - 2:50 PM. School hrs: 8 AM - 3 PM. Extended care hrs: 7 AM - 6 PM. App. deadline: February. Parent participation required. Accreditation: WASC, WCEA.

We strive to develop a community grounded in Gospel values, in which students learn and practice the principles of the Catholic faith; exercise the virtues; assume moral responsibility; and experience the importance of serving others. Our comprehensive academic program seeks to prepare members of society who are integrated individuals, capable of thinking critically and committed to life-long learning. We work in partnership with the parents, supporting their efforts to foster the unique development of each student. By honoring the funds of knowledge that the students bring from their homes, our school embraces the diversity inherent in our community.

SAINT LEO THE GREAT SCHOOL   San Jose
1051 West San Fernando Street, San Jose, CA 95126. Phone: 408-293-4846. www.stleos.pvt.k12.ca.us. Head: Phyllis Taurosa. Est. 1916. Nonprofit. Catholic. Uniforms.

Gr. K to 8. 260 students. Max class size: K, 30; gr. 1-3, 35; upper grades, 35. Aides in grades K-4. K Hrs: 8 AM - 11:30 AM, 9:30 AM - 12:30 PM. Elementary: 8 AM - 3 PM. Extended care hrs: 7 AM - 6 PM, $5/hr - $320/mo. Tuition: $4,796 - $5,546. Other fees: $425 - $550. Specialists: music, computer. Spanish. Computer lab, gym. PE, afterschool sports. Choir meets afterschool. App. deadline: February. Baptism certificate required. Parent participation required. 100% of teachers credentialed. Standardized tests administered. Accreditation: WASC, WCEA.

The mission of St. Leo the Great School is to create a Catholic environment and an academic atmosphere in which parents are recognized as the primary educators of their children. We encourage parents, faculty and staff to foster a love of learning, self-confidence, and a sense of responsibility, and to help the students discover and use their God-given potential.

SAINT MARTIN OF TOURS SCHOOL   San Jose

300 O'Connor Drive, San Jose, CA 95128. Phone: 408-287-3630. www.stmartinoftoursschool.org. Head: Karen De Monner. Est. 1955. Nonprofit. Catholic. Uniforms.

Gr. K to 8. 350 students. Max class size: 36. Aides in grades K-4. K Hrs: 8 AM - 3 PM. Elementary: 8 AM - 3 PM. Extended care hrs: 7 AM - 6 PM, $3.50/hr with a $25 registration. Tuition: $5,825 - $7,080. Other fees: $350. 6% receive fin. aid. Specialists: choir, instrumental music, lab science. French, Spanish. Large gymnasium, library, iMac computer lab, fine arts room, science lab, Learning Lab, extended care facilities. Volleyball, football, basketball, track, softball. Waiting list. Parent participation required. 95% of teachers credentialed. Standardized tests administered. Accreditation: WASC, WCEA, NCEA.

St. Martin of Tours Elementary School is a parish school rich in the tradition of Catholic education and committed to academic excellence. Together with the family and parish community, we are dedicated to creating an enthusiastic vision of the future, teaching the message of the gospels and formation of Christian values, embracing the uniqueness and dignity of each person and promoting a warm and welcoming community. It all begins here at St. Martins where students acquire a sound base of academic and critical thinking skills, a love of and a curiosity for learning and the confidence to take on new challenges.

SAINT PATRICK SCHOOL   San Jose

51 North 9th Street, San Jose, CA 95112. Phone: 408-283-5858. Fax: 408-283-5852. Head: Sister Rosemarie Carroll. Admissions: Sister Rosemarie Carroll. Est. 1925. Nonprofit. Catholic. Uniforms.

Gr. K to 8. 200 students. 1 to 8 teacher to student ratio. Max class size: K, 25; gr. 1-3, 30; upper grades, 35. Aides in grades K-1. K Hrs: 8 AM - 2:30 PM. Elementary: 8 AM - 2:45 PM. Early dismissals on Wednesdays. Extended care hrs: 7 AM - 6 PM. Tuition: $4,600. Other fees: $300. 30% receive fin. aid. Specialists: music, choir, PE. Computer lab, computers in each classroom. Volleyball, flag football, basketball, track. 3 applicants per space. App. deadline: April. Parent participation required. 90% of teachers credentialed. 30% of teachers have adv. degrees. Avg. yrs. teaching exp: 18. Standardized tests administered. Accreditation: WASC, WCEA.

St. Patrick School is a faith community where teachers and students pray together and are supported and united by their bond in Christ. We recognize our obligation to provide quality education, which will maximize the realization of each child's potential: spiritual, physical, intellectual, cultural, social.

SAINT STEPHEN'S SCHOOL   San Jose

420 Allegan Circle, San Jose, CA 95123. Phone: 408-365-2927. Fax: 408-365-3831. www.ststephenssj.com. Head: Rick Clarke. Admissions: Sue Nielsen. Est. 1978. Nonprofit. Episcopal. Uniforms.

Gr. Pre-K to 8. 180 students. 1 to 5 teacher to student ratio. Max class size: K, 22; gr. 1-3, 18; upper grades, 18. Aides in K. K Hrs: 8:30 AM - 11:30 AM, 8:30 AM - 2:30 PM. Elementary: 8:30 AM - 3 PM. Extended care hrs: 7:30 AM - 6 PM, $5/hour. Tuition: $4,000 - $7,700. Other fees: $150 application. 8% receive fin. aid. Specialists: technology, physical education. Latin, Spanish, Greek. Computer lab, homework center (after school), instructional facilities. Member of Silicon Valley Athletic League. 4 students per computer. 4,000 books in library. Drama, music programs available. App. deadline: February. Rolling admissions. Parent participation encouraged. 100% of teachers credentialed. 30% of teachers have adv. degrees. Avg. yrs. teaching exp: 7. 50% of teachers post HW online. Standardized tests administered. Thematic summer programs with social/moral expectations. Accreditation: CAIS, National Association of Episcopal Schools.

St. Stephen's School is committed to enriching our community with students confident in mind, body and spirit. In the Episcopal tradition, we will encourage our students to honor God and their responsibility to community. This will be realized in an environment of diversity, achievement, and trust. We will sustain a stimulating learning environment that provides the freedom for every child to fully develop his or her unique character and personality, ensuring that our children are thoughtful contributors to society, with a capacity to learn, to serve, and to lead.

SAINT TIMOTHY'S LUTHERAN SCHOOL   San Jose

5100 Camden Avenue, San Jose, CA 95124. Phone: 408-265-0244. www.st-tims-lutheran.org/DaySchool. Head: Mrs. Mickey Angerman. Est. 1979. Nonprofit. Lutheran. Uniforms.

Gr. Pre-K to 5. 156 students. Max class size: K, 20; gr. 1-3, 20; upper grades, 24. K Hrs: 9 AM - 12 PM, 9 AM - 3 PM. Elementary: 9 AM - 3 PM. Extended care hrs: 7:30 AM - 6 PM. Tuition: $2,600 - $6,100, early payment and sibling discounts available. Other fees: $280 - $490. 1% receive fin. aid. Specialists: choir, computer, robotics. Homework center, large library, computer lab. Chess club, science adventures, scouts. App. deadline: February. Rolling admissions. Admissions test. Parent participation encouraged. 100% of teachers credentialed. Standardized tests administered.

St. Timothy's Lutheran School is dedicated to nurturing, educating, and developing children in a Christ-centered environment to better understand and appreciate the world around us.

SAINT VICTOR SCHOOL   San Jose

3150 Sierra Road, San Jose, CA 95132. Phone: 408-251-1740. Fax: 408-251-1492. www.stvictor.org. Head: Patricia Wolf, Principal. Est. 1964. Nonprofit. Catholic. Uniforms.

Gr. K to 8. 318 students. 1 to 15 teacher to student ratio. Max class size: K, 30; gr. 1-3, 36; upper grades, 36. Aides in grades K-3. K Hrs: 8 AM - 11:15 AM, 10:30 AM - 2:45 PM. Elementary: 8 AM - 2:45 PM. Early dismissal on Wednesdays. Extended care hrs:

7 AM - 6 PM, $5/hr - $120/wk. Tuition: $5,000. Other fees: $775. 10% receive fin. aid. Specialists: art, music, PE, science. Spanish. Computer lab, science classroom. Football, basketball, volleyball, track, softball. 12 students per computer. 8,000 books in library. Choirs during school day, foreign languages and instrumentals after school. 2 applicants per space. App. deadline: February. Waiting list. Parent participation encouraged. 80% of teachers credentialed. 25% of teachers have adv. degrees. Avg. yrs. teaching exp: 13. 100% of teachers post HW online. Standardized tests administered. Accreditation: WASC, WCEA.

St.Victor is a Catholic School committed to teaching the Christian message, building a faith community, offering service for others, and providing academic excellence.

STRATFORD SCHOOL   San Jose
6670 San Anselmo Way, San Jose, CA 95119. Phone: 408-363-2130.

Please see complete listing under Los Gatos.

TOWER ACADEMY   San Jose
2887 McLaughlin Avenue, San Jose, CA 95121. Phone: 408-578-2830. Fax: 408-281-0541. www.toweracademy.com. Head: Gina Bence. Est. 1983. Uniforms.

Gr. Pre-K to 5. Max class size: 24. K Hrs: 8:30 AM - 3 PM. Elementary: 8:15 AM - 2:45 PM. School is open everyday in the year except for major holidays. Extended care hrs: 6:30 AM - 6 PM, cost included in tuition. Care open some holidays. Tuition: $6,136 - $7,548. Other fees: $290. Spanish. State of the art recreation room, computer lab. Afterschool and tutoring programs. App. deadline: March. Parent participation required. 50% of teachers credentialed. Avg. yrs. teaching exp: 15. Standardized tests administered. Summer program from mid July to mid August includes swimming, computer program, field trips.

Our mission is simple: to provide a warm, nurturing, extended family atmosphere while developing the highest standards of academic excellence and responsible behavior. We do this by developing a relationship with students and parents that is built on mutual respect, responsibility, trust and open communication.

VALLEY CHRISTIAN ELEMENTARY SCHOOL   San Jose
1500 Leigh Avenue, San Jose, CA 95125. Phone: 408-559-4400. Fax: 408-559-4022. www.valleychristian.net. Head: Shirley Hitchcock. Est. 1969. Nonprofit. Christian. Dress code.

Gr. K to 5. 1 to 12 teacher to student ratio. Max class size: K, 25; gr. 1-3, 28; upper grades, 28. K Hrs: 8:15 AM - 11:50 AM. Elementary: 8:15 AM - 2:45 PM. Extended care hrs: 7 AM - 6 PM, $2.50/hr. Tuition: $5,960 - $9,113, fin. aid avail. Other fees: $250 for enrollment. Specialists: art, choral music, computer science, dance, science, instrumental music, library, PE. Spanish. Computer lab, The Discovery Center provides assistance for students with learning difficulties. Basketball, track. Learning disabilities program. App. deadline: October. Admissions test. Reference from clergy or educator required, including statement regarding Judeo-Christian values of student. Standardized tests administered. Summer program June to August for school-age children. Accreditation: WASC, ACSI.

Valley Christian Schools' mission is to provide a nurturing environment offering quality education supported by a strong foundation of Christian Values in partnership with parents, equipping students to become leaders to serve God, their families, and to positively impact their communities and the world.

WILLOW VALE CHRISTIAN SCHOOL   San Jose

1730 Curtner Avenue, San Jose, CA 95125. Phone: 408-448-0656. Fax: 408-264-2817. www.wvministry.com. Head: Mrs. Carollyn Ellis. Admissions: Mrs. Carollyn Ellis. Est. 1998. Nonprofit. Free Methodist. Dress code.

Gr. Pre-K to 12. 144 students. 1 to 18 teacher to student ratio. Max class size: K, 18; gr. 1-3, 18; upper grades, 20. Aides in K. School hrs: 8:30 AM - 3 PM. Extended care hrs: 6:30 AM - 6 PM, $95/wk. Tuition: $4,500. Other fees: $75 new student application. Specialists: music, PE, and computer classes are a part of each child's learning experiences. Computer lab, homework center, large playground area with open space. Standardized tests administered. Summer Day Camp for K-gr.6.

ALPHA BEACON CHRISTIAN ELEMENTARY SCHOOL   San Mateo

525 West 42nd Avenue, San Mateo, CA 94403. Phone: 650-212-4222. Fax: 650-212-1026. www.alphabeacon.org. Head: Lillian G. Mark. Est. 1969. Nonprofit. Christian. Uniforms.

Gr. Pre-K to 12. 300 students. 1 to 15 teacher to student ratio. Avg. class size: 20. Max class size: 25. Elementary: 8:30 AM - 3 PM. Extended care hrs: 7 AM - 5:30 PM, $3.50/hr. Tuition: $4,400 - $6,400, fin. aid avail. Other fees: $200. Latin, Spanish. Multi-purpose room, library, computer with Internet in each class room. Bay Area Christian Athletic League (BACAL). Soccer, basketball, baseball, volleyball, softball. 12,000 books in library. Computer and laptop training programs. Parent participation required. 75% of teachers credentialed. Standardized tests administered. Accreditation: ACSI.

Our programs focus on the development of Christian character, leadership skills, social graces, and the appreciation for culture as expressed through the fine and performing arts. Our academic instruction includes training in several subject areas emphasizing the skills of reading, writing, and oral communication. Students are instructed in mathematical reasoning, computation and application. They are also trained to maintain proper levels of physical fitness.

CAREY SCHOOL   San Mateo

1 Carey School Lane, San Mateo, CA 94403. Phone: 650-345-8205. Fax: 650-345-2528. www.careyschool.com. Head: Eric Temple. Admissions: Lissa Fowler. Est. 1928. Nonprofit. Dress code.

Gr. Pre-K to 5. 180 students. 1 to 7 teacher to student ratio. Max class size: 22. Pre-K class size: 18. Aides in grades K-5. K Hrs: 8:30 AM - 12:30 PM. Elementary: 8:30 AM - 3 PM. Extended care hrs: 7 AM - 6 PM, $7/hr. Tuition: $10,000 - $15,000. 20% receive fin. aid. Specialists: art, music, PE, tech, science. French, Spanish. Computer lab. Organized basketball gr.4-5. 4 students per computer. Afterschool Adventures Program offers a variety of activities that combine learning and fun, taught by classroom teachers and outside experts in various fields. The program has included such classes as keyboarding, choir, science, cooking, art, computers, photography, drama, and sports. App. deadline: December. Waiting list. Parent participation encouraged. 90% of teachers credentialed. Avg. yrs. teaching exp: 17. Standardized tests administered. Accreditation: WASC (in process), CAIS, NAIS.

The mission of The Carey School is to inspire in our students a life-long love of learning and the pursuit of excellence within a diverse community that nurtures a deep sense of kindness, respect for others and personal responsibility.

GRACE LUTHERAN SCHOOL   San Mateo

2825 Alameda de las Pulgas, San Mateo, CA 94403. Phone: 650-345-9082. Fax: 650-377-4831. www.gracelutheranflashlcms.org. Head: Robert Meier. Est. 1984. Nonprofit. Lutheran. Uniforms.

Gr. K to 8. 90 students. 1 to 10 teacher to student ratio. Max class size: 22. K Hrs: 8:30 AM - 3:30 PM. Elementary: 8:30 AM - 3:15 PM. Extended care hrs: 7:30 AM - 6 PM, $3.25/hr. Care open some holidays. Tuition: $4,600. Other fees: $300. Wheelchair accessible; elevator. Volleyball, basketball, track & field. App. deadline: March. Rolling admissions. Parent participation encouraged. 100% of teachers credentialed. Avg. yrs. teaching exp: 20. Standardized tests administered. Summer Bible study.

SAINT GREGORY SCHOOL   San Mateo

2701 Hacienda Street, San Mateo, CA 94403. Phone: 650-573-0111. Fax: 650-573-6548. www.stgregs-sanmateo.org. Head: Linda Grund. Est. 1951. Nonprofit. Catholic. Uniforms.

Gr. K to 8. 324 students. 1 to 18 teacher to student ratio. Max class size: 36. School hrs: 8 AM - 3 PM. Extended care hrs: 7 AM - 6 PM, $4/hr. Tuition: $2,985. Specialists: science, computer, drama, PE, library, music. P.P.S.L.: baseball, volleyball, basketball, track. Parent participation required. Three week summer program. Accreditation: WASC, WCEA.

We are committed to the growth of the whole child. We challenge the spiritual, intellectual, social, physical and moral growth of our students. We offer a comprehensive, integrated curriculum in accordance with Archdiocesan guidelines. Cognizant of the need for student accountability, personal responsibility and integrity, teachers offer positive learning experiences that encourage each child to succeed. We believe that every student is unique and deserves to approach life with a sense of self-worth by being aware of his/her own gifts and special talents.

SAINT MATTHEW'S CATHOLIC SCHOOL   San Mateo

910 South El Camino Real, San Mateo, CA 94402. Phone: 650-343-1373. Fax: 650-343-2046. www.stmatthewcath.org. Head: Ken Boegel. Admissions: Jai Marino. Est. 1931. Nonprofit. Catholic. Uniforms.

Gr. K to 8. 599 students. Max class size: 35. Aides in grades K-4. Elementary: 8 AM - 3 PM. Extended care hrs: 7 AM - 6 PM, $240/mo or $4/hr drop in. Tuition: $4,150- $4,650. Other fees: $255. 25% receive fin. aid. Specialists: computer, PE, music. Spanish. Computer lab, media room, library. Baseball, basketball, volleyball, cheerleading. 11,000 books in library. App. deadline: January. Admissions test. Waiting list. Parent participation required. 88% of teachers credentialed. Avg. yrs. teaching exp: 15. Standardized tests administered. Accreditation: WASC, WCEA.

We commit ourselves to creating a peaceful and caring, Christian learning environment in which we recognize, respect, and celebrate the dignity and differences of individuals. Parent, parish, and school community work together to challenge students intellectually while nurturing them spiritually, physically, psychologically, and socially to prepare them to go forth into a diverse, technological world as active Christians with Catholic vision, persons with strong character, effective communicators, responsible citizens, and life-long learners who live according to the teachings of Christ.

SAINT MATTHEW'S EPISCOPAL DAY SCHOOL   San Mateo

16 Baldwin Avenue, San Mateo, CA 94401. Phone: 650-342-5436. Fax: 650-342-4019. www.smeds.info. Head: Mark C. Hale. Admissions: Linda Hanadalian. Est. 1953. Nonprofit. Episcopal. Uniforms.

Gr. Pre-K to 8. 230 students. 1 to 11 teacher to student ratio. Max class size: 22. Aides in grades K-3. K Hrs: 8:15 AM - 2:30 PM. Elementary: 8:15 AM - 3 PM. Supervised after school study hall with teaching support. Extended care hrs: 7:30 AM - 5 PM. Tuition: $7,875 - $17,800. 8% receive fin. aid. Specialists: technology, library, music, PE, art, drama, religion. Spanish. Flag football, basketball, volleyball, soccer, golf, swimming. 5 applicants per space. App. deadline: January. Admissions test. Waiting list. Standardized tests administered. Accreditation: CAIS, NAIS, NAES.

St. Matthew's offers an enriched academic program that includes a special focus on the social and moral development of young children. Best practices in curriculum and pedagogy are incorporated into a more traditional learning environment.

SAINT TIMOTHY SCHOOL — San Mateo

1515 Dolan Avenue, San Mateo, CA 94401. Phone: 650-342-6567. Fax: 650-342-5913. www.sttimothyschool.org. Head: Evelyn M. Nordberg. Est. 1961. Nonprofit. Catholic. Uniforms.

Gr. K to 8. 275 students. Max class size: 35. K Hrs: 8 AM - 3 PM. Elementary: 8 AM - 3 PM. Extended care hrs: 7 AM - 6 PM. Tuition: $3,175, fin. aid avail. Other fees: $225 for registration. Specialists: music, PE. Spanish. Computer lab, gym, library. Member of the PPSL: baseball, basketball, volleyball, track, cheerleading. Student faire, musicals, field trips. App. deadline: January. Admissions test. Parent participation required. Accreditation: WASC, WCEA.

St. Timothy School is an active Christian community dedicated to the education of the whole child. We acknowledge the parents as primary educators and expect ongoing participation from our school families. We work with the family to develop the spiritual, academic, psychological, social, and physical well-being of each child. We offer a comprehensive, student-centered academic curriculum and place special emphasis on teaching Catholic values. We teach the skills necessary to be productive, contributing citizens in a technological society.

ADVENTURES IN LEARNING SCHOOL — Santa Clara

890 Pomeroy Avenue, Bldg. E, Santa Clara, CA 95051. Phone: 408-247-4769. www.ainl.us. Head: Annegret Albrecht. Est. 1982. Uniforms.

Gr. K to 8. 50 students. 1 to 12 teacher to student ratio. Avg. class size: 20. Avg. class size K: 14. K Hrs: 8:30 AM - 2 PM. Elementary: 8:30 AM - 3 PM. Extracurricular activities (Karate, Science Adventures, Theater Workshop, Chess Club) 4 PM - 5 PM. Extended care hrs: 7 AM - 6 PM, no charge for morning care, $3/hr for afterschool. Tuition: $5,175 - $6,120. Other fees: $500 - $600/yr, materials, field trips as required. Specialists: music, drama, art, physical education, health. French. Library. Physical education, karate. App. deadline: September. Rolling admissions. 100% of teachers credentialed. Avg. yrs. teaching exp: 20. Summer child care plus 6-week academic review.

Adventures in Learning embodies characteristics that produce successful children and ultimately successful adults. In a multicultural environment, with many personalities and learning styles, children pursue academic studies, physical, social and creative development. In addition to achieving individual goals, children are encouraged to develop responsibility for their community.

CARDEN EL ENCANTO DAY SCHOOL — Santa Clara

615 Hobart Terrace, Santa Clara, CA 95051. Phone: 408-244-5041. Fax: 408-244-0684. www.cardenelencanto.com. Head: Mr. William A. Ries. Est. 1973. Uniforms.

Gr. Pre-K to 8. 320 students. 1 to 16 teacher to student ratio. Avg. class size: 20. Max class size: 24. Aides in K. K Hrs: 8:30 AM - 3 PM. Elementary: 8:30 AM - 3 PM. Extended care hrs: 7 AM - 6 PM, $2.75/day for am, $8/day for pm. Tuition: $9,700. Other fees: $600 admissions. 5% receive fin. aid. Specialists: physical education, music, art, drama. French, Latin. Computer lab, school library, art room, homework room. Volleyball, basketball, softball, flag football. 7,000 books in library. A variety of after school classes. Rolling admissions. Admissions test. Standardized tests administered. Carden El Encanto's summer program is designed to develop social, educational and recreational skills, as well as provide an interesting and enjoyable experience within Carden El Encanto's philosophy of behavioral standard. Accreditation: Carden Educational Foundation.

The mission of the Carden El Encanto Day School is to provide children with a solid foundation in the academic subjects, to awaken them to the beauty in nature, music, and art, to develop their characters as a basis for joyful and fulfilling lives, and to create leaders who will stand prepared to meet the challenges of the future with confidence.

CEDARWOOD SUDBURY ELEMENTARY SCHOOL   Santa Clara

2545 Warburtion Avenue, Santa Clara, CA 95051. Phone: 408-296-2072. www.cedarwoodsudbury.org. Head: Stuart Williams. Est. 1995. Nonprofit.

Gr. Pre-K to 12. 20 students. 9 AM - 4 PM flexible schedule for all grades. Students attend a minimum of 4 hours a day. Extended care hrs: 7:30 AM - 5 PM, $125/week. Tuition: $8,500, fin. aid avail. Other fees: $100. Given the opportunity, children spend much of their time learning to be adults-by doing things, talking, asking for help, reading, or observing and learning from those who know more than they do. Giving them that opportunity is why the school is there. Sometimes students request classes or individual instruction, but participation in such activities is voluntary; most do most or all of their self-educating outside of classes. Diplomas are given to students who can successfully show that they have adequately prepared themselves to be effective adults in the larger community. App. deadline: April.

This, a Sudbury-model school, is a completely different kind of school where students control their own time & activities. We respect each child's unique set of interests, goals and learning styles. The school is a nurturing and supportive environment where children practice the fine art of balancing freedom and responsibility in a democratic community. The school is governed democratically with students and staff members each getting one vote.

CHALLENGER SCHOOL   Santa Clara

890 Pomeroy Avenue, Santa Clara, CA 95051. Phone: 408-243-6190. Head: Bhavna Shah. Grades Pre-K to 5.

Please see complete listing under Palo Alto.

DELPHI ACADEMY
Santa Clara

890 Pomeroy Avenue, Santa Clara, CA 95051. Phone: 408-260-2300. Fax: 408-260-0693. www.delphi-sfb.org. Head: Nancy Hawkins. Admissions: Maria Director. Est. 1986. Nonprofit. Uniforms.

Gr. K to 8. 1 to 15 teacher to student ratio. Max class size: 20. Aides in grades K-2. K Hrs: 8:30 AM - 4:30 PM. School hrs: 8:30 AM - 4:30 PM. Extended care hrs: 8 AM - 4:30 PM. Tuition: $1,150. Other fees: $1,200. Specialists: science, art, music, math, geography, writing, reading, history. Science lab. Sports program offered. L. Ron Hubbard's written works on education and child development are applied within the school's program. Waiting list. Parent participation encouraged.

The Mission of Delphi Academy is to help young people become ever more certain that their lives and careers are their responsibility to build; and to help them develop the intellectual, ethical and productive tools they will need in building them.

GRANADA ISLAMIC SCHOOL
Santa Clara

3003 Scott Boulevard, Santa Clara, CA 95054. Phone: 408-980-1161. www.granadaschool.org. Head: Sharifah Alemoar. Est. 1988. Nonprofit. Muslim. Uniforms.

Gr. Pre-K to 8. 1 to 8 teacher to student ratio. Max class size: 22. School hrs: 8 AM - 3 PM. Extended care available afterschool until 6 PM., $4/hr. Tuition: $5,410 - $6,820. Other fees: $220. 8% receive fin. aid. Specialists: Islamic education. Arabic. Science lab, computer lab, library. Physical education. 5,000 books in library. Arabic language and Islamic studies for all grades. Afterschool soccer, gymnastics, drama, citizenship and Nasheed club. App. deadline: February. Admissions test. Parent participation required. Accreditation: WASC.

Our mission is to provide a nurturing and stimulating environment where the students will attain both a strong Muslim identity (according to Qur'an and Sunnah) and solid academic skills which will enable them to become successful adults living to please Allah.

JUBILEE ACADEMY
Santa Clara

2499 Homestead Road, Santa Clara, CA 95050. Phone: 408-244-9777. Fax: 408-244-9777. www.jubileeacademy.com. Head: Lola Perkins. Admissions: Sheba Lagasca. Est. 1992. Uniforms.

Gr. Pre-K to 5. 90 students. 1 to 12 teacher to student ratio. Max class size: K, 18; gr. 1-3, 22; upper grades, 22. Aides in K. K Hrs: 8:30 AM - 2:30 PM. Elementary: 8:15 AM - 3:15 PM. Extended care hrs: 7:30 AM - 4:30 PM. Tuition: $7,000. Other fees: $150 registration. 25% receive fin. aid. Specialists: music, PE, dance, gymnastics. Computers. Sport camps offered at specified times during the year. 2 students per computer. App. deadline: July. Parent participation encouraged. 4% of teachers have adv. degrees. Avg. yrs. teaching exp: 15. Standardized tests administered. Summer day camps and themes.

With a firm belief in the innate capacity of children to develop and fulfill their potential, we at Jubliee Academy dedicate ourselves to instilling the following : a wholesome, relevant, and well-rounded education to help our students develop basic skills.

NORTH VALLEY BAPTIST ELEMENTARY SCHOOL   Santa Clara

941 Clyde Avenue, Santa Clara, CA 95054. Phone: 408-988-8883. Fax: 408-980-1239. www.nvbschools.org. Head: Dan Azzarello. Est. 1977. Baptist. Dress code.

Gr. Pre-K to 8. School hrs: 7:30 AM - 4 PM. Tuition: $2,500 - $3,300, sibling discounts available. Specialists: photography, PE, computers, music, science, math, English. Laptops. Soccer, basketball, volleyball, roller hockey, baseball, cheerleading. Plays, science fair, concerts, carnivals. Admission open to students who are participating member of the church.

The purpose of North Valley Baptist Schools, based on Luke 2:52, is to educate and train the whole student -physically, socially, intellectually, and spriritually- for the gospel ministry.

ONE WORLD MONTESSORI SCHOOL   Santa Clara

2495 Cabrillo Ave, Santa Clara CA 95051. Phone: 408-615-1254. Fax: 408-615-1347. www.oneworldmontessori.org. Head: Rebecca Keith & Jeanette Montoto. Est. 1979. Nonprofit.

Please see complete listing under San Jose.

SAINT CLARE SCHOOL   Santa Clara

725 Washington Street, Santa Clara, CA 95050. Phone: 408-246-6797. Fax: 408-246-6726. www.stclareschool.org. Head: Kathy Almazol. Est. 1965. Nonprofit. Catholic. Uniforms.

Gr. K to 8. 315 students. Max class size: 35. K Hrs: 8:15 AM - 3 PM. Elementary: 8:15 AM - 3 PM. Extended care hrs: 7 AM - 6 PM. Tuition: $5,576 - $6,074. Specialists: religion, art. PE, computer, music. Spanish. App. deadline: March. Accreditation: WASC, WCEA.

St. Clare is committed to teaching the Good News to all students in grades K - 8. Integration of the gospel message through teaching, example, Christian service, and worshipping as a community distinguishes us among our neighboring schools. We offer quality Catholic education by encouraging all students to develop respect for self and others. In addition to a fine academic program, our faculty and staff believe our mission is to recognize that parents are partners in this educational process, while creating a community of faith and love.

SAINT JUSTIN SCHOOL   Santa Clara

2655 Homestead Road, Santa Clara, CA 95051. Phone: 408-248-1094. Fax: 408-246-0691. www.stjustinschool.org. Nonprofit. Catholic.

Gr. K to 8. 300 students. Max class size: 35. Aides in grades K-3. K Hrs: 8:15 AM - 11:50 PM. Elementary: 8:15 AM - 3 PM. Extended care hrs: 7 AM - 5:45 PM. Tuition: $4,515. Specialists: band, choir, drama, computer. Renovated gym, cross platform computer curricula w/ PCs and Macs. App. deadline: January. Parent participation encouraged. Accreditation: WASC, WCEA.

The school is committed to spreading the Gospel message of peace and justice. Students are asked to participate in parish & school programs benefiting those in need. St. Justin provides a warm nurturing environment and an excellent academic foundation with gifted teachers and staff.

SAINT LAWRENCE SCHOOL   Santa Clara

1971 Saint Lawrence Drive, Santa Clara, CA 95051. Phone: 408-296-2260. Fax: 408-296-1068. www.saintlawrence.org. Head: Priscilla Murphy. Est. 1961. Nonprofit. Catholic. Uniforms.

Gr. Pre-K to 8. 350 students. 1 to 17 teacher to student ratio. Max class size: 35. Aides in grades K-1. K Hrs: 8 AM - 2 PM. Elementary: 8 AM - 3 PM. Extended care hrs: 7:30 AM - 6 PM, $4.40/hr. Care open some holidays. Tuition: $6,100 - $6,500. Other fees: $375. 10% receive fin. aid. Specialists: physical education, art, music, science. Spanish. Computer lab, swimming pool, one-to-one Apple laptop initiative, homework center. Flag football, volleyball, basketball, soft ball, track. 6 students per computer. 10,000 books in library. Rolling admissions. Admissions test. Parent participation required. 90% of teachers credentialed. 50% of teachers have adv. degrees. Summer recreation, academic, study skills programs. Accreditation: WASC, WCEA.

The mission of St. Lawrence Elementary and Middle Schools is to provide a comprehensive Catholic education in which Gospel values are modeled, taught, and lived. Parents, faculty, staff and clergy work together to educate the whole child.

SANTA CLARA CHRISTIAN SCHOOL   Santa Clara

3421 Monroe Street, Santa Clara, CA 95051. Phone: 408-246-5423. Fax: 408-246-4883. www.scchristian.org. Head: Pastor Stuart Nice. Admissions: Lori Ferrante. Est. 1994. Nonprofit. Christian. Uniforms.

Gr. Pre-K to 5. 90 students. 1 to 20 teacher to student ratio. Max class size: 24. Aides in K. K Hrs: 8:30 AM - 12 PM, 8:30 AM - 3 PM. Elementary: 8:30 AM - 3 PM. Extended care hrs: 7:30 AM - 6 PM, $2,475. Care open some holidays. Tuition: $4,450 - $6,500. Other fees: $500. Specialists: music, P.E., computer. 1 student per computer. Admissions test. 100% of teachers credentialed. 100% of teachers have adv. degrees. Avg. yrs. teaching exp: 20. 25% of teachers post HW online. Standardized tests administered. Summer Spectacular: light academics, heavy on fun. Accreditation: ACSI.

We provide a quality classic education in a dynamic, Christian environment. We believe our role as a school is to partner with the family and church to help in education of the whole child, socially, physically, emotioinally, intellectually and spiritually

SIERRA SCHOOL   Santa Clara

220 Blake Avenue #B, Santa Clara, CA 95051. Phone: 408-247-4740. Fax: 408-247-0996. www.sierraschool.com. Head: Linda Wesley. Admissions: Linda Wesley/Sherryl Thomas. Est. 1974. Nonprofit. Dress code.

Gr. K to 12. 135 students. 1 to 20 teacher to student ratio. Max class size: 20. Each teacher has a full time assistant. School hrs: 9 AM - 3 PM. Extended care hrs: 7 AM - 6 PM, $16/day. Care open holidays. Tuition: $9,250 - $11,500. Other fees: one time $175 registration fee, $200 yearly materials fee. 20% receive fin. aid. Specialists: art, music, drama, choir, tap/ballet, martial arts, chess club. Spanish. Afterschool homework club, after school tutoring. P.E., after school martial arts. 4 students per computer. 500 books in library. Science fair, musical, student council, community service, field trips, spirit days, assemblies, a variety of fine arts, foreign language. Some learning disabilities can be accomodated due to small class size and one on one attention, as well as an individualized approach to learning. 5 applicants per space. App. deadline: August. Rolling admissions. Admissions test. Parent participation encouraged. 75% of teachers credentialed. 20% of teachers have adv. degrees. Avg. yrs. teaching exp: 5. 100% of teachers post HW online. Standardized tests administered. Summer academic re-enforcement and fun theme activities, full or half days. Accreditation: WASC (in process).

The basis of the Sierra program lies in the belief that balance is the key to a successful academic career. Students are placed at a level at which they are comfortable and proficient, and their academic program for the coming year is set from that point forward. Sierra School offers individualized instruction under a mastery system with an emphasis on high achievement. The curriculum focuses on a strong basic education, and through the mastery approach, students achieve thorough understanding of all material. Sierra offers a nurturing environment and focuses on building self-esteem.

SACRED HEART SCHOOL   Saratoga

13718 Saratoga Avenue, Saratoga, CA 95070. Phone: 408-867-9241. Fax: 408-867-9242. Head: Arlene Bertellotti. Est. 1957. Nonprofit. Catholic. Uniforms.

Gr. K to 8. 300 students. Max class size: K, 33; gr. 1-3, 33; upper grades, 37. Aides in grades K-5. Elementary: 8 AM - 3 PM. Extended care hrs: 7:30 AM - 6 PM. Tuition: $6,400. Other fees: $500. 10% receive fin. aid. Specialists: art, computer, science, PE, math, music, library. Spanish. Football, volleyball, basketball, baseball. 5,000 books in library. App. deadline: January. Waiting list. Parent participation required. Accreditation: WASC, WCEA.

Sacred Heart's students are encouraged to become participating members of the church and surrounding community. The faculty and clergy, in partnership with the parents, promote a community of faith and challenge students to achieve academic and personal excellence. Our philosophy reflects a thoroughness of instruction by addressing the intellectual, spiritual, cultural and physical needs of our students. We strive to help our students become independent thinkers who are able to apply learned skills to daily life. Through praise and positive reinforcement, we produce self-confident students who know the value of hard work, the joy of achievement and the responsibility of respecting others.

SAINT ANDREWS SCHOOL   Saratoga
13601 Saratoga Avenue, Saratoga, CA 95070. Phone: 408-867-3785. Fax: 408-741-1852. www.st-andrews.org. Head: Harry McKay, Jr. Admissions: Lani Mah. Est. 1961. Nonprofit. Episcopal. Uniforms.

Gr. Pre-K to 8. 380 students. Max class size: K, 15; gr. 1-3, 20; upper grades, 20. K Hrs: 8:15 AM - 3 PM. Elementary: 8:15 AM - 3 PM. Extended care hrs: 7:30 AM - 6 PM, $3/half hr. Tuition: $6,778 - $13,550. Specialists: art, PE, religion, computer, music/performing art. French, Spanish. Computer lab. Softball, cross country, volleyball. religious overview course required. App. deadline: February. Parent participation encouraged. Standardized tests administered. Accreditation: WASC, CAIS, NAEYC, NAIS.

The mission of Saint Andrew's School is to offer an enriched curriculum within the tradition and values of the Episcopal Church. We aim to educate the whole child, developing as fully as possible the intellectual, spiritual, social, and physical capacities of each student.

ALL SOULS ELEMENTARY SCHOOL   South San Francisco
479 Miller Avenue, South San Francisco, CA 94080. Phone: 650-583-3562. Fax: 650-952-1167. Head: Dr. Eileen Gorman. Est. 1949. Nonprofit. Catholic. Uniforms.

Gr. K to 8. 324 students. Avg. class size: 36. Max class size: 37. K Hrs: 8:15 AM - 12 PM, 9:30 AM - 1:15 PM. Elementary: 8:15 AM - 3 PM. Extended care hrs: 7:15 AM - 6 PM. Care open holidays. Tuition: $3,320. Other fees: $200 registration. Specialists: computer program, algebra, introduction to foreign languages. App. deadline: February. Admissions test. Waiting list. 100% of teachers credentialed. Avg. yrs. teaching exp: 10. Summer program for new kindergarteners. Accreditation: WASC, WCEA.

MATER DOLOROSA   South San Francisco
1040 Miller Avenue, South San Francisco, CA 94080. Phone: 650-588-8175. Fax: 650-588-0426. www.materdolorosa.net. Head: Ofelia Madriaga. Est. 1962. Nonprofit. Catholic. Uniforms.

Gr. K to 8. 270 students. 1 to 17 teacher to student ratio. Max class size: gr. 1-3, 33; upper grades, 33. School hrs: 8:25 AM - 2:50 PM. Extended care hrs: 7 AM - 6 PM. Tuition:

$3,450. Other fees: $200. Specialists: PE, religious education, computers. Baseball, basketball, volleyball, track. Drama, holiday musical. App. deadline: January. Admissions test. Waiting list. Parent participation required. 100% of teachers credentialed. Avg. yrs. teaching exp: 15. Accreditation: WASC, WCEA.

We, the Mater Dolorosa School Community, believe in the Catholic School as a form of education; unique because it integrates religious, academic, social and physical truths and values. Mater Dolorosa is a place where Christian values are modeled, expressed and incorporated into all activities, so that they are developed and nurtured in each person in accordance with the Gospel values. Our school exists to promote positive learning experiences that develop personal growth in the knowledge, skills, attitudes, and values.

ROGER WILLIAMS ACADEMY South San Francisco

600 Grand Avenue, South San Francisco, CA 94080. Phone: 650-589-1081. www.rogerwilliamsacademy.org. Head: Mrs. Rita Chavez. Admissions: Rev. Cynthia M. Smith. Est. 1946. Nonprofit. Baptist. Uniforms.

Gr. Pre-K to 12. 70 students. 1 to 15 teacher to student ratio. Max class size: K, 10; gr. 1-3, 15; upper grades, 20. K Hrs: 9 AM - 12 PM. School hrs: 8:30 AM - 3:30 PM. Extended care hrs: 7:30 AM - 5:30 PM, $5/hr. Tuition: $5,775. Other fees: $300. 5% receive fin. aid. Specialists: Etymology (Word Building or Spelling). Afterschool homework lab, Judo, Tae Kwan Do. 5 students per computer. 500 books in library. Educational therapist refers students as needed. 2 applicants per space. Rolling admissions. Admissions test. Parent participation encouraged. 5% of teachers credentialed. 2% of teachers have adv. degrees. Avg. yrs. teaching exp: 5. Standardized tests administered. Academic Summer Camp with morning study and afternoon activities. Accreditation: ACE Model School (in process).

We provide individual, tutorial instruction based on student needs, in an environment that fosters Christian character traits.

SAINT VERONICA CATHOLIC SCHOOL South San Francisco

434 Alida Way, South San Francisco, CA 94080. Phone: 650-589-3909. Fax: 650-589-2826. Head: Ms. Teresa J. Pallitto. Est. 1957. Nonprofit. Catholic. Uniforms.

Gr. K to 8. 318 students. 1 to 30 teacher to student ratio. Max class size: K, 36; gr. 1-3, 36; upper grades, 38. Aides in grades K-5. K Hrs: 8 AM - 12:05 PM, 9 AM - 1:45 PM. Elementary: 8 AM - 3 PM. Every third Monday, school is dismissed at 12:30 PM; early dismissal of 2 PM on Fridays. Extended care hrs: 6:45 AM - 5:45 PM, $3.50/hr. Tuition: $4,063, for a participating family. Other fees: $50 Men's Club, $25 Extended Care. 5% receive fin. aid. Specialists: music, P.E., computers, departmentalized junior high, parish children's choir. Spanish. Computer lab and wireless mobile unit, science lab, library. PPSL: volleyball, basketball, cheerleading, baseball, track. 2 students per computer. 1,000 books in library. Learning specialist provides a pull out program for students with learning differences and one-on-one instruction when necessary and sometimes meets with small groups when reinforcement is needed. Rolling admissions. Admissions test. Parent participation required. 100% of teachers credentialed. 35% of teachers have adv. degrees. Avg. yrs. teaching exp: 12. Standardized tests administered. Summer math camp for students entering grades seven and eight. Accreditation: WASC, WCEA.

St. Veronica Catholic School is committed to the education of the whole person based on the teachings of Jesus Christ. It promotes and sustains the spiritual, moral, social, intellectual, physical, and emotional growth of each student. In partnership with the family, the primary educator, and in collaboration with the parish community, we strive to provide a quality education centered in a Catholic environment in peace, security, and love. We enable students to achieve their goals as active Christians, life-long learners, effective communicators, problem solvers, self evaluators, and globally aware citizens.

CHALLENGER SCHOOL   Sunnyvale

1185 Hollenbeck Avenue, Sunnnyvale, CA 94087. Phone: 408-245-7170. Head: Traci Caton. Grades Pre-K to 8.

Please see complete listing under Palo Alto.

FRENCH-AMERICAN SCHOOL OF SILICON VALLEY   Sunnyvale

1522 Lewiston Drive, Sunnyvale, CA 94087. Phone: 408-746-0460. Fax: 408-735-8619. www.fassv.org. Head: Bernard Moreau. Admissions: Mariel Hall. Est. 1992. Nonprofit. Dress code.

Gr. Pre-K to 5. 125 students. 1 to 12 teacher to student ratio. Max class size: K, 24; gr. 1-3, 22; upper grades, 22. Aides in K. K Hrs: 8:30 AM - 3:30 PM. Elementary: 8:30 AM - 3:15 PM. Extended care hrs: 8 AM - 5 PM, $80/mo. Tuition: $12,550. Other fees: $940. 8% receive fin. aid. Specialists: art, music, P.E., technology. French. Computer lab, library. Curriculum includes both French and English instruction. App. deadline: December. Admissions test. Knowledge of French required. Avg. yrs. teaching exp: 8. Standardized tests administered. Accreditation: CAIS, French Ministry of Education.

The aim of the French-American School of Silicon Valley is to provide an academically excellent, French-American bilingual and bicultural education within a multicultural setting which fosters understanding and appreciation of all people.

RAINBOW MONTESSORI CHILD DEVELOPMENT CENTER   Sunnyvale

790 E. Duane, Sunnyvale, CA 94086. Phone: 408-738-3261. Fax: 408-738-0239. www.rainbow-montessori.com. Head: Ms. Spyroula Rodenborn. Est. 1975. Dress code.

Gr. Pre-K to 6. 350 students. 1 to 18 teacher to student ratio. K Hrs: 8 AM - 4 PM. School hrs: 6 AM - 6 PM. Tuition pays for 10 hrs at school each day. Tuition: $5,850 - $6,030. Specialists: science, art, computers, and physical education. Chinese, Spanish, Hindi. Computer lab, science lab. swimming, gymnastics Tae Kwon Do, tennis. Dance, photography. Rolling admissions. 100% of teachers credentialed. Accreditation: American Montessori.

Our mission here at Rainbow Montessori is to facilitate the total development of the child's unique style of learning by providing a safe, healthy, stimulating, and loving environment in which physical, intellectual, personal, moral, and social growth flourishes. Montessori education provides the foundation for the child's natural inner discipline and control. A feeling of caring and respect for ones self, others, and the environment is fostered in the Montessori classroom. A Montessori education prepares a child for life. We commit to do whatever is within our talents and capacity to protect the rights of each child to have the freedom and opportunity to develop to his or her full potential.

RESURRECTION ELEMENTARY SCHOOL   Sunnyvale

1395 Hollenbeck Avenue, Sunnyvale, CA 94087. Phone: 408-245-4571. Fax: 408-733-7301. www.resparish.org/school. Head: Sr. Georgianna Coonis, SND. Admissions: Sr. Georgianna Coonis, SND. Est. 1965. Nonprofit. Catholic. Uniforms.

Gr. Pre-K to 8. 285 students. 1 to 15 teacher to student ratio. Max class size: 32. Aides in grades K-5. K Hrs: 8 AM - 3 PM. Elementary: 8 AM - 3 PM. Wednesdays dismissal at 12:30 PM. Extended care hrs: 7:30 AM - 6 PM, $4/hr. Care open some holidays. Tuition: $3,745 - $7,710. Other fees: $350 annual registration/book fee. 11% receive fin. aid. Specialists: PE, music, computers, library, science lab, afterschool sports. Spanish. Computer lab, library, state of the art science lab, Extended Care with homework room, 10 acre campus, band program through the music school next door. Flag football, soccer, basketball and baseball, softball, volleyball. 6,900 books in library. App. deadline: February. Baptism certificate required. 95% of teachers credentialed. Avg. yrs. teaching exp: 8. Standardized tests administered. Summer camp and summer school programs. Accreditation: WASC, WCEA.

Our mission is to educate students in a Christ-centered, peace-filled, family-oriented environment, recognizing the value and uniqueness of the individual child. We believe parents are the primary educators in the formation of their children's Christian values, and the teachers and staff of the school support, enhance and complement this role.

SAINT CYPRIAN SCHOOL   Sunnyvale

195 Leota Avenue, Sunnyvale, CA 94086. Phone: 408-738-3444. Fax: 408-733-3730. www.saintcyprianschool.org. Head: Mrs. Maureen Velasquez. Est. 1968. Nonprofit. Catholic. Uniforms.

Gr. K to 8. 195 students. 1 to 30 teacher to student ratio. Max class size: K, 25; gr. 1-3, 30; upper grades, 30. Aides in grades K-5. K Hrs: 8 AM - 2:50 PM. Elementary: 8 AM - 3 PM. Extended care hrs: 7:30 AM - 6 PM, hourly rates. Tuition: $5,000 - $6,400. Other fees: $400 - $450. 5% receive fin. aid. Specialists: PE, art, music, computers, library. Full computer lab, library, science lab. Afterschool sports. 1 student per computer. 4,000 books in library. Band program, athletics, Mad Science. Rolling admissions. Admissions test. Parent participation encouraged. 100% of teachers credentialed. 75% of teachers have adv. degrees. Avg. yrs. teaching exp: 15. Standardized tests administered. Summer JefunIra Camp. Accreditation: WASC, WCEA.

St. Cyprian Catholic School provides a spiritually based education to its students in a multicultural environment founded in an atmosphere of respect that is family oriented and supports the needs of today's family. We strive to meet the needs of local and commuter families and are committed to the individual growth of each student- spiritually, academically, physically, socially, and morally.

SAINT MARTIN SCHOOL   Sunnyvale
597 Central Avenue, Sunnyvale, CA 94086. Phone: 408-736-5534. Fax: 408-736-3104. www.stmartinsun.org. Head: Genie Florczyk. Est. 1953. Nonprofit. Catholic. Uniforms.

Gr. Pre-K to 8. 225 students. 1 to 17 teacher to student ratio. Max class size: K, 30; gr. 1-3, 35; upper grades, 35. Aides in grades K-3. K Hrs: 8:05 AM - 3 PM. Elementary: 8 AM - 3 PM. Wednesday dimissal at 2 PM or 12:30 PM. Extended care hrs: 7:30 AM - 6 PM, $4/hr. Tuition: $5,071. Other fees: $355. 6% receive fin. aid. Specialists: music and computers. Computer lab, state-of-the-art science lab. Flag football, basketball, volleyball, soccer, softball, track meet, swim meet. 6 students per computer. 1,500 books in library. Music department offers band. Rolling admissions. Admissions test. Parent participation required. 81% of teachers credentialed. 13% of teachers have adv. degrees. Avg. yrs. teaching exp: 10. Standardized tests administered. Accreditation: WASC, WCEA.

In partnership with family and church, the St.Martin School community creates an atmosphere of learning that will encourage the growth of knowledgeable, creative, self-assured, Christian individuals with a desire for life-long learning.

SILICON VALLEY ACADEMY   Sunnyvale
1095 Dunford Way, Sunnyvale, CA 94087. Phone: 408-243-9333. www.svagroup.net. Head: Mariam Jamil. Est. 1996. Nonprofit. Muslim. Uniforms.

Gr. Pre-K to 9. 120 students. 1 to 6 teacher to student ratio. Max class size: 15. K Hrs: 8:30 AM - 3 PM. Elementary: 8:30 AM - 3 PM. Tuition: $3,500 - $4,000. Other fees: $250. 25% receive fin. aid. Specialists: art, PE. Arabic. 30 acre campus with four soccer fields and a student cooperative garden. Our Arabic programs are based on Quran, Hadith and daily Islamic expressions. Rolling admissions. Summer fun and learning program.

We believe school life should maximize the opportunity to learn and practice Islam, while taking advantage of the latest technology and resources in the field of education. We use the Guided Language Acquisition Design (GLAD) learning model to help our children reach their highest potential. We present a complete academic program to all children without discrimination on the basis of color, ethnic background, national origin, race, religion, gender or economic status. We provide social development through a well balanced range of studies and encourage our children to be productive members of society with high achievement in their professional careers and in community service.

SOUTH PENINSULA HEBREW DAY SCHOOL   Sunnyvale

1030 Astoria Drive, Sunnyvale, CA 94087. Phone: 408-738-3060. Fax: 408-738-0237. www.sphds.org. Head: Rabbi Avi Schochet. Admissions: Barbara Spielman. Est. 1972. Nonprofit. Jewish.

Gr. Pre-K to 8. 300 students. 1 to 6 teacher to student ratio. Avg. class size: 15. School hrs: 8:15 AM - 3:40 PM., $2,500/yr or $7/hr. Tuition: $4,600 - $8,950. 13% receive fin. aid. Specialists: PE, fine arts, computer. Hebrew. Computer center, science lab, library. Afterschool martial arts and gymnastics. App. deadline: May. Parent participation required. Avg. yrs. teaching exp: 15.

SPHDS provides a rigorous Jewish and General Studies education and encourages our children to grow in the learning of Torah, and to identify with the Jewish people and with the State of Israel.

STRATFORD SCHOOL   Sunnyvale

1196 Lime Drive, Sunnyvale, CA 94087. Phone: 408-732-4424.

820 W. McKinley Avenue, Sunnyvale, CA 94086. Phone: 408-737-1500.

Please see complete listing under Los Gatos.

SUNNYVALE CHRISTIAN SCHOOL   Sunnyvale

445 South Mary Avenue, Sunnyvale, CA 94086. Phone: 408-736-3286. Fax: 408-736-3549. www.sunnyvalechristianschool.com. Head: Mr. Jerry Ingalls. Est. 1979. Nonprofit. Christian. Uniforms.

Gr. Pre-K to 5. 187 students. 1 to 16 teacher to student ratio. Max class size: K, 22; gr. 1-3, 22; upper grades, 24. Aides in grades K-5. K Hrs: 8:30 AM - 2:30 PM. Elementary: 8:30 AM - 3 PM. Extended care hrs: 7 AM - 6 PM. Tuition: $5,938. Other fees: $300 - $350. Specialists: PE, computer. Computer lab. 1 student per computer. App. deadline: March. Avg. yrs. teaching exp: 15. Standardized tests administered. Summer program includes field trips and more.

The school strives to initiate and nurture our relationship with Jesus Christ in ourselves, our community, our church, our family, and wherever our influence extends.

PRIVATE HIGH SCHOOLS
IN SAN MATEO, SANTA CLARA AND
SAN FRANCISCO COUNTIES

MENLO SCHOOL
Atherton

50 Valparaiso Avenue, Atherton, CA 94027. Phone: 650-330-2001. Fax: 650-330-2002. www.menloschool.org. Head: Norman Colb. Admissions: Dectora Jeffers, Upper School; Lisa Schiavenza, Middle School. Est. 1915. Nonprofit. No dress code. Open campus.

Gr. 6 to 12. 754 students. 1 to 11 teacher to student ratio. Avg. class size: 16. School hrs: 8 AM - 3 PM. Drama and sports practices take place daily from 3:30 until 5:30. 7 period day. Tuition: $26,000. Other fees: $1,500 - $2,500, depending on grade. 14% receive fin. aid. French, Japanese, Latin, Spanish. 21 AP classes. Pool and a full complement of athletic facilities, computer labs, writing center, photography dark room. Football, baseball, track, cross country, lacrosse, golf, soccer, basketball, tennis, swimming, water polo, softball, volleyball. 20 students per computer. 20,000 books in library. Independent study, biotechnology research, history lab, and multi-media internship. Coordinator of Academic Support assists documented LD students. 5 applicants per space. 80 service hrs. req'd. 100% take SAT. Avg. SAT math: 650-699. Avg. SAT verbal: 600-649. 2% attend 2 yr. college. 98% attend 4 yr. college. 100% students fulfill UC req. 80% of teachers have adv. degrees. Avg. yrs. teaching exp: 15. 20% of teachers post HW online. Standardized tests administered. Summer courses provided to students who need to repeat courses. Summer program for high potential students who are coming to Menlo with weak academic preparation. Accreditation: WASC, CAIS, WAIS.

Menlo School offers a rigorous and engaging academic curriculum and an array of outstanding athletic, fine arts and extracurricular programs designed to give all students opportunities to explore and expand their passions and discover their talents. Menlo values integrity, initiative and appreciation for the richness of human diversity. The school encourages students to take responsibility for themselves and their education and to develop a sense of service to purposes larger than themselves. It prizes the bond of mutual respect and inspiration between students and teachers. Through challenge and support, the school seeks to promote in students the courage to stretch themselves, raise questions and, above all, live ethically and engage in the life-long pursuit of learning.

SACRED HEART PREPARATORY SCHOOL
Atherton

150 Valparaiso Avenue, Atherton, CA 94027. Phone: 650-322-1866. www.shschools.org. Head: Richard Dioli. Admissions: Carl Dos Remedios. Est. 1898. Nonprofit. Catholic. Dress code. Closed campus.

Gr. 9 to 12. 473 students. Avg. class size: 20. School hrs: 7:50 AM - 2:30 PM. 6 period day. Tuition: $22,000. 35% receive fin. aid. Specialists: drama, music. French, Latin,

Spanish. 13 AP classes. Computer lab, library, science labs, sports center, pool, gym, theater. Cross country, soccer, football, water polo, tennis, volleyball, basketball, baseball, golf, lacrosse, swimming, track and field, softball. App. deadline: January. Admissions test. 100 service hrs. req'd. Avg. SAT math: 600-649. Avg. SAT verbal: 600-649. 1% attend 2 yr. college. 99% attend 4 yr. college. 80% of teachers credentialed. Standardized tests administered. Wide variety of summer programs. Accreditation: WASC, CAIS, Religious of Sacred Heart NCOG.

An education at Sacred Heart Schools is strong in studies, serious in principles and rich in the spirit of life and love. It is the essence of a Sacred Heart School that it be deeply concerned for each student's total development: spiritual, intellectual, emotional and physical.

NOTRE DAME HIGH SCHOOL (BELMONT)   Belmont

1540 Ralston Avenue, Belmont, CA 94002. Phone: 650-595-1913. Fax: 650-595-2116. www.ndhsb.org. Head: Rita Gleason. Admissions: Lynn Stieren. Est. 1851. Nonprofit. Catholic. Uniforms. Closed campus.

Gr. 9 to 12. 720 girls. 1 to 16 teacher to student ratio. Avg. class size: 25. School hrs: 8 AM - 3 PM. Tuition: $12,500. 35% receive fin. aid. French, Spanish, ASL. 10 AP classes. Library, pool. Cross country, basketball, soccer, softball, swimming, tennis, track, golf, volleyball, water polo. Strong visual arts program. Special needs counselor. App. deadline: January. 100 service hrs. req'd. 100% take SAT. Avg. SAT math: 500-549. Avg. SAT verbal: 550-599. 12% attend 2 yr. college. 88% attend 4 yr. college. 100% of teachers credentialed. 40% of teachers have adv. degrees. Avg. yrs. teaching exp: 15. Standardized tests administered. Academic summer programs. Accreditation: WASC, WCEA.

Notre Dame High School is an independent Catholic college preparatory school dedicated to the educational mission of St. Julie Billiart and the Sisters of Notre Dame de Namur. We are a caring and compassionate community committed to justice and peace while developing responsible young women of active faith, strong intellect, and Christian leadership. We develop the gifts and talents of each student and foster Gospel values in an environment of academic excellence and mutual respect.

MERCY HIGH SCHOOL   Burlingame

2750 Adeline Drive, Burlingame, CA 94010. Phone: 650-343-3631. Fax: 650-343-2316. www.mercyhsb.com. Head: Laura Held. Admissions: Ellen Williamson. Est. 1931. Nonprofit. Catholic. Uniforms. Closed campus.

Gr. 9 to 12. 470 girls. 1 to 12 teacher to student ratio. Avg. class size: 25. Tuition: $11,825. Other fees: $550 registration. 20% receive fin. aid. French, Spanish, ASL. 12 AP classes. Tennis courts, swimming pool, library, 3 study centers, multimedia lab, physics, chemistry, biology labs. Cross country, tennis, golf, volleyball, water polo, basketball, soccer, gymnastics, swimming, softball, track and field, lacrosse. Learning assistance program for a limited number of students who need extra support. App. deadline: December. 98% take SAT. Avg. SAT math: 500-549. Avg. SAT verbal: 550-599. 99% attend 4 yr. college. 79% of teachers have adv. degrees. Summer program. Accreditation: WASC.

Mercy High School, a Catholic college preparatory school, is dedicated to educating young women of all cultural and economic backgrounds for academic excellence, compassionate service, Christian leadership, global awareness, and life-long learning. Rooted in Catherine McAuley's unique vision for women and the poor, Mercy High School is sponsored by the Sisters of Mercy. The faculty and staff work in collaboration with the Sisters of Mercy to create a Christian community which values hospitality and the dignity of each person. Mercy High School challenges its faculty, staff and students to act with integrity and work for justice.

VERITAS CHRISTIAN ACADEMY   Campbell

400 Llewellyn Avenue, Unit 2, Campbell, CA 95008. Phone: 408-984-1255. Fax: 408-871-7929. www.veritaschristian.org. Head: David Wallace. Est. 2004. Nonprofit. Protestant. Dress code. Closed campus.

Gr. 6 to 12. Avg. class size: 6. Academic courses limited to 16 students. School hrs: 8 AM - 3:15 PM. Doors open at 7:30 AM and close at 5 PM. 7 period day. Tuition: $8,492 - $8,998. Other fees: $350. 50% receive fin. aid. Specialists: Bible, logic, rhetoric. Latin. Afterschool study hall is available until 5 PM M-F. We welcome families who wish to pioneer a small but competitive athletic program. Two Saturday study skills sessions are required for incoming students. 50% of teachers credentialed. Standardized tests administered.

Veritas Christian Academy offers Christ-centered instruction through time-tested classical methods. We help you train your children to think and act biblically and excel academically. The fear of the Lord is the beginning of wisdom. (Proverbs 9:10) We equip your children with the tools of learning to enable them to pursue whatever God calls them to pursue in life. We also offer support to home-schoolers.

EASTSIDE COLLEGE PREPARATORY SCHOOL   East Palo Alto

2101 Pulgas Avenue, East Palo Alto, CA 94303. Phone: 650-688-0850. www.eastside.org. Head: Chris Bischof. Est. 1996. Nonprofit. Dress code. Closed campus.

Gr. 6 to 12. 210 students. Avg. class size: 16. School hrs: 8 AM - 5 PM. Tuition: $15,000. 100% receive fin. aid. Spanish. 5 AP classes. Computer lab (open until 10 PM), science lab, gymnasium. Basketball, volleyball, soccer, track and field, fitness and conditioning. Journalism, drama, theater design and production, photography, mock trial, piano, band, choral ensemble. Learning resource specialists on-site. 3 applicants per space. App. deadline: January. Eastside also offers motivated students a summer enrichment program where students study on college campuses, participate in outdoor leadership programs, obtain summer internships and more. Accreditation: WASC.

Eastside College Preparatory School is committed to opening new doors for students historically underrepresented in higher education. Eastside takes an innovative approach to working with students from underserved backgrounds. With small class sizes, extended days, a personalized approach to learning, and intensive college guidance services, students have the resources and support they need to complete a rigorous high school curriculum and succeed in college and beyond. One hundred percent of Eastside graduates have enrolled in college, and 97% of these students are the first in their families to go to college. Eastside students are paving the way for a brighter future for themselves, their families, and their community.

ANCHORPOINT CHRISTIAN HIGH SCHOOL   Gilroy

8095 Kelton Drive, Gilroy, CA 95020. Phone: 408-846-6642. Fax: 408-848-4426. www.anchorpointgilroy.org. Head: Stephen Malone. Est. 1999. Open campus.

Gr. 9 to 12. Tuition: $4,950. Other fees: $400. Auditorium, counseling center, printing press, swimming pool, science lab, computer lab, 2 gymnasiums, golf course. Basketball, tennis, volleyball, swimming, soccer, baseball, golf.

Our mission is to provide a Christ-centered education to enable each student to acquire knowledge with understanding and wisdom, and a biblical worldview as evidenced by a lifestyle of character, leadership, service, stewardship and worship and to live with purpose to affect a difference in the world for the glory of God.

CRYSTAL SPRINGS UPLANDS SCHOOL   Hillsborough

400 Uplands Drive, Hillsborough, CA 94010. Phone: 650-342-4175. Fax: 650-342-7611. www.csus.com. Head: Amy C. Richards. Admissions: Abby H. Wilder. Est. 1952. Nonprofit. Dress code. Closed campus.

Gr. 6 to 12. 350 students. 1 to 9 teacher to student ratio. Avg. class size: 14. School hrs: 8:05 AM - 3 PM. School ends at 2:20 PM on Fridays. 8 period day. Tuition: $24,560. Other fees: $1,125. 19% receive fin. aid. Specialists: studio art, graphic design. French, Spanish. Computer lab, gym, fitness center, soccer field, theater. Learning specialist from the Children's Health Council on contract. 5 applicants per space. 100% take SAT. 100% attend 4 yr. college. 100% students fulfill UC req. 50% of teachers have adv. degrees. Summer academic camps, sports camps, enrichment, Gateway. Accreditation: WASC, CAIS.

We believe that students learn best in an environment that: promotes learning in diverse ways about a complex world, stimulates intellectual and creative development, nurtures the individual within a community of mutual trust, caring, and respect, balances academic and extracurricular interests and accomplishments. We encourage: critical thinking and intellectual risk-taking, responsibility for one's ideas and actions, personal integrity, ethical awareness, and multicultural understanding, individual leadership and cooperative interaction, respect for one's self and for the views of others. We endeavor to equip students with: a spirit of inquiry, a respect for human potential, a sense of responsibility for the environment and to the global community, a feeling of joy in lifelong learning.

PINEWOOD HIGH SCHOOL   Los Altos Hills

26800 Fremont Road, Los Altos Hills, CA 94022. Phone: 650-941-1532. Fax: 650-941-4727. www.pinewood.edu. Head: Mark Gardner. Admissions: Dafna Brown. Est. 1981. Nonprofit. Dress code. Closed campus.

Gr. 7 to 12. 300 students. 1 to 7 teacher to student ratio. Avg. class size: 12. School hrs: 8 AM - 3 PM. 8 period day. Tuition: $14,800 - $16,800. Other fees: $850. 1% receive fin. aid. French, Spanish. 13 AP classes. Computer lab, science lab, gym, theater, pool. Cross country, baseball, basketball, volleyball, softball, swimming, soccer, tennis. Student government, yearbook and journalism, drama, debate, Interact, Model Congress, various service and honor clubs. 20 service hrs. req'd. 100% take SAT. Avg. SAT math: 600-649. Avg. SAT verbal: 600-649. 90% of teachers credentialed. Standardized tests administered. Summer program includes academics, arts, theater, music, sports, engineering. Accreditation: WASC.

Pinewood is dedicated to providing its students with the environment most conducive to learning and growing. The dedicated faculty and staff know and care for each student. Their goal is to provide the skills necessary for students to be successful not only at school but also throughout life by emphasizing the importance of critical thinking, writing, reading, speaking, research and organizational skills. Pinewood is committed to offering a full complement of honors and advanced placement classes. Small classes allow for individual instruction, encouragement, and guidance in every subject. Pinewood offers a well-rounded, stimulating, and creative agenda for all.

MID-PENINSULA HIGH SCHOOL   Menlo Park

1340 Willow Road, Menlo Park, CA 94025. Phone: 650-321-1991. Fax: 650-321-9921. www.mid-pen.com. Head: Douglas Thompson, Ph.D. Admissions: Chloe Kamprath. Est. 1980. Nonprofit. No dress code. Closed campus.

Gr. 9 to 12. 135 students. 1 to 12 teacher to student ratio. Avg. class size: 12. School hrs: 9:30 AM - 3:10 PM. 6 period day. Tuition: $21,158. Other fees: $750. 24% receive fin. aid. Spanish. Fully equipped science labs, art studio, photo lab, technology-based enrichment center, student center, full-size gymnasium, weight room, locker rooms, music rehearsal room. Basketball, baseball, cross-country, soccer, volleyball, softball. 3 students per computer. We support students who have been pushed too far by extremely competitive schools, learn differently, feel they don't fit in socially, or feel they don't have a voice in their education. On-site learning specialist. 40 service hrs. req'd. 58% take SAT. Avg. SAT math: 550-599. Avg. SAT verbal: 550-599. 50% attend 2 yr. college. 50% attend 4 yr. college. 50% students fulfill UC req. 64% of teachers credentialed. 43% of teachers have adv. degrees. Avg. yrs. teaching exp: 17. Standardized tests administered. Accreditation: WASC, CAIS.

Mid-Peninsula High School, a community for learning, offers students a stimulating, nurturing, safe environment that empowers them to reach their full academic and social potential. As a small, caring educational community, we work to strengthen relationships between the students, their families, and the school. We recognize and understand unique styles and create flexible academic programs designed to meet each student's needs. It is our expectation that Mid-Peninsula High School students will become capable, self-directed individuals who care about themselves, their families, and their communities.

GIRLS' MIDDLE SCHOOL   Mountain View

180 North Rengstorff Avenue, Mountain View, CA 94043. Phone: 650-968-8338. Fax: 650-968-4775. www.girlsms.org. Head: Margaret Scott. Admissions: Holly Zuklie. Est. 1998. Nonprofit. Uniforms. Closed campus.

Gr. 6 to 8. 114 girls. Avg. class size: 20. School hrs: 8:30 AM - 3:20 PM. Tuition: $16,500. Spanish. Volleyball, basketball, soccer. The Entrepreneurial Program offers seventh grade students the opportunity to experience firsthand the excitement of starting and running a business. App. deadline: January. Admissions test. Parent participation required. 70% of teachers credentialed. Avg. yrs. teaching exp: 5. Accreditation: WASC.

The Girls' Middle School nurtures, empowers, and educates girls during a pivotal time in their lives. Our project-based, hands-on curriculum encourages girls to collaborate, think critically, and experience the joy of learning. Through practice, girls grow to value their voices, develop empathy, and set and reach their personal goals. By offering non-traditional educational opportunities, respecting teachers' independence, and assessing students authentically, we create a community in which girls take risks, expand their horizons and realize their potential. By intentionally recruiting a diverse group of high-achieving girls, we work toward a more equitable world.

MOUNTAIN VIEW ACADEMY   Mountain View

360 South Shoreline Boulevard, Mountain View, CA 94041. Phone: 650-967-2324. www.mtnviewacademy.org. Head: Stanely Baldwin. Admissions: Alyce Schales. Est. 1922. Nonprofit. Seventh-Day Adventist. Dress code. Closed campus.

Gr. 9 to 12. 150 students. Avg. class size: 20. School hrs: 8:15 AM - 3:30 PM. Tuition: $6,900, fin. aid for SDA students. Other fees: $600 - $700 for books. Spanish. 2 AP classes. College prep. Limited spaces for special needs students. 15% attend 2 yr. college. 80% attend 4 yr. college. 100% of teachers credentialed. Avg. yrs. teaching exp: 10. Accreditation: WASC.

An education is only as valuable as the efforts that go into teaching and learning. Mountain View Academy believes that an education should be centered in the Source that created that opportunity to educate and learn. Therefore science cannot be learned without its Origin, law without a Standard, language without Love, humanity without its Heavenly Father, and the arts without The Creator. We believe the Best Teacher is God, through His example, Jesus Christ. Mountain View Academy places itself as an active medium for education: mentally, physically, socially, and spiritually inspired by the Word of God.

SAINT FRANCIS HIGH SCHOOL   Mountain View

1885 Miramonte Avenue, Mountain View, CA 94040. Phone: 650-968-1213.
Fax: 650-968-1706. www.sfhs.com. Head: Patricia Tennant. Admissions: Mike Speckman.
Est. 1954. Nonprofit. Catholic. Dress code. Closed campus.

Gr. 9 to 12. 1,500 students. 1 to 15 teacher to student ratio. Avg. class size: 28. School hrs:
7 AM - 2:30 PM. College-style block schedule. Classes meet for 85 minutes every other
day. 4 period day. Tuition: $9,840. 12% receive fin. aid. Extensive computer graphics
program, including graphic arts, advanced digital photography, flash animation, clay animation and video editing. French, German, Spanish. 16 AP classes. Olympic sized-pool
and aquatic facility. Over 280 student computers, with 15 computer labs, including PC,
Mac and mobile laptops. Saint Francis holds more Central Coast Championships than
any other school in the section. Each season, at least one non-cut sport, including cross-
country, wrestling, track and swimming. Lunchtime intramurals open to everyone. 4 students per computer. 50 service hrs. req'd. 100% take SAT. Avg. SAT math: 650-699. Avg.
SAT verbal: 600-649. 7.3% attend 2 yr. college. 91.9% attend 4 yr. college. 100% students fulfill UC req. 47% of teachers credentialed. Avg. yrs. teaching exp: 12. Accreditation: WASC.

*Saint Francis High School educates the whole person in the tradition of Holy Cross.
Saint Francis provides an environment which encourages students to achieve their highest potential through spiritual development, which imparts Christian values and promotes community service; through intellectual development, which fosters academic
achievement and lifelong learning; and through social development, which provides
exposure to a broad range of activities and experiences.*

ALMA HEIGHTS CHRISTIAN ACADEMY- HIGH SCHOOL   Pacifica

1030 Linda Mar Boulevard, Pacifica, CA 94044. Phone: 650-355-1935. Fax: 650-355-3488.
www.almaheights.org. Head: David Gross. Admissions: Jackie Flynn. Est. 1955. Christian.
Uniforms. Closed campus.

Gr. K to 12. 300 students. 1 to 10 teacher to student ratio. Avg. class size: 23. School hrs:
8:15 PM - 3:15 AM. Tuition: $6,930. Other fees: $630 registration and student fees.
Spanish. Gymnasium, library, media and science center. Bay Area Christian Athletic
League (BACAL): baseball, basketball, soccer, softball, volleyball. App. deadline: June.
Rolling admissions. Admissions test. Waiting list. Avg. SAT math: 550-599. Avg. SAT
verbal: 500-549. 70% of teachers credentialed. Avg. yrs. teaching exp: 10. Summer
soccer, academic camps, and a reading program. Accreditation: WASC, ASCI, Western
Association of Christian Schools.

*Education is the search for truth and all truth ultimately derives from God, especially
through the Bible. Our wish is to guide students in the pursuit of a sound traditional
educational program, in an atmosphere of Christian love and care for the individual.*

CASTILLEJA SCHOOL   Palo Alto

1310 Byrant Street, Palo Alto, CA 94301. Phone: 650-328-3160. Fax: 650-326-8036. www.castilleja.org. Head: Joan Lonergan. Admissions: Jill Lee. Est. 1907. Nonprofit. Uniforms. Closed campus.

Gr. 6 to 12. 415 girls. 1 to 6 teacher to student ratio. Avg. class size: 15. School hrs: 8 AM - 3:15 PM. 7 period day. Tuition: $24,500. 14% receive fin. aid. French, Latin, Spanish. 18 AP classes. Open enrollment for AP classes. Digital language lab, computer lab, computer media lab, theater, athletic facilites: softball field, competition pool, dance studio, gym. Softball, swimming, soccer, track and field, volleyball, tennis, basketball, waterpolo, cross country, lacrosse, golf. 60 service hrs. req'd. 100% take SAT. Avg. SAT math: 650-699. Avg. SAT verbal: 650-699. 100% attend 4 yr. college. 100% students fulfill UC req. 80% of teachers have adv. degrees. Summer camp for elementary aged girls. Accreditation: WASC, CAIS.

Castilleja School is dedicated to providing a rigorous college preparatory education for young women in grades six through twelve. It is the only non-sectarian all-girls middle and high school in the San Francisco Bay Area. Castilleja's philosophy is shaped by both tradition and current research that affirm the academic and personal advantages of all-girls education. We demonstrate this conviction in the conscious attention we pay to the needs, issues, pedagogies, and opportunities particular to girls. While emphasis is on the development of the intellect, Castilleja is committed to the education of the whole person: heart, body, and spirit as well as mind.

KEHILLAH JEWISH HIGH SCHOOL   Palo Alto

3900 Fabian Way, Palo Alto, CA 94303. Phone: 650-213-9600. Fax: 650-213-9601. www.kehillahhigh.org. Head: Rabbi Reuven Greenvald. Admissions: Marily Lerner. Est. 2001. Nonprofit. Jewish. Dress code. Closed campus.

Gr. 9 to 12. 100 students (plans to grow to 250-300 students). 1 to 7 teacher to student ratio. Avg. class size: 15. School hrs: 8 AM - 4 PM. 5 period day. Tuition: $24,000. Other fees: $1,350 activities fee. 30% receive fin. aid. Hebrew, Japanese, Spanish. 10 AP classes. Brand new, state of the art building with Smart Boards and science labs. Volleyball, soccer, basketball, tennis. 2 students per computer. 1,000 books in library. Robotics, dance, theater. 80 service hrs. req'd. 100% students fulfill UC req. 95% of teachers credentialed. 50% of teachers have adv. degrees. Avg. yrs. teaching exp: 10. 100% of teachers post HW online. Accreditation: WASC (in process), CAIS (in process).

Kehillah Jewish High School offers a four year college preparatory course of study blending the arts, sciences, humanities, and social sciences with a deep exploration of Jewish sources, values, and practices in an intimate community setting. A community-based school, Kehillah welcomes students of all Jewish ideological backgrounds.

PALO ALTO PREPARATORY SCHOOL   Palo Alto

4000 Middlefield Road Ste H2, Palo Alto, CA 94303. Phone: 650-493-7071. www.paloaltoprep.com. Head: Christopher Keck. Admissions: Lisa O'hearn-Keck. Est. 1987. Nonprofit. Open campus.

Gr. 8 to 12. 60 students. 1 to 8 teacher to student ratio. Avg. class size: 10. School hrs: M-Th 9 AM - 3 PM. Fri 9-12:30. Friday hours for students to catch up on work. 6 period day. Tuition: $15,000. Spanish. 5 AP classes. Open enrollment for AP classes. Backpacking, skiing, scuba diving, ocean kayaking. 3 students per computer. Educational trips to Europe and the southern U.S. On-site learning specialist. Rolling admissions. 48 service hrs. req'd. 95% take SAT. 15% attend 2 yr. college. 85% attend 4 yr. college. 90% students fulfill UC req. 100% of teachers credentialed. Avg. yrs. teaching exp: 8. 100% of teachers post HW online. Academic program during summer where students may earn a semester of high school credit. We offer a 10 day backpacking trip in the high Sierras. Accreditation: WASC.

Palo Alto Prep is a truly unique high school environment. We are a closely-knit community of individuals who respect and like each other. We build fun and variety into our learning experiences, and we strive to understand and appreciate our differences. No two people at Palo Alto Prep look or think exactly alike; our attitudes range from conservative to cutting edge, and our fashion sense includes both the funky and the refined. We successfully combine structure and flexibility while we maintain an unrelenting focus on academic success.

WOODSIDE PRIORY SCHOOL   Portola Valley

302 Portola Road, Portola Valley, CA 94028. Phone: 650-851-8223. Fax: 650-851-2839. www.woodsidepriory.com. Head: Timothy J. Molak, Head of School. Admissions: Al D. Zappelli. Est. 1957. Nonprofit. Roman Catholic. Dress code. Closed campus.

Gr. 6 to 12. 350 students. 1 to 6 teacher to student ratio. Avg. class size: 15. Some upper division high school classes can be as low as 5 to 6 students. School hrs: 8:30 AM - 3:30 PM. Special classes for Performing Arts may be held at 7:30 am. 6 period day. Tuition: Day: $25,617 Boarding: $34,932. Other fees: Day and Boarding: $400, Student Store Deposit/ Boarding $700, weekend activities. 20% receive fin. aid. French, Japanese, Latin, Spanish. 18 AP classes. Olympic size pool, Briggs Science Center: 20 wireless laptops and 28 PCs, two electron microscopes, telescopes, equipment for genetics study. Library resources: 16 computers, scanner, printers, and 20 wireless laptops. Fine Arts Center: equipment for ceramics, photography, metalwork, glass, digital multimedia production and storage, space for large-scale projects. Soccer, volleyball, basketball, swimming, cross country, track and field, baseball, golf, tennis. 18,000 books in library. Boarding program. Resource Center. 3 applicants per space. App. deadline: January. 80 service hrs. req'd. 100% take SAT. Avg. SAT math: 650-699. Avg. SAT verbal: 600-649. 100% attend 4 yr. college. 100% students fulfill UC req. Standardized tests administered. Summer Camp Unique, www.campunique.com. Accreditation: WASC, CAIS, WCEA, NCEA.

Woodside Priory School is an independent, Catholic, college preparatory school in the Benedictine tradition. Our mission is to assist students of promise in becoming lifelong learners who will productively serve a world in need of their gifts.

WHERRY ACADEMY HIGH SCHOOL   Redwood City
452 Fifth Avenue, Redwood City, CA 94063. Phone: 650-367-6791. Est. 1983. Dress code. Closed campus.

40 students. 1 to 10 teacher to student ratio. Avg. class size: 10. School hrs: 8:30 AM - 2 PM. Tuition: $5,900. Other fees: $100 registration, $20/mo for materials. 10% receive fin. aid. French. remedial program. Rolling admissions. Admissions test. 100% of teachers credentialed. Avg. yrs. teaching exp: 19. Summer enrichment and remedial programs.

Each student is an individual. With that in mind, Wherry Academy offers a full program and the student benefits in every area. We welcome all students with acceptable behavior. They will progress as far toward college preparation as possible.

WEST BAY HIGH SCHOOL   San Carlos
1561 Laurel Street, Suite A, San Carlos, CA 95070. Phone: 650-595-5022. Fax: 650-595-5042. www.westbayhigh.org. Head: Larry Krusemark. Admissions: Gloria Senteney. Est. 1974. Nonprofit. Dress code. Closed campus.

Gr. 9 to 12. 50 students. 1 to 12 teacher to student ratio. All grades taught together. School hrs: 9 AM - 1 PM. Tuition: $4,380. French, Spanish. 3 students per computer. Career Pathway program available and students can enroll in Regional Occupation Program (ROP) classes or community college classes concurrently. Our methods assist students in accepting the responsibility for their own progress, We provide individual attention and extend the opportunity to graduate to students including those with special circumstances or needs. This includes students who were not functioning in an appropriate manner at previous high schools. 67% of teachers credentialed. 33% of teachers have adv. degrees. Avg. yrs. teaching exp: 3. Standardized tests administered. Accreditation: WASC, National Private School Accreditation Alliance.

West Bay High School emphasizes the importance of a minimum distraction, respectful learning environment, in which students have the opportunity to make individual progress according to their abilities. To create such a positive and wholesome setting for the benefit of each individual, we stress the need for respect, both among students and for the teachers. Students are encouraged to move forward using their potential to the greatest degree possible while maintaining a high ethical standard. Our school provides an atmosphere in which students can feel secure and motivated to develop the confidence they will need to be responsible members of their community with integrity.

ARCHBISHOP RIORDAN HIGH SCHOOL   San Francisco

175 Phelan Avenue, San Francisco, CA 94112. Phone: 415-586-8200. Fax: 415-587-1310. www.riordanhs.org. Head: Gabriel A. Crotti. Admissions: Dion Sabalvaro. Est. 1949. Nonprofit. Catholic. Dress code. Closed campus.

Gr. 9 to 12. 750 boys. Avg. class size: 27. School hrs: 7:45 AM - 2:35 PM. Early dismissal Wednesdays. 4 period day. Tuition: $10,400. Other fees: $600 registration fee. 30% receive fin. aid. Spanish, Italian, ASL. 13 AP classes. Member of WCAL: cross-country, football, basketball, soccer, wrestling, golf, tennis, track and field, baseball, swimming. Limited Resource Specialist Program for students with mild to moderate needs. 4 applicants per space. 100 service hrs. req'd. 100% take SAT. 26% attend 2 yr. college. 74% attend 4 yr. college. 100% students fulfill UC req. 90% of teachers credentialed. Avg. yrs. teaching exp: 15. Standardized tests administered. summer freshman intro program. Accreditation: WASC.

Archbishop Riordan High School is an urban Catholic high school for boys, owned by the Roman Catholic Archdiocese of San Francisco and conducted by the Society of Mary, Marianists, who are assisted by lay men and women. Archbishop Riordan strives to be a Christian community of faculty, students, parents, and others associated with its programs, who by example, instruction, and concerns, mutually support and assist one another to develop Christian values of love of God, love of oneself and love of others.

BAY SCHOOL OF SAN FRANCISCO   San Francisco

682 Schofield Road, San Francisco, CA 94129. Phone: 415-561-5800. Fax: 415-561-5808. www.bayschoolsf.org. Head: Malcolm H. Manson. Admissions: Nancy Wheeler. Est. 2004. Open campus.

Gr. 9 to 12. 400 students. 1 to 10 teacher to student ratio. Avg. class size: 16. Tuition: $27,375, financial aid available. Chinese, French, Latin, Spanish. 8 AP classes. Library/media center, science labs, IT lab, art studio. Dance, martial arts, soccer, basketball, baseball, softball, volleyball, cross country. Admissions test.

The Bay School is committed to helping the whole person develop in the intellectual, aesthetic, physical, social, and spiritual domains.

BRIDGEMONT HIGH SCHOOL   San Francisco

777 Brotherhood Way, San Francisco, CA 94132. Phone: 415-333-7600. Fax: 415-333-7603. www.bridgemontschool.org. Head: Mr. Peter Tropper. Admissions: Tiffany L. Mann. Est. 1975. Nonprofit. Christian. Dress code. Closed campus.

Gr. 6 to 12. 100 students. 1 to 8 teacher to student ratio. Avg. class size: 12. School hrs: 8:30 AM - 2:55 PM. 7 period day. Tuition: Junior High $9,985, High School $10,985. Other fees: registration: JH $350, HS $400, student fee: JH $315, HS $415. 65% receive fin. aid. French, Spanish. 3 AP classes. Volleyball, basketball, softball, soccer, baseball.

100 service hrs. req'd. 98% take SAT. Avg. SAT math: 550-599. Avg. SAT verbal: 550-599. 10% attend 2 yr. college. 85% attend 4 yr. college. 100% students fulfill UC req. 50% of teachers credentialed. Avg. yrs. teaching exp: 7. Standardized tests administered. Accreditation: WASC, ACSI.

Bridgemont is a Christian, non-denominational, fully accredited college preparatory school with a low student to teacher ratio. Our well-qualified and caring faculty develop the whole student through challenging academic curriculum and biblical studies.

CONVENT OF THE SACRED HEART HIGH SCHOOL   San Francisco

2222 Broadway Street, San Francisco, CA 94115. Phone: 415-563-2900. Fax: 415-929-0553. www.sacredsf.org. Head: Douglas Grant. Admissions: Caitlin Curran. Est. 1887. Nonprofit. Catholic. Uniforms. Closed campus.

Gr. 9 to 12. 200 girls. Avg. class size: 11. Tuition: $22,475, fin. aid avail. Chinese, French, Japanese, Latin, Spanish. 21 AP classes. Computer lab, student center, auditorium, library, full gymnasium, science labs, art studios. Elevator access. Volleyball, cross-country, golf, tennis, basketball, swimming, soccer, track badminton, fencing. App. deadline: December. Admissions test. 100 service hrs. req'd. 100% take SAT. Avg. SAT math: 600-649. Avg. SAT verbal: 600-649. Wide selection of summer academic and sports programs for K-12. Accreditation: WASC, CAIS.

Schools of the Sacred Heart, San Francisco remain committed to academic excellence, to the endowment of spiritual and ethical values, to the continued representation of the ethnic, religious and socio-economic diversity of the Bay Area and to single-sex education. While clearly Catholic in philosophy, the Schools strive to maintain a global, ecumenical perspective enhancing the experience of all constituents. The curriculum and extracurricular activities recognize the unique talents and viewpoints of every individual, providing superior programs in academics, arts, athletics and community service.

CORNERSTONE ACADEMY   San Francisco

501 Cambridge Street, San Francisco, CA 94134. Phone: 415-585-5183. Fax: 415-469-9600. www.cornerstone-academy.net. Head: Mr. Derrick Wong. Closed campus.

Gr. 5 to 12. School hrs: 8 AM - 2:30 PM. 8 period day. Tuition: $5,300 - $6,200. Chinese, Spanish. Computer lab, gym.

The instructional program not only sets high standards, but also recognizes student diversity in learning styles and rate of achievement. The goal of developing students to their highest potentials is achieved by making explicit intended outcomes of the course work, delineating the building blocks to reach those outcomes, consistently assessing student progress towards the outcomes, and giving assistance as needed. Our curriculum and recommended course of study exceed most minimum requirements of most major colleges and universities. The school wants to provide a comprehensive education for the student.

DREW COLLEGE PREPARATORY SCHOOL — San Francisco

2901 California Street, San Francisco, CA 94115. Phone: 415-409-3739. www.drewschool.org. Head: Samual M. Cuddeback III. Admissions: Tearon Joseph. Est. 1908. Nonprofit. Open campus.

Gr. 9 to 12. 250 students. Avg. class size: 12. Tuition: $17,500. 33% receive fin. aid. French, Spanish. 7 AP classes. Theater, courtyard. Soccer, volleyball, tennis, basketball, baseball. Drew Education for Active Lifelong Learning (DEALL) exposes students to experiences that are educational, broadening and enjoyable. On-site learning specialist. App. deadline: January. Rolling admissions. Admissions test. 99% attend 4 yr. college. 90% of teachers have adv. degrees. Standardized tests administered. Drew's summer program offers full-credit courses in a broad range of disciplines in one four-week session. Accreditation: WASC, CAIS.

Drew is a small, supportive college preparatory high school community. We have a global outlook, but focus on the individual student. Our mission is to enhance the academic talents and self-esteem of our students and better enable them to meet the challenges and opportunities of being international citizens.

HEBREW ACADEMY OF SAN FRANCISCO — San Francisco

645 14th Avenue, San Francisco, CA 94118. Phone: 415-752-7333. Fax: 415-752-5851. www.hebrewacademy.com. Head: Rabbi Pinchas Lipner. Admissions: Mimi Real. Est. 1969. Nonprofit. Jewish. Dress code. Closed campus.

Gr. Pre-K to 12. 190 students. Avg. class size: 15. School hrs: 8:30 AM - 3:30 PM. 9 period day. Tuition: varies. Other fees: $600 building fee; book fee. 88% receive fin. aid. Hebrew, Italian. 10 AP classes. 7,000 books in library. Drama, student council. 30 service hrs. req'd. 100% take SAT. 1% attend 2 yr. college. 99% attend 4 yr. college. 100% students fulfill UC req. 75% of teachers credentialed. 75% of teachers have adv. degrees. Avg. yrs. teaching exp: 14. Standardized tests administered. Summer academic program. Accreditation: Torah Umesorah.

Educating a child is a responsibility best shared between the home and school. The Hebrew Academy is a Jewish day school, which strives to provide an excellent academic and Jewish education. We endeavor to expose our children to an intensive appreciation of their religious and ethical responsibilities.

IMMACULATE CONCEPTION ACADEMY — San Francisco

3625 24th Street, San Francisco, CA 94110. Phone: 415-824-2052. www.icacademy.org. Head: Sr. Janice Therese Wellington. Admissions: Gina Espinal. Est. 1883. Nonprofit. Catholic. Closed campus.

Gr. 9 to 12. 252 girls. 1 to 10 teacher to student ratio. Avg. class size: 23. Tuition: $6,600. Other fees: $420. 65% receive fin. aid. Extensive technology curriculum. French, Spanish. 3 AP classes. Computer lab, library, auditorium. Tennis, cross country, volleyball, basketball, soccer and softball. Retreats, Dominican Preaching Conference. App. deadline: February. 100 service hrs. req'd. 100% of teachers credentialed. Avg. yrs. teaching exp: 18. Summer program. Accreditation: WASC.

Immaculate Conception Academy, founded by the Dominican Sisters of Mission San Jose, has been committed for more than a century to the education of young women in the San Francisco Bay Area. Our faculty and staff of dedicated sisters and lay colleagues collaborate with the community of families, alumnae and benefactors to enable each student to realize her God-given potential and become a lifelong seeker of Truth. Within a loving, spirited and nurturing environment, we are dedicated to academic excellence and responsible global citizenship, challenging our students to grow as compassionate individuals, joyfully living the Gospel of Jesus Christ.

INTERNATIONAL HIGH SCHOOL   San Francisco
150 Oak Street, San Francisco, CA 94102. Phone: 415-558-2093. Fax: 415-558-2085. www.ihs.fais.org. Head: Jane Camblin. Admissions: Betsy Brady Albertazzi. Est. 1976. Nonprofit. No dress code. Open campus.

Gr. Pre-K to 12. 325 students. 1 to 16 teacher to student ratio. Avg. class size: 18. School hrs: 8:15 AM - 4:20 PM. 8 period day. Tuition: $23,790. Other fees: $2,000 Enrollment Fee. 25% receive fin. aid. Chinese, French, German, Spanish, Italian. Computer lab, gymnasium. Soccer, basketball, baseball, swimming, golf, tennis, cross-country, volleyball. 6 applicants per space. App. deadline: January. Rolling admissions. Admissions test. Writing sample. 150 service hrs. req'd. 95% attend 4 yr. college. 95% of teachers credentialed. 80% of teachers have adv. degrees. Avg. yrs. teaching exp: 12. Accreditation: WASC, CAIS, IBO, CIS, AEFE.

Guided by the priniples of academic vigor and diversity, the International High School offers programs of study in French and English to prepare its graduates for a world in which the ability to think critically and to communicate across cultures is of paramount importance.

JEWISH COMMUNITY HIGH SCHOOL OF THE BAY   San Francisco
1835 Ellis Street, San Francisco, CA 94115. Phone: 415-345-9777. Fax: 415-345-1888. www.jchsofthebay.org. Head: Dr. Sheldon Dorph, Rabbi. Admissions: Dana Goldberg. Est. 2001. Nonprofit. Jewish. Dress code. Closed campus.

Gr. 9 to 12. 160 students. 1 to 7 teacher to student ratio. Avg. class size: 15. Individual classes do not exceed 19 students. School hrs: 8:15 AM - 3:15 PM. 4 period day. Tuition: $24,155. 48% receive fin. aid. Judaic studies, pilates, photography, Tefillah. Hebrew, Spanish. 7 AP classes. Open enrollment for AP classes. 62,000 square foot campus with library, art studio, dance studio, three state-of-the-art science labs, catering kitchen. Students get iBook laptops. Volleyball, soccer, basketball, track and field, tennis, baseball. 2

students per computer. 23,000 books in library. student government, recycling/composting programs. Director of Educational Support provide support for various learning styles and provide professional development opportunities. 3 applicants per space. App. deadline: January. Admissions test. Jewish Professional recommendation required. Waiting list. 100% take SAT. 8% attend 2 yr. college. 92% attend 4 yr. college. 20% of teachers credentialed. 75% of teachers have adv. degrees. Standardized tests administered. Summer Talmud, health courses. Accreditation: WASC, CAIS, BAAD, BAIHS, ISBOA, BALD, BAISSC, SSBL.

The Jewish Community High School of the Bay (JCHS) is a co-educational day school providing a rigorous, college preparatory curriculum in general and Judaic studies. We are committed to an extensive enrichment program, including the arts and athletics. JCHS serves the San Francisco Bay Community and is open to all Jewish students regardless of prior Jewish educational experience. JCHS is guided by the rhythms of the Jewish calendar, culture and tradition and by an inextricable link to the land of Israel. Our goal is to provide our students with the education necessary to gain acceptance into the finest colleges and universities and to engage in life-long Jewish learning.

LICK-WILMERDING HIGH SCHOOL　　　　　　　San Francisco
755 Ocean Avenue, San Francisco, CA 94112. Phone: 415-333-4021. Fax: 415-333-9443. www.lwhs.org. Head: Al Adams. Admissions: Jane W. Faller. Est. 1874. Nonprofit. Open campus.

Gr. 9 to 12. 380 students. Avg. class size: 16. School hrs: 8 AM - 2:45 PM or 3:15 PM. 6 period day. Tuition: $25,700. Other fees: Books and other fees included; one time facilities use fee of $1,000. 42% receive fin. aid. French, Spanish. Technical arts shop, student center. Tennis, volleyball, cross country, basketball, swimming, soccer, track and field, baseball, lacrosse. Learning Service Center works with students with learning differences. App. deadline: December. Admissions test. 100% take SAT. Summer academic programs. Accreditation: WASC, CAIS.

Lick-Wilmerding's central mission is to offer its students a distinctive and exemplary education, the key ingredients of which are: the school's head, heart, and hands curriculum, the inclusive nature of its community, and its commitment to society beyond the campus. From the beginning, Lick-Wilmerding served young people from all segments of society, honored work with the hands as well as the head, and committed to contributing to the common good.

LYCEE FRANCAIS LA PEROUSE　　　　　　　San Francisco
755 Ashbury Street, San Francisco, CA 94117. Phone: 415-661-5232. Fax: 415-661-0246. www.lelycee.org. Head: Patrick Frebet. Admissions: Isabelle Desmole. Est. 1967. Nonprofit. Dress code. Closed campus.

Gr. Pre-K to 12. 600 students. Avg. class size: 20. School hrs: 9 AM - 3:30 PM. Tuition: $12,930 - $15,975. 10% receive fin. aid. Specialists: Lycée Français La Pérouse is a total immersion French school, all subjects are taught in French; however, some courses taught by native speakers of English. French, German, Japanese. Auditorium, library, 2 computer labs, 3 science labs, shower rooms, gymnastic room. Afterschool sports, music, theater, and arts programs. App. deadline: January. Knowledge of French required. Avg. SAT math: 600-649. Avg. SAT verbal: 550-599. 90% of teachers credentialed. Avg. yrs. teaching exp: 6. Standardized tests administered. Accreditation: WASC, CAIS, French Ministry of Education.

The Lycée Français La Pérouse provides international-minded families of the greater Bay Area an academically rigorous curriculum in a fully bilingual French/English environment. Based on the French national education system, the preschool-12 innovative program prepares students for completion of the educational requirements of both France and the United States and provides an excellent preparation for both European and North American colleges and universities. The diverse and international nature of the student body and faculty fosters a spirit of community and prepares students to be contributing citizens of the world.

MERCY HIGH SCHOOL   San Francisco
3250 19th Avenue, San Francisco, CA 94132. Phone: 415-334-0525. Fax: 415-334-9726. www.mercyhs.org. Head: Dr. Dorthy McCrea. Admissions: Liz Belonogoff. Est. 1952. Nonprofit. Catholic. Uniforms. Closed campus.

Gr. 9 to 12. 525 girls. 1 to 13 teacher to student ratio. Avg. class size: 21. School hrs: 8 AM - 3 PM. 5 period day. Tuition: $10,900. Other fees: $500. 35% receive fin. aid. French, Spanish, ASL. 13 AP classes. Theater, dance studio, multi-purpose facility for athletics. Basketball, volleyball, tennis, cross country, soccer, softball, track. 5 students per computer. 900 books in library. Honors and AP classes: science, math, social studies, world languages, English. Counselors have training for learning disabilities and will adjust time for exams. 12 applicants per space. App. deadline: January. Admissions test. 100 service hrs. req'd. 100% take SAT. Avg. SAT math: 550-599. Avg. SAT verbal: 550-599. 40% attend 2 yr. college. 60% attend 4 yr. college. 70% students fulfill UC req. 100% of teachers credentialed. 88% of teachers have adv. degrees. Avg. yrs. teaching exp: 25. 40% of teachers post HW online. Standardized tests administered. Summer school for enrichment and sports. Accreditation: WASC, WCEA.

Mercy educates young women for college placement and seeks to develop leaders who will make a difference in the world. We want to give our students their voice as young women.

SACRED HEART CATHEDRAL PREPARATORY   San Francisco
1055 Ellis Street, San Francisco, CA 94109. Phone: 415-775-6626. Fax: 415-931-6941. www.shcp.edu. Head: Dr. Kenneth Hogarty. Admissions: Timothy M. Burke. Est. 1852. Nonprofit. Catholic. Dress code. Closed campus.

Gr. 9 to 12. 1,200 students. 1 to 12 teacher to student ratio. Avg. class size: 26. School hrs: 7:55 AM - 2:20 PM. 7 period day. Tuition: $12,550, fin. aid avail. Specialists: visual and performing arts. French, Japanese, Spanish. 10 AP classes. Gymnasium, chapel, library, computer lab. Baseball, basketball, cross country, football, golf, soccer, softball, swimming, tennis, track & field volleyball, wrestling. 21,000 books in library. The SHCP Club Program provides students with an assortment of special interest opportunities that allow our students to grow and mature while providing an atmosphere of community, fun and service. Academic resource specialist for learning disablities. 100% take SAT. 12% attend 2 yr. college. 87% attend 4 yr. college. 100% of teachers credentialed. 42% of teachers have adv. degrees. Standardized tests administered. Academic summer school and sport camp; enrichment camps for drama, arts and sciences. Accreditation: WASC.

Inspired by the traditions of St. John Baptist de La Salle and St. Vincent de Paul, Sacred Heart Cathedral Preparatory is a Catholic, college preparatory school which educates young men and women in the heart of San Francisco. We are an inclusive and multicultural community which values the intrinsic dignity of each person. We foster a student-centered approach which integrates a challenging academic curriculum and a dynamic co-curricular program. Within a nurturing and disciplined environment, we prepare our students to become service-oriented individuals with a commitment to living the Gospel.

SAINT IGNATIUS COLLEGE PREPARATORY   San Francisco

2001 37th Avenue, San Francisco, CA 94116. Phone: 415-731-7500. www.siprep.org. Head: Charles Dullea. Admissions: Kevin Grady. Est. 1855. Nonprofit. Catholic. Dress code. Closed campus.

Gr. 9 to 12. 1,415 students. Avg. class size: 26. Tuition: $12,480. Other fees: $800 registration, $400 for books. 20% receive fin. aid. French, German, Japanese, Latin, Spanish. Science lab, computer lab, pool, library, wireless Internet access throughout the school. Cross country, soccer, field hockey, basketball, football, golf, tennis, volleyball, water polo, baseball, crew, lacrosse, softball, swimming, track and field. Academic, social, service clubs. 3 applicants per space. App. deadline: November. 100 service hrs. req'd. 100% take SAT. Avg. SAT math: 550-599. Avg. SAT verbal: 600-649. 3% attend 2 yr. college. 97% attend 4 yr. college. Standardized tests administered. Summer academic and sports programs. Accreditation: WASC.

St. Ignatius is a Catholic, college preparatory school in the Jesuit tradition serving the San Francisco Bay Area. St. Ignatius strives to develop young women and men of competence, conscience, and compassion through an integrated program of academic, spiritual, and extra-curricular activities. St. Ignatius seeks to develop students who strive toward the Jesuit ideal of the magis: a thirst for the more, for the greater good, for the most courageous response to the challenges of our time in the fullest development of students' talents, and for a life-long disposition to serve.

SAINT JOHN OF SAN FRANCISCO ORTHODOX ACADEMY   San Francisco

6210 Geary Boulevard, San Francisco, CA 94121. Phone: 415-221-3484. Fax: 415-386-4368. www.stjohnsacademysf.org. Head: His Eminence Kyrill, Archbishop of San Francisco and Western America. Russian Orthodox. Uniforms. Closed campus.

Gr. K to 12. Tuition: $5,000. Other fees: $250 registration. French, Latin, Russian. Parent participation required. Orthodox Summer Camp offers a fun and engaging program for children six years and up.

Saint John of San Francisco Orthodox Academy is a Russian Orthodox coeducational, non-profit, full-time day school for grades K-12, scheduled around the old calendar of Orthodox feast days and services. Saint John of San Francisco Orthodox Academy intends to provide its pupils an excellent education in its curriculum, participating with the parents in the development of Orthodox children who are both well trained in secular sciences, and are equipped with that knowledge of Orthodox faith and ethics, which shall enable them to live a proper Orthodox lifestyle in today's mostly secular society.

SAN FRANCISCO UNIVERSITY HIGH SCHOOL   San Francisco

3065 Jackson Street, San Francisco, CA 94115. Phone: 415-447-3104. Fax: 415-447-5802. www.sfuhs.org. Head: Dr. Michael Diamonti. Admissions: Karen N. Kindler. Est. 1973. Nonprofit. No dress code. Open campus.

Gr. 9 to 12. 389 students. 1 to 8 teacher to student ratio. Avg. class size: 15. School hrs: 8 AM - 3:05 PM or 3:30 PM. 7 period day. Tuition: $25,850. Other fees: $210 Student Activities Fee. 22% receive fin. aid. French, Latin, Spanish. 18 AP classes. Computer labs, science laboratories, library, student center, gymnasium, photography dark room, ceramics studio, state of the art theater. Soccer, cross country, track, field hockey, tennis, volleyball, basketball, sailing, badminton, fencing, baseball, golf, lacrosse, swimming, softball. 4 students per computer. 15,000 books in library. Independent study program, school year abroad, community service program, outdoor education. On-site learning specialist. 5 applicants per space. 150 service hrs. req'd. 100% take SAT. Avg. SAT math: 650-699. Avg. SAT verbal: 650-699. 100% attend 4 yr. college. 98% students fulfill UC req. 100% of teachers credentialed. 72% of teachers have adv. degrees. Avg. yrs. teaching exp: 15.5. 33% of teachers post HW online. Standardized tests administered. Accreditation: WASC, CAIS, NAIS, College Entrance Examination Board, The Secondary Admissions Test Board.

San Francisco University High School, a college preparatory secondary school, offers an intellectually stimulating, personally enriching and academically challenging program in the liberal arts and sciences to an able and diverse student body. Standards of excellence guide all aspects of our program and the people engaged in it. We seek to instill in students the skills and the attitudes of the lifelong learner and the responsible, engaged and productive citizen.

SAN FRANCISCO WALDORF HIGH SCHOOL   San Francisco

245 Valencia Street, San Francisco, CA 94103. Phone: 415-431-2736. www.sfwaldorf.org. Head: Joan Caldarera. Admissions: Barbara Allen. Est. 1997. Nonprofit. Dress code. Closed campus.

Gr. 9 to 12. 120 students. 1 to 12 teacher to student ratio. Avg. class size: 25. School hrs: 8:20 AM - 3:25 PM. 6 period day. Tuition: $16,590, fin. aid avail. Other fees: $650. German, Spanish. Science labs, arts and crafts studio, library/media center. Basketball, baseball, soccer, volleyball, track and field, cross country. Field trips, internships, international exchange program. Eurythmy therapist. App. deadline: January. 40 service hrs. req'd. 100% take SAT. 8% attend 2 yr. college. 85% attend 4 yr. college. 100% of teachers credentialed. Six-week kindergarten introduction and summer day camp. Accreditation: WASC.

The arts and practical work are the bedrock out of which Waldorf education nourishes creativity, thinking, feeling life, self discipline and health in its students. At the San Francisco Waldorf School, our deeply committed faculty works together to foster each child's sense of self-reliance, social responsibility and moral purpose. By educating the whole child in these rich and creative ways, we hope to encourage young people to bring the highest human capacities into their adult lives as they become citizens of the future.

STUART HALL HIGH SCHOOL   San Francisco

1715 Octavia Street, San Francisco, CA 94109. Phone: 415-345-5811. Fax: 415-931-9161. www.sacredsf.org. Head: Gordon Sharafinski. Admissions: Tony Farrell. Est. 2000. Nonprofit. Catholic. Dress code. Open campus.

Gr. 9 to 12. 170 boys. 1 to 8 teacher to student ratio. School hrs: 8 AM - 3 PM. Tuition: $22,475. 45% receive fin. aid. French, Japanese, Latin, Spanish, ASL. Computer lab, library, gymnasium, art studio, science lab, student center. Soccer, basketball, tennis, lacrosse, golf, baseball. App. deadline: December. Admissions test. 100 service hrs. req'd. 90% of teachers credentialed. Avg. yrs. teaching exp: 7. Wide selection of summer academic and sports programs for K-12. Driver's Ed. Accreditation: WASC, CAIS, Network of Sacred Heart Schools.

Schools of the Sacred Heart, San Francisco remain committed to academic excellence, to the endowment of spiritual and ethical values, to the continued representation of the ethnic, religious and socio-economic diversity of the Bay Area and to single-sex education. While clearly Catholic in philosophy, the Schools strive to maintain a global, ecumenical perspective enhancing the experience of all constituents. The curriculum and extracurricular activities recognize the unique talents and viewpoints of every individual, providing superior programs in academics, arts, athletics and community service.

URBAN SCHOOL OF SAN FRANCISCO   San Francisco

1563 Page Street, San Francisco, CA 94117. Phone: 415-626-2919. Fax: 415-626-1125. www.urbanschool.org. Head: Mark Salkind. Admissions: Angela Brown. Est. 1966. Nonprofit. Closed campus.

Gr. 9 to 12. 250 students. 1 to 8 teacher to student ratio. Tuition: $26,600, fin. aid avail. French, Spanish. Laptop for each student, campus-wide wireless T1 high speed Internet access. Cross country, soccer, tennis, volleyball, basketball, baseball, softball, golf, dance, fencing, yoga, capoeira. Field trips, plays, outdoor education. On-site learning specialist. App. deadline: December. Admissions test. Standardized tests administered. Accreditation: WASC.

An Urban education is a joyful process of discovery: students learn to ask questions, to search for their own answers, to voice their opinions, to think critically and independently, and to discern with their hearts as well as their minds. Urban believes that high school is an important experience in its own right, not merely a stepping stone to college, and we aim to educate the whole student through a broad and rich academic and co-curricular program balancing the intellectual, artistic, physical, emotional, and social development of each student.

WOODSIDE INTERNATIONAL SCHOOL   San Francisco

1555 Irving Street, San Francisco, CA 94122. Phone: 415-564-1063. www.wissf.com. Head: John S. Edwards. Admissions: Janet McClelland. Est. 1976. No dress code. Open campus.

Gr. 6 to 12. 105 students. Avg. class size: 14. Tuition: $14,720, fin. aid avail. Other fees: $800. Chinese, French, Japanese, Spanish, Russian. 4 AP classes. Recreation room, study halls. Rolling admissions. 100 service hrs. req'd. 98% of teachers credentialed. Avg. yrs. teaching exp: 10. 100% of teachers post HW online. Summer school. Accreditation: WASC.

As educators, our goal is to ensure that each one of our students progresses academically, socially, and personally. We realize that for real learning to take place, students require individual attention, personal freedom, structure, and an open intellectual climate.

ARCHBISHOP MITTY HIGH SCHOOL   San Jose

5000 Mitty Way, San Jose, CA 95129. Phone: 408-252-6610. Fax: 408-252-0518. www.mitty.com. Head: Timothy Brosnan. Admissions: Latanya Johnson. Est. 1964. Nonprofit. Catholic. Dress code. Closed campus.

Gr. 9 to 12. 1,665 students. 1 to 17 teacher to student ratio. Avg. class size: 27. School hrs: 7:50 AM - 2:35 PM. Tuition: $10,405. Other fees: $600. 12% receive fin. aid. French, Spanish. 12 AP classes. Computer lab, library, gym. Volleyball, football, cross country, water polo, field hockey, tennis, golf, basketball, wrestling, soccer, badminton, golf, swimming, track and field, baseball. State-of-the-art technology center. Math & science tutorial centers. 3 applicants per space. App. deadline: February. Admissions test. 25

service hrs. req'd. 100% take SAT. Avg. SAT math: 550-599. Avg. SAT verbal: 550-599. 20% attend 2 yr. college. 80% attend 4 yr. college. 56% of teachers have adv. degrees. Standardized tests administered. Accreditation: WASC, National Catholic Education Association.

Archbishop Mitty High School is the Catholic, coeducational, college preparatory school of the Diocese of San Jose. We embrace the Catholic educational mission of developing community, teaching the message of the Gospels, and promoting service, peace, and justice. Through our rigorous academic program, we seek to prepare our students for college and for responsible leadership in the global society of the 21st century. We celebrate and affirm our diverse cultural community and encourage students to respond to their world with competence, insight, understanding, courage, and compassion based on a tradition of faith and moral values.

BELLARMINE COLLEGE PREPARATORY SCHOOL   San Jose

850 Elm Street, San Jose, CA 95126. Phone: 408-294-9224. www.bcp.org. Head: Mark Pierotti. Admissions: Bill Colucci. Est. 1851. Nonprofit. Catholic. Dress code. Closed campus.

Gr. 9 to 12. 1,440 boys. Avg. class size: 26. Tuition: $9,745. 15% receive fin. aid. French, Latin, Spanish, Mandarin. 19 AP classes. Classrooms equipped with computers and LCD projectors. Carney Science Center, Leontyne Chapel, Schott Center for counseling and guidance, outdoor pool, gymnasium. Baseball, basketball, cross country, football, golf, lacrosse, soccer, swimming, tennis, track, volleyball, water polo, wrestling. 41 honors & AP classes. 50+ clubs and organizations, many electives for juniors and seniors. Brother 2 Brother Program (older students serve as friends and mentors to freshmen). On-site learning specialist. 2 applicants per space. Admissions test. 100 service hrs. req'd. 5% attend 2 yr. college. 95% attend 4 yr. college. Standardized tests administered. Summer academic and enrichment courses range from remedial courses to top-level honors programs. Accreditation: WASC.

Bellarmine College Preparatory is a community gathered together by God for the purpose of educating the student to seek justice and truth throughout his life. We are a Catholic school in the tradition of St. Ignatius of Loyola, the Founder of the Society of Jesus. As such, our entire school program is dedicated to forming men for others — persons whose lives will be dedicated to bringing all their God-given talents to fullness and to living according to the pattern of service inaugurated by Jesus Christ.

HARKER SCHOOL – MIDDLE SCHOOL   San Jose

3800 Blackford Avenue, San Jose, CA 95117. Phone: 408-248-2510. Fax: 408-248-2502. www.harker.org. Head: Christopher Nikoloff. Admissions: Nan Nielsen. Est. 1893. Nonprofit. Uniforms. Closed campus.

Gr. 6-8. 465 students. 1 to 16 teacher student ratio. Avg. class size: 16. Max class size: 22. School hours: 7:50 AM - 3:35 PM. 9 period day. Tuition: $22,174 - $23,952 Other fees: $400-$1000. 10% receive financial aid. Specialists: art, science, PE, computer, performing arts, music. French, Spanish, Japanese, Latin. Computer labs, library, art center, gymnasium, pool, dance/music room. Flag football, volleyball, basketball, baseball, softball, soccer, swimming. 28,500 books in library. App. deadline: February. Admissions test. Interview required. 100% of teachers credentialed. Standardized tests administered.

HARKER SCHOOL – HIGH SCHOOL   San Jose

500 Saratoga Avenue, San Jose, CA 95129. Phone: 408-249-2510. Fax: 408-984-2325. www.harker.org. Head: Christopher Nikoloff. Admissions: Nan Nielsen. Est. 1893. Nonprofit. Uniforms. Closed campus.

Gr. 9 to 12. 640 students. 1 to 11 teacher student ratio. Avg. class size: 13. Max class size: 18. School hrs: 8:30 AM - 3:20 PM. 9 period day. Tuition: $24,968. Other fees: $400 - $1000. 10% receive fin. aid. French, Japanese, Latin, Spanish. 23 AP classes. State-of-the-art Library & Technology Center, pool, music/dance room, 14 science labs, wireless network, gym. Football, volleyball, soccer, tennis, golf, cross country, basketball, wrestling, track, swimming, softball, baseball, water polo, lacrosse. 28,500 books in library. App. deadline: January. Admissions test. Interview required. 40 service hrs. req'd. 100% take SAT. Avg. SAT math: 700-749. Avg. SAT verbal: 650-699. 100% attend 4 yr. college. 100% of teachers credentialed. 80% of teachers have adv. degrees. Standardized tests administered. Summer academic and enrichment courses. Accreditation: WASC, CAIS, ACA, WAIC.

The Harker School is a coeducational, non-sectarian, college preparatory day school serving grades Kindergarten through twelfth. Our goal is to develop well-rounded global citizens and lifelong learners. Through comprehensive programs of sound academics and character development, Harker provides a challenging and balanced education for college-bound students.

LIBERTY BAPTIST HIGH SCHOOL   San Jose

2790 South King Road, San Jose, CA 95122. Phone: 408-274-5613. www.libertybaptist.org. Head: Russel Barnes. Est. 1968. Christian. Closed campus.

Liberty Baptist is a K-12 school. Please see complete listing under Santa Clara elementary schools.

NOTRE DAME HIGH SCHOOL   San Jose

596 South 2nd Street, San Jose, CA 95112. Phone: 408-294-1113. Fax: 408-288-8185. www.ndsj.org. Head: Diane Saign. Admissions: Mary Beth Riley. Est. 1851. Nonprofit. Catholic. Uniforms. Closed campus.

Gr. 9 to 12. 615 girls. 1 to 15 teacher to student ratio. Avg. class size: 27. School hrs: 7:50 AM - 2:45 PM. Dismissal at 1:25 PM on Fridays. 7 period day. Tuition: $10,000. Other fees: $400 registration, $60 application, books and uniform. 15% receive fin. aid. French, Spanish. 12 AP classes. Ceramics lab, photo lab, walking distance from city center: museums, theaters, SJSU, civic community. Volleyball, tennis, golf, cross country, soccer, basketball, track and field, swimming, softball, intramurals. 6 students per computer. 11,383 books in library. Internship program with downtown businesses, museums and theaters; Community Service Learning Program. 100 service hrs. req'd. 100% take SAT. Avg. SAT math: 550-599. Avg. SAT verbal: 550-599. 15% attend 2 yr. college. 85% attend 4 yr. college. 85% students fulfill UC req. 85% of teachers credentialed. 65% of teachers have adv. degrees. Avg. yrs. teaching exp: 10. Standardized tests administered. Summer enrichment for in-coming 9th grade students. Accreditation: WASC.

Teach them what they need to know for life -St. Julie Billiart

PRESENTATION HIGH SCHOOL   San Jose

2281 Plummer Avenue, San Jose, CA 95125. Phone: 408-264-1664. www.pres-net.com. Head: Ms. Mary Miller. Admissions: Susan Mikacich. Est. 1962. Nonprofit. Catholic. Uniforms. Closed campus.

Gr. 9 to 12. 750 girls. Avg. class size: 28. School hrs: 7:30 AM - 2:10 PM. Tuition: $9,485. 11% receive fin. aid. French, Spanish. 5 AP classes. Three computer labs, T1 high speed Internet throughout the school, online access to libraries and student files. WCAL sports: cross country, water polo, golf, tennis, volleyball, basketball, soccer, softball, track and field, swimming. 4 students per computer. 23 on campus clubs: community service, public awareness, math, science, speech and debate, computer, music, dance, Big/Little Sister program. 100% take SAT. 15% attend 2 yr. college. 85% attend 4 yr. college. 100% of teachers credentialed. 62% of teachers have adv. degrees. Avg. yrs. teaching exp: 11. Standardized tests administered. Accreditation: WASC.

Presentation High School is a secondary school for girls whose purpose and direction flow from the teaching mission of the Catholic Church and the educational ministry of the Sisters of the Presentation. This school strives to infuse the entire educational experience with the vision of life found in the Gospels. Each student is challenged to become a woman of faith, dedicated to working with others, intellectually competent and committed to her personal growth.

SCHOOL OF CHOICE   San Jose

3800 Blackford Road, San Jose, CA 95117. Phone: 408-887-5108. www.schoolofchoice.com. Head: Suzanne C. Arnes, Robert C. Arnes. Est. 1999. Dress code. Open campus.

Gr. 6 to 12. 1 to 10 teacher to student ratio. Max class size: 10. School hrs: 8:30 AM - 3 PM. 7 period day. Tuition: $12,000. Spanish. 13 AP classes. Gym, tennis courts, swimming pool, auditorium. Afterschool sports and PE. ADD, ADHD dealt with in small classes.

The School of Choice actively engages gifted and motivated students in rigorous scholarship while developing their aesthetic and athletic talents; their success builds confidence that, in turn, raises expectations and boosts results. Supportive instructors teach a classical curriculum which helps students mature into responsible, creative leaders — successful adults who have learned integrity and wisdom, who live passionately and lead with justice and compassion.

VALLEY CHRISTIAN JR. HIGH AND HIGH SCHOOLS   San Jose

100 Skyway Drive, San Jose, CA 95111. Phone: 408-513-2460 (junior high) 408-513-2400 (high school). Fax: 408-513-2424. www.valleychristian.net. Head: Robert Bridges, Joel Torode. Est. 1969. Nonprofit. Christian. Dress code. Open campus.

Gr. 6 to 12. 506 students. Avg. class size: 22. Tuition: $9,000 - $11,000, financial aid available. Other fees: $350 for enrollment. French, Japanese, Latin, Spanish, ASL. 11 AP classes. Computer lab, photo lab, 2 gyms, playing fields, dance studio, theater, aquatic center, radio station, video studio. Football, cross country, water polo, volleyball, tennis, basketball, soccer, wrestling, baseball, golf, track and field, softball. Discovery Center West offers private therapy sessions with a trained, qualified learning specialist. On-site learning specialist. Standardized tests administered. Summer sports program. Accreditation: WASC, ACSI.

Valley Christian Schools' mission is to provide a nurturing environment offering quality education supported by a strong foundation of Christian Values in partnership with parents, equipping students to become leaders to serve God and. their families, and to positively impact their communities and the world.

WILLOW VALE CHRISTIAN MIDDLE AND HIGH SCHOOL   San Jose

1730 Curtner Avenue, San Jose, CA 95118. Phone: 408-448-0656. Fax: 408-264-2817. www.wvministry.com. Head: Mrs. Carollyn Ellis. Free Methodist. Dress code. Closed campus.

Gr. 9 to 12. 144 students. 1 to 18 teacher to student ratio. Avg. class size: 18. School hrs: 8:30 AM - 3 PM. Tuition: $4,500. Other fees: $75 new student application. Computer lab, homework center, large playground area with open space. Laptop for each student.

Our purpose is to provide a safe, loving and stimulating Christian environment for children while away from their primary caregivers. We believe that Christian principles, based on the Holy Bible help assure a strong self image, wholesome personality growth and a solid value system which ultimately strengthens both the individual and the family unit. We believe every child is of inestimable worth in God's eyes and deserving of respect and dignity.

ALPHA BEACON HIGH SCHOOL   San Mateo

525 W. 42nd Avenue, San Mateo, CA 94403. Phone: 650-212-4222. www.alphabeacon.org. Head: Lillian G. Mark. Admissions: Jeannie Chiari. Est. 1969. Nonprofit. Closed campus.

Alpha Beacon is a K-12 school. Please see complete listing under San Mateo elementary schools.

JUNIPERO SERRA HIGH SCHOOL   San Mateo

451 West 20th Avenue, San Mateo, CA 94403. Phone: 650-345-8207. Fax: 650-573-6638. www.serrahs.com. Head: Lars Lund. Admissions: Randy Vogel. Est. 1944. Nonprofit. Catholic. Dress code. Closed campus.

Gr. 9 to 12. 999 boys. 1 to 2 teacher to student ratio. Avg. class size: 25. School hrs: 8:10 AM - 2:50 PM, 9 AM - 1:15 PM on Friday. 8 period day. Tuition: $11,500. Other fees: $400 approx. for books. 20% receive fin. aid. Specialists: theology, visual and performing arts. French, German, Spanish. 22 AP classes. Pool, chapel, Campus Ministry Center, art building, band room, fully staffed library, college and career center, resource center, 3 computer labs, auditorium, gymnasium, newly renovated baseball, football and track fields. Cross country, football, water polo, wrestling, soccer, basketball, baseball, golf, tennis, crew, volleyball, swimming, track. 18,000 books in library. Academic Resource Center to assist students. 80 service hrs. req'd. 90% take SAT. 25% attend 2 yr. college. 75% attend 4 yr. college. 100% students fulfill UC req. 100% of teachers credentialed. 75% of teachers have adv. degrees. Avg. yrs. teaching exp: 16. Standardized tests administered. Summer academic summer school, recreation camps, swim school, summer instructional camps in baseball, crew, football, and soccer. Accreditation: WASC.

Junipero Serra High School is the Archdiocesan Catholic school educating the young men of San Mateo County. We are an academic high school with a strong college preparatory curriculum. Our mission is to develop the gifts and talents of each student and foster Gospel values in an environment with academic excellence and mutual respect.

ODYSSEY SCHOOL   San Mateo

201 Polhemus Road, San Mateo, CA 94402. Phone: 650-548-1500. Fax: 650-548-0500. www.odysseyms.org. Head: Steve Smuin. Admissions: Shane Smuin. Est. 1997. Nonprofit. Dress code. Closed campus.

Gr. 6 to 8. 45 students. 1 to 10 teacher to student ratio. Avg. class size: 15. School hrs: 8:15 AM - 3:10 PM. Afterschool care until 5 PM. Tuition: $20,000. 20% receive fin. aid. Japanese. Each student is given a laptop Apple computer. Individual, life-time sports. 5 week intersession. 5 applicants per space. 30 service hrs. req'd. 100% of teachers credentialed. 90% of teachers have adv. degrees. Avg. yrs. teaching exp: 10. Standardized tests administered. Accreditation: Educational Records Bureau, National Middle School Association, Round Square Schools, Pacific Rim Association.

Odyssey School, an adventure in middle school education, is the only co-ed, independent school for gifted and talented 6-8th graders in the area. The curriculum is highly integrated, academically challenging and art enriched. Building a sense of community and teaching emotional intelligent skills provide the foundation for this unique environment.

CEDARWOOD SUDBURY HIGH SCHOOL   Santa Clara

2545 Warburtion Avenue, Santa Clara, CA 95051. Phone: 408-296-2072. www.cedarwoodsudbury.org. Head: Stuart Williams. Est. 1995. Closed campus.

Cedarwood Sudbury is a K-12 school. Please see complete listing under Santa Clara elementary schools.

NORTH VALLEY BAPTIST HIGH SCHOOL   Santa Clara

941 Clyde Avenue, Santa Clara, CA 95054. Phone: 408-988-8883. Fax: 408-980-1239. www.nvbschools.org. Head: Dan Azzarello. Est. 1977. Baptist. Dress code. Closed campus.

Gr. 9 to 12. School hrs: 7:30 AM - 4 PM. Tuition: $2,500 - $3,300, sibling discounts available. Laptops. Soccer, basketball, volleyball, roller hockey, baseball, cheerleading. Plays, science fair, concerts, carnivals. Admission open to students who are participating members of the church.

The purpose of North Valley Baptist Schools, based on Luke 2:52, is to educate and train the whole student -physically, socially, intellectually, and spriritually- for the gospel ministry.

SAINT LAWRENCE ACADEMY   Santa Clara

2000 Lawrence Court, Santa Clara, CA 95051. Phone: 408-296-3013. Fax: 408-296-3794. www.saintlawrence.org. Head: Christy Filios. Admissions: Jennifer Giorgianni. Est. 1960. Nonprofit. Catholic. Uniforms. Closed campus.

Gr. 9 to 12. 330 students. 1 to 20 teacher to student ratio. Avg. class size: 25. School hrs: 8:10 AM - 2:45 PM. 6 period day. Tuition: $9,780. Other fees: $900. French, Spanish, ASL. 10 AP classes. Cross country, football, soccer, tennis, volleyball, basketball, baseball, golf, softball, swimming, track and field. Academic and social clubs. Zacchaeus Program: college preparatory program, run by an educational psychologist, designed for high functioning students with documented learning disabilities. App. deadline: February. Admissions test. 100% take SAT. 1% attend 2 yr. college. 99% attend 4 yr. college. 50% of teachers credentialed. Accreditation: WASC, WCEA.

In cooperation with students and parents, we seek to encourage our students' moral and spiritual potential. Saint Lawrence Academy recognizes the uniqueness and dignity of the individual. We help develop our students' intellectual, emotional, social and physical growth, and encourage them to achieve their fullest potential. Throughout our curriculum, we promote the growth of the whole student in a school with a diverse population. We empower the students to become responsible leaders who will fully share their gifts and talents with family, church, and local and global communities.

SIERRA SCHOOL- HIGH SCHOOL   Santa Clara

220 Blake Avenue, Santa Clara, CA 95051. Phone: 408-247-4740. Fax: 408-247-0996. www.sierraschool.com. Head: Linda Wesley. Admissions: Linda Wesley/Sherryl Thomas. Est. 1974. Dress code. Closed campus.

Sierra is a K-12 school. Please see complete listing under Santa Clara elementary schools.

ROGER WILLIAMS ACADEMY   South San Francisco

600 Grand Avenue, South San Francisco, CA 94080. Phone: 650-589-1081. www.rogerwilliamsacademy.org. Head: Mrs. Rita Chavez. Admissions: Rev. Cynthia M. Smith. Est. 1946. Nonprofit. Baptist. Uniforms.

Roger Williams Academy is a K-12 school. Please see complete listing under San Mateo elementary schools.

KING'S ACADEMY   Sunnyvale

562 Britton Avenue, Sunnyvale, CA 94085. Phone: 408-481-9900. Fax: 408-481-9932. www.tka.org. Head: Bob Kellogg. Admissions: Jackie LaFrance. Est. 1991. Nonprofit. Christian. Dress code. Closed campus.

Gr. 6 to 12. 707 students. 1 to 14 teacher to student ratio. Avg. class size: 23. School hrs: 8 AM - 2 PM TF, 3 PM MWTh. Extended care available until 5:30 PM, $4/hr, minimum of one hour. 6 period day. Tuition: $7,656 - $9,152. Other fees: $600 student fee. 10% receive fin. aid. French, Spanish. 6 AP classes. 10,000 sq. ft. theater, large spiritual life building, three computer labs, multi-media center, art center, library, two chemistry labs, physics lab, biology lab, 2 gyms. Volleyball, soccer, cross country, track, swimming, basketball, football, baseball, wrestling, softball, tennis. Leagues: California Interscholastic Federation, the Central Coast Section and the Private School Athletic League. Annual trip to build houses in Tijuana Mexico, annual trip to Woodleaf Young Life Camp, leadership training, weekly mentoring sessions, teacher and peer tutoring, Shepherding Program. full-time Student Services Director: meets with student's educational testing evaluator, evaluates progress, coordinates conferences between student/parent/teacher. 40 service hrs. req'd. 100% take SAT. Avg. SAT math: 600-649. Avg. SAT verbal: 550-599. 20% attend 2 yr. college. 80% attend 4 yr. college. 75% of teachers credentialed. Avg. yrs. teaching exp: 4. Standardized tests administered. Summer Knights Sports Camps, SAT Prep, chemistry/math/english prep. Accreditation: WASC, ACSI.

The King's Academy is a Christ-centered college preparatory middle and senior high school for students who have teachable hearts and coachable spirits. We offer a loving, family environment where students are encouraged to grow in their relationships with Jesus, their family, teachers and others. We are committed to developing God's best for each student spiritually, academically, morally and socially through every program and activity.

SPECIAL EDUCATION SCHOOLS
IN SAN MATEO AND SANTA CLARA COUNITES

CHARLES ARMSTRONG SCHOOL   Belmont

1405 Solana Drive, Belmont, CA 94002. Phone: 650-592-7570. Fax: 650-592-0780. www.charlesarmstrong.org. Head: Rosalie Whitlock, Ph.D. Admissions: Christy Chochran. Est. 1968. Nonprofit. Dress code.

Gr. 1 to 8. 248 students. School serves dyslexic learners whose educational needs couldn't be met in more traditional schools. 1 to 8 teacher to student ratio. Avg. class size: 16. School hrs: 8:30 AM - 3:30 PM. Tuition: $22,400. 26% receive fin. aid. 3% paid for by public school district. Specialists: music, art, science, drama, PE. Multimedia library. Flag football, basketball, fencing, soccer, gymnastics, volleyball, lacrosse, archery, street hockey, wrestling, tennis, bowling. 1 student per computer. Outdoor Experiential Learning Program, Student Mentor Program. Dyslexia remediation. Waiting list. Parent participation encouraged. 100% of teachers credentialed. 50% of teachers post HW online. Two three-week summer academic programs. Accreditation: WASC, CAIS (in process), NAIS.

The mission of the Charles Armstrong School is to serve the dyslexic learner by providing an appropriate educational experience which not only enables the student to acquire language skills, but also instills a joy of learning, enhances self-worth, and allows each the right to identify, understand and fulfill personal potential.

BRIDGE SCHOOL   Hillsborough

545 Eucalyptus Avenue, Hillsborough, CA 94010. Phone: 650-696-7295. Fax: 650-342-7598. www.bridgeschool.org. Head: Catherine Sementelli. Est. 1987. Nonprofit.

Gr. K to 8. 14 students. School serves children with speech or physical impairment. 1 to 3 teacher to student ratio. Avg. class size: 6. School hrs: 8:30 AM - 2:30 PM. 40% receive fin. aid. 60% paid for by public school district. Educational team comprised of special education teachers, speech-language pathologists, an assistive technologist, a psychologist, and a highly talented group of paraeducators. App. deadline: January. Building Bridges Camp and Training Institute: provides a summer camp experience for Augmentative & Alternative Communication users 5 -17 years of age, offers training opportunities for individuals who work with AAC users, and support for siblings. Certified by the State Dept. of Education.

The Bridge School is a non-profit organization whose mission is to ensure that individuals with severe speech and physical impairments achieve full participation in their communities through the use of augmentative & alternative means of communication

(AAC) and assistive technology (AT) applications and through the development, implementation and dissemination of innovative life-long educational strategies. Professional staff works together to teach a communication-based curriculum, which includes art, communication skill development, community trips and field experiences, computer literacy, expressive language and written communication, leisure management, literature and reading, mathematics, movement integration, science, sensory integration, social studies and history.

ACHIEVEKIDS SPECIAL EDUCATION SCHOOL   Palo Alto

3860 Middlefield Road, Palo Alto, CA 94303. Phone: 650-494-1200. Fax: 650-494-1243. www.achievekids.org. Head: Tom Drechsler. Est. 1960. Nonprofit.

Ages 6-22. 60 students. We serve students with autism, mental retardation, pervasive developmental delay, Asperger's Syndrome, depression, anxiety, PTSD, ADHD, bipolar disorder, or schizophrenia. 1 to 3 teacher to student ratio. Avg. class size: 7. Ungraded class rooms. School hrs: 9 AM - 2:30 PM, Wednesdays 9 AM - 1:30 PM. 100% paid for by public school district. We provide school-based mental health therapy, outpatient   counseling, speech and language therapy, behavior modification, vocational training,   transition services, psychiatric services. Two-month summer sessions. Certified by State Department of Education.

Helping our students reintegrate into their community and public schools while becoming self-reliant in their families is and has been our goal for over 44 years. We achieve this by addressing each student's disability with our intensive programs and individualized services—allowing our students to overcome the challenges they face while reaching their fullest potential throughout their lives.

ESTHER B. CLARK SCHOOL   Palo Alto

650 Clark Way, Palo Alto, CA 94304. Phone: 650-322-3065. Fax: 650-322-4329. www.chconline.org/sp_school.htm. Head: Karen A. Breslow, M.A. Est. 1950.

Gr. 1 to 10. 82 students. The EBC School program is designed for children between the ages of 7 and 16, who have difficulty functioning at home or school due to one or more of the following conditions: behavior disorders, social and emotional problems, specific learning disabilities, speech or language disorders, or neurological problems. 1 to 4 teacher to student ratio. School hrs: 8:15 AM - 3:05 PM. 100% paid for by public school district. Special Education Teacher and Teaching Assistant, Clinician, Behavioral Specialist.

The Esther B. Clark (EBC) School is a certified non-public school for children ages 7-16, who have significant learning, behavioral, and emotional challenges. The full-day program combines academics, behavior management, and therapy in an individualized classroom format.

JEAN WEINGARTEN PENINSULA
ORAL SCHOOL FOR THE DEAF   Redwood City

3518 Jefferson Avenue, Redwood City, CA 94062. Phone: 650-365-7500. Fax: 650-365-7500. www.oraldeafed.org. Head: Kathleen Daniel Sussman. Admissions: Kathy Berger. Est. 1969. Nonprofit. No dress code.

Gr. Pre-K to 4. 80 students. Children with severe to profound hearing loss are given an intensive training that focuses on the development of cognitive processes. 1 to 2 teacher to student ratio. Avg. class size: 5. Teaching methods focus on the training of the residual hearing of each child, using amplification equipment such as power hearing aids and cochlear implants. On-site monitoring of each child's amplification equipment, and the availability of loaner hearing aids ensures that every child is given the opportunity to listen everyday. School hrs: 8:40 AM - 2:30 PM. Tuition: $24,000. 8% receive fin. aid. 92% paid for by public school district. Specialists: art, physical education. 5 speech and language pathologists, 2 part-time audiologists, an occupational therapist. Parent participation encouraged. 100% of teachers credentialed. 98% of teachers have adv. degrees. Avg. yrs. teaching exp: 15. Standardized tests administered. 15 day summer camp, includes individual speech and language therapy; siblings are invited. Certified by State Dept. of Education.

Every child at JWPOSD gains from a planned teaching strategy that promotes his own ability to think; to express feelings and sensitivities through oral and written communication; to acquire speech and language from the manipulation of ideas; and to listen with increasing skill and sophistication. Every parent at JWPOSD gains from the close partnership that exists between them and the child's therapist and teacher as they learn together how to meet each child's special needs during daily therapy and class. Parent education and counseling are a key focus of the school's total program as the school strives to empower each family with the information they need to understand their child's hearing loss and to become informed advocates for their child's future needs.

STERNE SCHOOL   San Francisco

2690 Jackson Street, San Francisco, CA 94115. Phone: 415-922-6081. Fax: 415-922-1598. www.sterneschool.org. Est. 1976.

Gr. 5 to 12. 60 students. School serves children with learning disabilities. Avg. class size: 13. Computer lab. Daily physical education classes and weekly elective classes such as bowling, digital movie making and urban hiking. High school students participate in PathFinders, a career and education transition program. Parent participation encouraged. Accreditation: WASC. Certified by State Dept. of Education.

Sterne School provides an educational community where young people with specific learning disabilities realize their individual academic potential. They are encouraged to achieve mastery of basic skills through an information-rich curriculum. In a warm, respectful atmosphere, Sterne students become confident, disciplined, responsible citizens ready to meet the challenges of further learning and society.

199

ACHIEVEKIDS SPECIAL EDUCATION SCHOOL   San Jose

1212 McGinness Avenue, San Jose, CA 95127. Head: Skye Cary.

Please see complete listing under Palo Alto.

BEACON SCHOOL   San Jose

5670 Camden Avenue, San Jose, CA 95124. Phone: 408-265-8611. Fax: 408-265-7324. www.beaconschool.com. Head: Teresa Malekzadeh. Est. 1970.

Gr. 1 to 12. 40 students. Beacon serves students categorized as emotionally disturbed, developmentally disabled, or learning disabled. 1 to 3 teacher to student ratio. Avg. class size: 8. School hrs: 8:30 AM - 1:30 PM. 100% paid for by public school district. Physical education. Curriculum includes academics as well as hands-on experiences like computer instruction, art, woodshop, ceramics, jewelry making, outdoor leadership, and cooking. Behavioral counseling, vocational training. 100% of teachers credentialed. 6 wk. summer program with emphasis on math, language arts, and special programs. Certified by State Dept. of Education.

Beacon School provides a therapeutic educational setting designed to meet the needs of special education students. Beacon School provides a safe supportive environment that will help each student to develop independent living skills, academic achievement consistent with his or her potential, and the opportunity to gain sufficient maturity and judgment to be successful in daily living. A full curriculum is offered for students grades six through twelve, and all students are required to participate in prevocational and independent living skills course.

SECOND START-PINE HILL SCHOOL   San Jose

3002 Leigh Avenue, San Jose, CA 95124. Phone: 408-979-8210. Fax: 408-979-8223. www.pinehillschool.com. Head: David Gerster. Est. 1976. Nonprofit. Dress code.

Gr. K to 12. 100 students. Specialists serve students with learning disabilities, social-cognitive difficulties and emotional problems. 1 to 4 teacher to student ratio. Avg. class size: 10. School hrs: 8 AM - 2:30 PM. 75% paid for by public school district. Computer lab. 3-on-3 basketball. Multilevel behavioral approach. Offers prescriptive academics, multi-sensory reading programs, computer resources, counseling services, speech therapy, and vocational training/placement. Slingerland instruction provided. Serves students from 25 schools districts and from the Santa Clara County of Education. Behavior, crisis, and therapeutic counselors on staff. Six-week summer school program with project-based academic classes and PE. Certified by State Dept. of Education.

Pine Hill staff is committed to the belief that each student can achieve to his/her fullest potential when provided with a safe, nurturing supportive, and a developmentally therapeutic environment that will enrich the quality of life for youths with academic, behavioral, social and emotional needs.

RUSSELL BEDE SCHOOL San Mateo

446 Turner Terrace, San Mateo, CA 94401. Phone: 650-579-4400. Fax: 650-579-4402. www.russellbedeschool.com. Head: Dr. John Piper. Est. 1983. Nonprofit. Uniforms.

Gr. 2 to 5. 18 students. School serves students who have average to above average ability, but are challenged by dyslexia, receptive and expressive language disorders, Dyscalculia, Asperger's Syndrome, or Auditory processing disorders. 1 to 6 teacher to student ratio. Avg. class size: 5. School hrs: 8:30 AM - 2:15 PM. Tuition: $16,250 - $19,000. Specialists: PE, drama, music. Learning specialists in speech and language. Parent participation encouraged. 100% of teachers credentialed. Avg. yrs. teaching exp: 20. Four-weeks summer program focused on academics in a more relaxed setting. Certified by State Dept. of Education.

The mission of Russell Bede School is to teach and remediate young students who are having difficulty succeeding in a regular education classroom. As soon as feasible, students return to mainstream education with the capabilities required to be successful. Teaching and remediation includes academic skill development, promoting appropriate learning behaviors, active learning, and independent learning skills.

STANBRIDGE ACADEMY San Mateo

515 East Poplar Avenue, San Mateo, CA 94401. Phone: 650-375-5860. Fax: 650-375-5861. www.stanbridgeacademy.org. Head: Marty Procaccio. Est. 1982. Nonprofit. Dress code.

Gr. K to 12. 80 students. Serves students with Attention Deficit Disorder (ADD), Attention Deficit Disorder with Hyperactivity (ADHD), Dyslexia, Dysgraphia, Discalcula, Nonverbal Learning Disability (NLD), Central Auditory Processing Disorder, Anxiety disorder, Obsessive-Compulsive Disorder, Central Auditory Processing Disorder, Tourette's Disorder, Asperger's Disorder. 1 to 10 teacher to student ratio. Avg. class size: 7. Max class size: 10. School hrs: 8:30 AM - 3 PM. Tuition: $21,700, fin. aid avail. Other fees: $750 supplies and equipment. 12% paid for by public school district. Field trips, community service. Waiting list. Accreditation: WASC.

Stanbridge Academy is a private, non-profit school for students with specific learning disabilities, primary grades through high school. We provide an experientially-based educational environment which fosters creativity, challenge, safety, and individual growth for students and staff. We strive to prepare our students to succeed academically and socially to their full potential.

WINGS LEARNING CENTER San Mateo

49 North San Mateo Drive, San Mateo, CA 94401. Phone: 650-342-8753. Fax: 650-342-8763. www.wingslearningcenter.org. Head: Irma E. Velasquez. Est. 1999.

Gr. Pre-K to 4. School serves academic and social needs of children with autism spectrum disorder. 1 to 3 teacher to student ratio. Avg. class size: 6. School hrs: 8:30 AM

- 2:30 PM. Speech pathologist, special education teacher, occupational therapist, play and social skills facilitator. Parent participation encouraged. 100% of teachers credentialed.

At Wings, students work in an individualized, small group setting where the curriculum provides opportunities for each child to be challenged and to excel. Teachers use language-based, multi-sensory and interactive teaching methods to make learning accessible for every child. Our goal is to help each student to be the best that he or she can be, capable of living independently as a member of the society. If at all possible, we strive to transition each student to an appropriate public or private school classroom with the necessary skills and strategies to be a successful and independent learner.

MORGAN CENTER   Santa Clara

400 North Winchester Boulevard, Santa Clara, CA 95050. Phone: 408-241-8161. www.morgancenter.org. Head: Jennifer Sullivan. Est. 1969. Nonprofit.

50 students. Special education program for children and adults with Autism, Asperger's Disorder, Pervasive Developmental Disorder, and related neurological and learning disorders. Many students have accompanying disabilities, such as epilepsy, cerebral palsy, chromosomal disorders, and visual/hearing impairment. All students demonstrate significant deficits in perception, communication, learning and behavior, and function below their age levels in most areas. Class size ranges from 4-7, teacher/student ratio 1:1. School hrs: 9 AM - 2:30 PM. 100% paid for by public school district. Specialists: art, music, PE. Daily schedule includes speech/language therapy, academics ranging from basic cognitive skills to reading, writing, composition and math. Play and social skills, physical education, as well as enrichment activities are also provided individually by appropriately credentialed staff. Waiting list. Certified by State Dept. of Education.

The Morgan Center's mission is to help every child and adult in its care to maximize his or her potential; to be in a dignified, positive, and loving environment, to remain in the community, and to lead a productive and happy life.

PACE SCHOOL (PACIFIC AUTISM CENTER FOR EDUCATION)   Sunnyvale

572 Dunholme Way, Sunnyvale, CA 94087. Phone: 408-245-3408. Fax: 408-245-3449. www.pacificautism.org. Head: Marcia Goldman. Admissions: Marquis Zane. Est. 1989. Nonprofit. No dress code.

Gr. K to 12. 53 students. PACE school serves students with autism, related developmental disabilities, and other disabilities and conditions. 1 to 7 teacher to student ratio. Avg. class size: 7. Class sizes range from 5 to 10 students. School hrs: 9:15 AM - 2:15 PM. 95% paid for by public school district. Indoor swimming facility, computers throughout the school, classroom devoted to occupational therapy. A skilled and energetic instructor visits the school several times each week to incorporate music and dance into the classrooms and get the students moving to the rhythm. Year-round school. Three full-time speech and language pathologists provide service to students with communication disorders through a Total Communication Approach. Three full-time occupational therapists provide group, individual, and consultative services. Certified State Dept. of Education.

Our teaching philosophy is based on a child-centered approach, allowing each child to work on his/her specific learning needs by utilizing their strengths and interests. Our students experience an age-appropriate academic curriculum, taught individually and in small groups. The three-step vocational and independent life skills program prepares our students to achieve independence and workplace success in the future. Leisure and social skills are addressed throughout the week through group learning and play and community activities. Our goal is to address each student's specific needs, to help them to learn and grow, and to provide an atmosphere that is both loving and supportive while equally intense and productive.

APPENDIX

CALIFORNIA DISTINGUISHED SCHOOL AWARDS

Since 1986 the California Department of Education has annually recognized schools as a reward for achievement and as a motivation for other schools to strive for excellence. Awards are given in alternate years to elementary and high schools. Award-winning schools are recognized for four years. Approximately five percent of California's public schools are selected each year.

To be eligible, schools must score in the top half of the statewide distribution of the Academic Performance Index (API) scores, and if the school's API is less than 800, the school must have also met its target growth at the school and subgroup levels from the previous year. Schools are selected for the award on the basis of statewide quality indicators. The criteria established by the California Department of Education are revised from year to year. Characteristics used to select winning schools in 2005 included:

- Dedicated and collaborative school leadership

- High academic expectations for all students, based on state-adopted curriculum and performance standards, and rigorous graduation standards

- Varied teaching strategies that meet the instructional needs of all students and accommodate all learning styles

- Academically competent and caring teachers, and strong professional development aligned to standards-based instructional materials

- Comprehensive guidance and counseling programs for all students

- Active family involvement and business and community partnerships

- A safe school culture that supports inclusion of all students and promotes positive character traits

Not all eligible schools choose to apply for the award. The application is detailed, and schools may choose not to expend their efforts on pursuing this kind of recognition. Award-winning schools are encouraged to mentor other schools applying for the award and may reapply for the award after their official four-year recognition period has concluded, provided they meet the eligibility criteria for that year.

SAN MATEO COUNTY DISTINGUISHED SCHOOLS

DISTRICT	SCHOOL	YEAR
Belmont-Redwood	Cipriani	2004
	Central Elem.	1995
	Fox Elem.	1997
	Nesbit	1997
	Ralston Mid.	1994
Burlingame	Burlingame Int.	1988, 1994, 2003
	Franklin	2002
	Lincoln	1989
Cabrillo Unified	El Granada	1997
	Farallone	1993
	Kings Mountain	1989
Hillsborough	Crocker Mid.	1988, 1992, 1994, 1999, 2003
	North	1995, 2000, 2004
	South	1987, 1993, 1997, 2000, 2004
	West	1987, 1993, 1997, 2000, 2004
Jefferson Elem.	Colma	1989, 2002
	Franklin Int.	1996, 2001
	Kennedy	1989
	Rivera Int.	2001
	Westlake	1989
Jefferson High	Terra Nova H.S.	1990
La Honda-Pescadero	La Honda	1995
Laguna Salada	Ortega Mid.	1996
(now Pacifica)	Vallemar	1997
Las Lomitas	La Entrada Mid.	1988, 1990, 1992, 1994, 1999
	Las Lomitas	1989, 1997, 2002
Menlo Park	Encinal Mid.	1990
	Hillview Mid.	1986, 1990, 1992, 1994, 1999, 2005
Millbrae	Lomita Park	1987
	Spring Valley.	1995
	Taylor Mid.	1986, 1994, 2001

Portola Valley	Corte Madera (Mid)	1988, 1992, 2001
	Ormondale	1987, 1997, 2000
Ravenswood	Flood Science	1993
Redwood City	Clifford	1998
	Kennedy Mid.	1994
	Roy Cloud	1997
San Bruno Park	Crestmoor	1987
San Carlos	Arundel	1998
	Brittan Acres	1997
	Central Mid.	2005
	San Carlos Charter	1997
San Mateo-Foster City	Abbott Mid.	1988
	Audobon	1997
	Bayside Middle	2001
	Baywood	1987
	Borel Mid.	1996
	Bowditch	2005
	Fiesta Gardens	2000
	Foster City	1998
	Highlands	1987
	Parkside	1987
	Turnbull Academy	1995
San Mateo Union High	Aragon H.S.	1988
	Capuchino	1994
	Mills H.S.	1988, 1996
Sequoia	Carlmont H.S.	1988, 1990
	Menlo Atherton H.S.	1986
	Sequoia H.S.	1986
	Woodside	1994
So. San Francisco	El Camino	1990
Woodside	Woodside	1987, 1993, 1997

SANTA CLARA COUNTY DISTINGUISHED SCHOOLS

DISTRICT	SCHOOL	YEAR
Alum Rock	Dorsa	1998
	George Mid.	1988, 1992
	Linda Vista	2004
	Lyndale	2004
Berryessa	Northwood	1987
	Piedmont Mid.	2003
	Ruskin	1987
'	Sierramont Mid.	2003
Cambrian	Bagby.	1995
	Fammatre	1997
	Farnham	2000
	Price Mid.	1990, 1996
	Sartorette	1998, 2002
Campbell Elem.	Blackford	1993, 1997
	Campbell Mid.	1990, 1999
	Castlemont	2000, 2004
	Forest Hill.	1997
	Hazelwood	1989, 2000
	Lynhaven	1987
	Marshall Lane	1993, 2004
	Monroe Mid.	1994, 1999, 2005
	Rolling Hills Mid.	1988, 2001, 2005
	Rosemary	1987, 1998
	Sherman Oaks	1998
Campbell High	Leigh H.S.	1999, 2003
	Prospect H.S	1996
	Westmont H.S	1996, 2005
Cupertino	Blue Hills	1989
	Collins	1987
	Cupertino Int.	1990
	DeVargas	1995
	Eisenhower	1989
	Faria	1989
	Hyde Jr. High	1994
	Kennedy Jr. High	1990, 1992
	Lincoln.	1987, 2000
	McAuliffe	1993
	Miller Mid.	1986, 1990, 1992

Cupertino	Montclaire.	1987
	Muir	1989
	Nimitz.	1993
	Regnart	1987
	Stevens Creek	1987
	West Valley	1989
East Side Union H.S.	Andrew Hill H.S.	1996
	Independence H.S.	1994
	Oak Grove H.S.	1999
	Overfelt H.S.	1988
	Piedmont Hills H.S.	2003
	Silver Creek H.S.	1999
Evergreen	Cadwaller	1995, 2004
	Cedar Grove	1993
	Chaboya Mid.	1994, 1999, 2003
	Dove Hill	1995, 2004
	Evergreen	1995, 2000
	Holly Oak	1995, 2004
	Laurelwood	1995, 2002
	Leyva Mid.	1990, 1994, 1999
	Matsumoto	2002
	Millbrook	1993, 1997
	Montgomery	1995, 2000
	Norwood Creek	1989, 1993
	Quimby Oak Int.	1992, 1996, 2001
	Silver Oak	1997, 2004
	Smith, (James)	2004
	Smith (Katherine)	1987, 2002
	Whaley	1989, 1997, 2004
Franklin-McKinley	Kennedy	1998
	Meadows	1993
Fremont Union H.S.	Cupertino H.S.	1990, 1994
	Fremont H.S.	1996, 2003
	Homestead H.S.	1990, 1994, 2003
	Lynbrook H.S.	1990, 1994, 1999, 2003
	Monte Vista H.S.	1988, 1990, 1996, 2003
Gilroy	Gilroy H.S.	1994
	Glen View	1997
Lakeside	Lakeside	2000
Loma Prieta	English Mid.	1988, 1990, 1992
Los Altos	Almond	1989
	Blach Int.	1990, 1992
	Bullis-Purisima	1989

Los Altos	Egan Mid.	1988, 1990
	Loyola.	1989
	Oak Ave.	1989
	Santa Rita	1989
	Springer	1989
Los Gatos	Daves Ave.	1995
.	Fisher J.H.	1988, 1990
	Van Meter	1989
Los Gatos-Sar. H.S.	Los Gatos H.S.	1986, 1990
	Saratoga H.S.	1986, 1990, 1992
Milpitas	Joseph Weller	1989, 2000
	Rancho Milpitas	2005
	Russell Mid.	1994, 1999, 2005
	Spangler	2004
	Zanker	2004
Moreland	Anderson	1987, 1995
	Baker	1987, 1995
	Castro Mid.	1988, 1990, 1996, 2001
	Country Lane	1989, 1997, 2002
	Easterbrook	1987, 2000
	Latimer	1989, 1993
	Moreland Disc.	1998, 2002
	Payne	1993, 2002
	Rogers Mid.	1988, 1990, 1992, 1994
Morgan Hill	Encinal	1989
	Jackson	1997
	Nordstrom	1995, 2004
	Walsh	1993
Mount Pleasant	Foothill Int.	1998
	Valle Vista	2000
Mountain View	Bubb.	1987, 2000
	Graham Mid.	1986, 1990, 1992
	Landels	1987
(Awarded when	Crittenden Mid.	1990, 1992
part of the	Monte Loma	1987
Whisman School	Theuerkauf	1987
District.)	Whisman	1997
Mt. View- Los Altos	Los Altos H.S.	1986, 1996
	Mtn. View H.S.	1988, 1994, 2003
Oak Grove	Anderson	2002
	Baldwin	1989, 2000
	Bernal Int.	1990, 2003

Oak Grove	Blossom Valley	2000
	Davis Int.	1990, 1999
	Edenvale	2004
	Hayes.	1987, 2002
	Herman Int.	2003
	Ledesma	2002
	Oak Ridge	2004
	Parkview	1989
	San Anselmo	2002
	Santa Teresa	2002
	Taylor	2000
Palo Alto Unified	Gunn H.S.	1988, 1990, 1992
	Palo Alto H.S.	1986, 1990, 1992
	Stanford Mid.	1988, 1990, 1992, 1994
San Jose Unified	Booksin	2000
	Bret Harte Mid.	1990, 1992, 1994, 2001
	Canoas	2004
	Carson	2002
	Castillero Mid.	1999
	Cory	2002
	Erikson Academy	2002
	Graystone	2000
	Hacienda	2000
	Leland H.S.	1990, 2003
	Lincoln H.S.	1992, 1996, 2005
	Los Alamitos	2000
	Muir Mid.	1999, 2003
	Pioneer H.S.	1992, 2001
	Randol	1997
	Reed	2002
	River Glen	2000
	San Jose Academy	1990
	Schallenberger	2002
	Simonds	2000
	Terrell	2000
	Williams	1998
Santa Clara Unified	Bowers	1998
	Braly	2000
	Mayne	1993
	Milliken	1989, 1995
	Laurelwood	1998
	Ponderosa	1997, 2004
	Santa Clara H.S.	1988, 2001
	Washington Open	2000, 2004
	Westwood	1987, 1993
	Wilcox H.S.	2005

Saratoga	Argonaut	1987, 1993
	Foothill	1989, 1995
	Redwood Mid.	1990, 1992
	Saratoga	1987, 1993
Sunnyvale	Bishop	1989
	Cherry Chase	1989, 2002
	Columbia Com.	1989
	Cumberland	1987, 2004
	Fairwood	2004
	Hollenbeck	1987
	San Miguel	2000
	Sunnyvale Mid.	1992, 1999
	Vargas	2004
Union	Alta Vista	2000
	Dartmouth Mid.	1999
	Guadalupe	1987, 1995
	Lietz	1987
	Lone Hill	1987, 2002
	Noddin	1997
	Oster	2004
	Union Mid.	1999

NATIONAL SCHOOL RECOGNITION PROGRAM

The No Child Left Behind Blue Ribbon Schools Program honors public and private K-12 schools that are either academically superior in their states or that demonstrate dramatic gains in student achievement. Before 2002, the federal government's blue ribbon awards were granted on the basis of a number of criteria, including evidence of family involvement and clear vision and sense of mission, and required schools to fill out a very long application. Now that the award is part of the NCLB program, the criteria for determining which schools win is based primarily on testing data. Public schools are nominated by each state's department of education. There are two categories of nominations:

- Dramatically improving schools that have made adequate yearly progress (AYP) as defined by their state and in which at least 40 percent of their students come from disadvantaged backgrounds.

- High performing schools that are in the top 10 percent of all schools on state assessment scores in both reading (language arts or English) and mathematics, regardless of their demographics. These schools must also meet AYP goals.

Private schools that administer state tests and nationally normed tests may apply for the award through the Council for American Private Education (CAPE).

WINNERS OF NATIONAL SCHOOL RECOGNITION PROGRAM

San Mateo County Schools

DISTRICT	SCHOOL	YEAR
Hillsborough	Crocker Mid.	1983, 1989, 1995, 2004
Hillsborough	South Hillsborough	1997
Hillsborough	West Hillsborough	1994
Las Lomitas	Las Lomitas	2003
Menlo Park	Hillview Mid.	2000
Millbrae	Taylor Mid.	1995
Portola Valley	Corte Madera	2002
Private school	Nueva	1988, 1997
San Mateo-Foster City	Borel Mid.	1984
San Mateo-Foster-City	Bowditch Middle	1993
San Mateo Union High	Hillsdale H.S.	1993
San Mateo Union High	San Mateo H.S.	1991
Sequoia	Menlo Atherton H.S.	1987
Woodside	Woodside Elem.	1994

Santa Clara County Schools

DISTRICT	SCHOOL	YEAR
Berryessa	Northwood	2004
Campbell Elem.	Forest Hill	1999
Campbell Elem.	Rolling Hills Mid.	1989, 1993
Campbell H.S.	Westmont H.S.	1998
Cupertino	Collins Elem.	1988
Cupertino	Garden Gate Elem.	1986
Cupertino	Hyde Jr. High	1989
Cupertino	Kennedy Jr. High	1993
Cupertino	Miller Jr. High	1987
Cupertino	Regnart Elem.	1988
Cupertino	Stevens Creek Elem.	1988
Cupertino	West Valley Elem.	1986
Evergreen	Cadwallader Elem.	1997
Evergreen	Cedar Grove Elem.	1997
Evergreen	Dove Hill	1997
Evergreen	Holly Oak	1997

DISTRICT	SCHOOL	YEAR
Evergreen	K.R. Smith Elem.	1988
Evergreen	Levya Jr. High	1983
Evergreen	Matsumoto	2004
Evergreen	Millbrook Elem.	1997
Evergreen	Norwood Creek	1994
Evergreen	O.B. Whaley	1990
Evergreen	Silver Oak	2001
Fremont	Cupertino	1995
Fremont	Homestead H.S.	1987, 2004
Fremont	Monte Vista H.S.	1998
Los Altos	Bullis-Purissima	1992
Los Altos	Santa Rita	1992
Los Gatos	Fischer Jr. High	1989
Los Gatos-Saratoga	Los Gatos H.S.	1987, 1991
Los Gatos-Saratoga	Saratoga H.S.	1989
Moreland	Anderson Elem.	1988
Moreland	Moreland Discovery	2003
Moreland	Rogers Mid.	1993
Morgan Hill	Jackson	1999
Mtn. View-Los Altos	Mountain View H.S.	1989
Oak Grove	Davis Int.	1993
Palo Alto	Palo Alto H.S.	1987
Private School	Valley Christian H.S.	2004
Private School	St. Francis H.S.	1991, 1995
Private School	St. Simon	1992
San Jose	Bret Harte Mid.	2002
San Jose	Castillero Mid.	2000
San Jose	Graystone	1992, 2001
San Jose	Leland	2004
San Jose	Lincoln H.S.	1998
San Jose	Los Alamitos	2001
San Jose	Randol	1999
San Jose	Simonds	2001
San Jose	Williams	1999
Santa Clara	Westwood	1994
Saratoga	Argonaut	1994
Saratoga	Foothill	1992
Sunnyvale	Cherry Chase	2003
Sunnyvale	Sunnyvale Mid.	2000
Union	Noddin	1999

Source: California Department of Education

EXPLANATION OF THE
ACADEMIC PERFORMANCE INDEX

The pages that follow list the Academic Performance Index (API) rankings released in March 2005. (See the Explanation of Statewide Testing at the beginning of this book for a more complete explanation of the API and STAR testing and the debate surrounding these tests.) Based on the results of the STAR (SAT-9) tests given in the 2003-2004 school year, each school was given a score on a scale from 200 to 1000. The statewide target for all schools is 800. Schools scoring below 800 are expected to reach a set target growth goal each year. Those that continually fail to meet their goals may face state intervention.

The first column shows the number of students tested. The second column shows the API score and the next the school's statewide ranking. Schools with a ranking of 2 are in the bottom 20% and those with rankings of 10 are in the top 10%. The fourth column indicates how the school's API score compares to scores of similar schools, based on a number of characteristics including student mobility, ethnicity, socioeconomic status, percentage of fully credentialed teachers, and percentage of students who are English learners. The last column gives the percentage of students categorized as disadvantaged because of socioeconomic factors.

Schools that are part of the Alternative Schools Accountability Model (ASAM) do not receive state or similar schools ranking. An asterisk indicates that a school had fewer than 100 students taking the test and therefore the scores may be unreliable.

You can obtain API scores for years after 2004 at **www.ed-data.k12.ca.us.** or at **http://api.cde.gov.**

SANTA CLARA COUNTY
2004 ACADEMIC PERFORMANCE INDEX
(API) BASE

ALUM ROCK UNION	Number of Students Included in the 2004 API	2004 API Base	2004 Statewide Rank	2004 Similar Schools Rank	Percentage of Disadvantaged Students
Elementary Schools					
Arbuckle (Clyde) Elementary	310	691	4	8	85
Cassell (Sylvia) Elementary	365	717	5	8	76
Chavez (Cesar) Elementary	482	623	2	4	87
Cureton (Horace) Elementary	339	694	4	8	70
Dorsa (A. J.) Elementary	377	592	1	4	93
Goss (Mildred) Elementary	305	580	1	1	82
Hubbard (O. S.) Elementary	272	642	2	4	85
Linda Vista Elementary	363	717	5	6	57
Lyndale Elementary	354	696	4	8	72
McCollam (Millard) Elementary	367	791	8	10	66
Meyer (Donald J.) Elementary	343	666	3	7	77
Painter (Ben) Elementary	327	750	6	8	69
Rogers (William R.) Elementary	264	643	2	1	67
Ryan (Thomas P.) Elementary	281	684	4	7	76
San Antonio Elementary	385	705	4	9	78
Shields (Lester W.) Elementary	352	631	2	1	76
Slonaker (Harry) Elementary	289	616	1	2	85
Middle Schools					
Fischer (Clyde L.) Middle	692	596	2	3	82
George (Joseph) Middle	530	632	3	2	66
Mathson (Lee) Middle	443	613	2	5	87
Ocala Middle	693	649	4	3	63
Pala Middle	545	617	2	2	71
Sheppard (William L.) Middle	582	643	3	2	67
Small Schools					
Miller (Grandin) Elementary	13	628 *	2 *	N/A	85

	Number of Students Included in the 2004 API	2004 API Base	2004 Statewide Rank	2004 Similar Schools Rank	Percentage of Disadvantaged Students
BERRYESSA UNION					
Elementary Schools					
Brooktree Elementary	353	801	8	3	35
Cherrywood Elementary	345	760	7	1	34
Laneview Elementary	356	765	7	1	33
Majestic Way Elementary	342	765	7	1	35
Noble Elementary	347	791	8	1	23
Northwood Elementary	250	784	7	5	53
Ruskin Elementary	431	847	9	1	21
Summerdale Elementary	335	753	6	1	40
Toyon Elementary	293	690	4	1	42
Vinci Park Elementary	491	744	6	1	36
Middle Schools					
Morrill Middle	882	761	8	4	36
Piedmont Middle	1,000	750	7	3	29
Sierramont Middle	977	788	9	5	24
CAMBRIAN					
Elementary Schools					
Bagby Elementary	375	867	10	8	15
Fammatre Elementary	259	837	9	7	25
Farnham Charter School	236	814	8	5	28
Sartorette Charter School	250	860	9	10	24
Middle Schools					
Price Charter Middle School	893	823	9	9	16
CAMPBELL UNION ELEMENTARY					
Elementary Schools					
Blackford Elementary	282	702	4	4	55
Capri Elementary	244	854	9	10	31
Castlemont Elementary	413	804	8	5	27
Forest Hill Elementary	319	849	9	6	14
Hazelwood Elementary	220	739	6	2	40
Lynhaven Elementary	288	758	7	7	44
Marshall Lane Elementary	333	902	10	6	3
Rosemary Elementary	200	657	3	4	80
Sherman Oaks Elementary	273	644	2	4	80
Middle Schools					
Campbell Middle	802	666	4	1	40
Monroe Middle	795	724	7	6	36
Rolling Hills Middle	912	813	9	3	9

CAMPBELL UNION HIGH	Number of Students Included in the 2004 API	2004 API Base	2004 Statewide Rank	2004 Similar Schools Rank	Percentage of Disadvantaged Students
High Schools					
Branham High	967	722	8	4	8
Leigh High	1,198	747	9	2	3
Prospect High	818	679	6	2	24
Westmont High	1,270	704	7	1	13
ASAM Schools					
Boynton High	72	393 *	B *	B	28
CUPERTINO UNION					
Elementary Schools					
Blue Hills Elementary	367	956	10	9	0.5
Collins Elementary	486	934	10	6	2
De Vargas Elementary	336	837	9	2	26
Dilworth Elementary	283	964	10	10	1
Eaton (C.B.) Elementary	293	925	10	5	3
Eisenhower Elementary	352	874	10	2	8
Faria Elementary	374	993	10	10	1
Garden Gate Elementary	449	955	10	9	3
Lincoln Elementary	529	925	10	5	3
Meyerholz Elementary	286	875	10	1	10
Montclaire Elementary	328	944	10	8	2
Muir Elementary	353	881	10	1	6
Murdock-Portal Elementary School	302	985	10	10	1
Nimitz Elementary	295	800	8	2	29
Regnart Elementary	425	953	10	9	2
Sedgwick Elementary	362	864	9	2	17
Stevens Creek Elementary	456	915	10	4	4
Stocklmeir (Louis V.) Elementary	409	926	10	5	2
West Valley Elementary	496	911	10	3	2
Middle Schools					
Cupertino Middle	1,063	896	10	9	7
Hyde (Warren E.) Middle	988	829	9	2	7
Kennedy (John F.) Middle	1,392	941	10	10	2
Miller (Joaquin) Middle	1,160	938	10	10	3
EAST SIDE UNION					
Elementary Schools					
Escuela Popular Accelerated Family	103	446	1	1	99

EAST SIDE UNION	Number of Students Included in the 2004 API	2004 API Base	2004 Statewide Rank	2004 Similar Schools Rank	Percentage of Disadvantaged Students
High Schools					
Brooktree Elementary	353	801	8	3	35
Cherrywood Elementary	345	760	7	1	34
Laneview Elementary	356	765	7	1	33
Majestic Way Elementary	342	765	7	1	35
Noble Elementary	347	791	8	1	23
Northwood Elementary	250	784	7	5	53
Ruskin Elementary	431	847	9	1	21
Summerdale Elementary	335	753	6	1	40
Toyon Elementary	293	690	4	1	42
Vinci Park Elementary	491	744	6	1	36
Middle Schools					
Morrill Middle	882	761	8	4	36
Piedmont Middle	1,000	750	7	3	29
Sierramont Middle	977	788	9	5	24
EVERGREEN					
Elementary Schools					
Cadwallader Elementary	272	797	8	9	48
Cedar Grove Elementary	546	780	7	6	38
Dove Hill Elementary	502	740	6	8	70
Evergreen Elementary	441	877	10	5	14
Holly Oak Elementary	542	769	7	8	52
Laurelwood Elementary	312	820	8	10	39
Matsumoto (Tom) Elementary	544	913	10	3	6
Millbrook Elementary	536	836	9	9	35
Montgomery (John J.) Elementary	522	758	7	8	52
Norwood Creek Elementary	488	851	9	5	27
Silver Oak Elementary	555	939	10	9	1
Smith (James Franklin) Elementary	335	940	10	7	2
Smith (Katherine R.) Elementary	523	778	7	10	68
Whaley (O.B.) Elementary	478	773	7	10	78
Middle Schools					
Chaboya Middle	1,072	825	9	10	26
Leyva (George V.) Intermediate	872	732	7	8	50
Quimby Oak Intermediate	1,092	775	8	9	32

FRANKLIN-MCKINLEY	Number of Students Included in the 2004 API	2004 API Base	2004 Statewide Rank	2004 Similar Schools Rank	Percentage of Disadvantaged Students
Elementary Schools					
Captain Jason M. Dahl	428	653	3	4	85
Franklin Elementary	413	695	4	5	87
Hellyer (G. W.) Elementary	459	745	6	3	69
Kennedy (Robert F.) Elementary	444	700	4	6	86
Los Arboles Elementary	441	635	2	3	86
McKinley Elementary	338	555	1	1	97
Meadows (Jeanne R.) Elementary	440	715	5	5	74
Santee Elementary	419	594	1	2	96
Seven Trees Elementary	418	627	2	2	88
Shirakawa (George) Sr. (Elementary	519	688	4	2	75
Stonegate Elementary	457	744	6	5	66
Windmill Springs Elementary	416	723	5	2	65
Middle Schools					
Fair (J. Wilbur) Junior High	705	648	4	3	79
Sylvandale Junior High	886	640	3	2	73
FREMONT UNION HIGH					
High Schools					
Cupertino High	1,102	795	10	4	7
Fremont High	1,284	683	6	7	34
Homestead High	1,337	810	10	6	10
Lynbrook High	1,233	892	10	10	3
Monta Vista High	1,670	912	10	10	2
GILROY UNIFIED					
Elementary Schools					
Aprea (Luigi) Elementary	463	824	9	7	18
Ascencion Solorsano Middle School	211	712	5	4	51
Del Buono (Antonio) Elementary	417	753	6	8	58
El Roble Elementary	349	683	4	4	68
Eliot Elementary	222	679	3	2	68
Glen View Elementary	384	656	3	4	82
Kelley Rod Elementary	463	709	5	4	53
Las Animas Elementary	350	640	2	4	81
Rucker Elementary	271	721	5	3	45
Middle Schools					
Brownell Middle School	927	703	6	5	41
South Valley Middle School	924	656	4	4	61
High Schools					
Gilroy High	1,611	655	5	4	38
MACSA El Portal Leadership Academy	109	472	1	1	92

	Number of Students Included in the 2004 API	2004 API Base	2004 Statewide Rank	2004 Similar Schools Rank	Percentage of Disadvantaged Students
LAKESIDE JOINT ELEM.					
Small Schools					
Lakeside Elementary	69	836 *	9 *	N/A	3
LOMA PRIETA JOINT UNION ELEM.					
Elementary Schools					
Loma Prieta Elementary	261	877	10	4	2
Middle Schools					
English (C. T.) Middle	256	875	10	8	1
LOS ALTOS					
Elementary Schools					
Almond Elementary	392	959	10	10	2
Covington Elementary	370	948	10	10	2
Loyola Elementary	382	959	10	10	1
Oak Avenue Elementary	309	945	10	8	1
Santa Rita Elementary	358	949	10	10	5
Springer Elementary	298	950	10	9	0
Middle Schools					
Blach (Georgina P.) Intermediate	430	948	10	10	1
Egan (Ardis G.) Intermediate	494	928	10	10	2
LOS GATOS UNION ELEM.					
Elementary Schools					
Blossom Hill Elementary	383	898	10	5	2
Daves Avenue Elementary	317	886	10	5	4
Louise Van Meter Elementary	258	884	10	5	5
Middle Schools					
Raymond J. Fisher Middle	988	874	10	6	3
Small Schools					
Lexington Elementary	94	886 *	10 *	N/A	1
LOS GATOS-SARATOGA HIGH					
High Schools					
Los Gatos High	1,104	863	10	9	2
Saratoga High	900	909	10	10	1
LUTHER BURBANK					
Elementary Schools					
Luther Burbank Elementary	267	661	3	6	86

223

	Number of Students Included in the 2004 API	2004 API Base	2004 Statewide Rank	2004 Similar Schools Rank	Percentage of Disadvantaged Students
MILPITAS UNIFIED					
Middle Schools					
Burnett (William) Elementary	405	776	7	2	40
Curtner Elementary	451	844	9	2	24
Pomeroy (Marshall) Elementary	456	846	9	1	18
Randall (Robert) Elementary	312	720	5	3	67
Rose (Alexander) Elementary	325	734	6	5	60
Sinnott (John) Elementary	468	842	9	3	26
Spangler (Anthony) Elementary	386	788	8	5	40
Weller (Joseph) Elementary	304	806	8	8	43
Zanker (Pearl) Elementary	267	795	8	2	32
Middle Schools					
Rancho Milpitas Junior High	659	766	8	8	39
Russell (Thomas) Junior High	758	804	9	5	27
High Schools					
Milpitas High	1,924	722	8	3	29
ASAM Schools					
Calaveras Hills Continuation H	63	407 *	B *	B	46
Milpitas Community Day	12	447 *	B *	B	42
MONTEBELLO ELEMENTARY					
Small Schools					
Montebello Elementary	31	799 *	8 *	N/A	39
MORELAND					
Elementary Schools					
Anderson (Leroy) Elementary	248	634	2	2	77
Baker (Gussie M.) Elementary	299	855	9	9	23
Country Lane Elementary	311	877	10	1	9
Easterbrook Elementary	176	806	8	8	34
Latimer Elementary	329	816	8	5	24
Moreland Discovery (Elem)	225	901	10	5	7
Payne (George C.) Elementary	250	803	8	3	26
Middle Schools					
Castro (Elvira) Middle	742	815	9	6	21
Rogers (Samuel Curtis) Middle	666	781	8	5	29
MORGAN HILL UNIFIED					
Elementary Schools					
Barrett Elementary	324	720	5	1	38
Burnett Elementary	252	684	4	1	50
Charter School of Morgan Hill	227	819	8	5	10
El Toro Elementary	384	786	7	3	25

	Number of Students Included in the 2004 API	2004 API Base	2004 Statewide Rank	2004 Similar Schools Rank	Percentage of Disadvantaged Students
MORGAN HILL UNIFIED					
Elementary Schools					
Jackson Elementary	348	782	7	4	30
Los Paseos Elementary	379	801	8	3	24
Nordstrom Elementary	425	859	9	9	17
Paradise Valley/Machado Elementary	345	799	8	3	21
San Martin/Gwinn Elementary	363	701	4	3	53
Walsh (P. A.) Elementary	262	718	5	4	46
Middle Schools					
Britton (Lewis H.) Middle	1,091	716	6	1	26
Murphy (Martin) Middle	768	737	7	2	20
High Schools					
Live Oak High	1,055	729	8	6	17
ASAM Schools					
Central High (Cont.)	20	348 *	B *	B	60
MOUNTAIN VIEW-LOS ALTOS UNION					
High Schools					
Los Altos High	1,117	791	10	8	19
Mountain View High	1,230	806	10	6	10
ASAM Schools					
Alta Vista High (Cont.)	40	417 *	B *	B	20
MOUNTAIN VIEW-WHISMAN ELEM.					
Elementary Schools					
Bubb (Benjamin) Elementary	273	840	9	7	23
Castro (Mariano) Elementary	255	635	2	5	85
Huff (Frank L.) Elementary	233	926	10	9	9
Landels (Edith) Elementary	259	805	8	8	41
Monta Loma Elementary	271	779	7	6	38
Slater (Kenneth N.) Elementary	231	728	5	4	52
Theuerkauf Elementary	299	707	5	4	60
Middle Schools					
Crittenden Middle	522	737	7	8	47
Graham (Isaac Newton) Middle	676	767	8	9	38
MT. PLEASANT ELEMENTARY					
Elementary Schools					
Foothill Intermediate	789	730	5	9	67
Mt. Pleasant Elementary	195	716	5	10	82
Sanders (Robert) Elementary	227	703	4	7	69
Valle Vista Elementary	209	811	8	10	61

	Number of Students Included in the 2004 API	2004 API Base	2004 Statewide Rank	2004 Similar Schools Rank	Percentage of Disadvantaged Students
MT. PLEASANT ELEM.					
Middle Schools					
Boeger (August) Junior High	575	683	5	8	64
OAK GROVE ELEMENTARY					
Elementary Schools					
Anderson (Alex) Elementary	392	752	6	3	32
Baldwin (Julia) Elementary	392	780	7	7	35
Christopher Elementary	348	687	4	7	81
Del Roble Elementary	366	723	5	4	51
Edenvale Elementary	376	701	4	9	83
Frost (Earl) Elementary	315	736	6	3	43
Glider Elementary	409	795	8	3	28
Hayes Elementary	361	753	6	3	33
Ledesma (Rita) Elementary	314	779	7	6	37
Miner (George) Elementary	336	722	5	7	68
Oak Ridge Elementary	347	833	9	9	25
Parkview Elementary	442	799	8	8	38
Sakamoto Elementary	368	868	10	9	12
Santa Teresa Elementary	423	799	8	8	31
Stipe (Samuel) Elementary	325	692	4	8	87
Taylor (Bertha) Elementary	435	820	8	5	23
Middle Schools					
Bernal Intermediate	820	781	8	6	25
Davis (Caroline) Elementary	824	710	6	6	57
Herman (Leonard) Intermediate	746	751	7	4	27
ASAM Schools					
The Academy	18	435 *	B *	B	61
ORCHARD ELEMENTARY					
Elementary Schools					
Orchard Elementary	566	687	4	1	57
PALO ALTO UNIFIED					
Elementary Schools					
Addison Elementary	250	915	10	8	6
Barron Park Elementary	148	844	9	4	25
Briones (Juana) Elementary	173	850	9	5	23
Duveneck Elementary	304	939	10	10	5
El Carmelo Elementary	222	884	10	6	9
Escondido Elementary	254	879	10	4	15
Fairmeadow Elementary	236	882	10	2	8
Hays (Walter) Elementary	334	921	10	6	4
Hoover (Herbert) Elementary	242	958	10	10	5

PALO ALTO UNIFIED	Number of Students Included in the 2004 API	2004 API Base	2004 Statewide Rank	2004 Similar Schools Rank	Percentage of Disadvantaged Students
Elementary Schools					
Nixon (Lucille M.) Elementary	248	946	10	10	3
Ohlone Elementary	264	907	10	8	6
Palo Verde Elementary	245	890	10	5	6
Middle Schools					
Jordan (David Starr) Middle	875	905	10	9	6
Stanford (Jane Lathrop) Middle	786	889	10	8	6
Terman Middle	547	912	10	9	6
High Schools					
Gunn (Henry M.) High	1,157	881	10	9	3
Palo Alto High	1,070	878	10	9	4
SAN JOSE UNIFIED					
Elementary Schools					
Allen Elementary	239	718	5	3	52
Almaden Elementary	230	633	2	1	72
Bachrodt (Walter L.) Elementar	302	624	2	1	72
Booksin Elementary	451	864	9	8	14
Canoas Elementary	183	735	6	9	66
Carson (Rachel) Elementary	250	757	6	2	39
Cory (Benjamin) Elementary	125	701	4	5	70
Darling (Anne) Elementary	466	573	1	1	82
Empire Gardens Elementary	174	622	2	1	73
Erikson Elementary	196	705	4	4	65
Ernesto Galarza Elementary	264	624	2	1	75
Gardner Elementary	249	601	1	5	96
Grant Elementary	316	633	2	2	78
Graystone Elementary	534	904	10	2	3
Hacienda Science/Environmental Mag	438	831	9	1	8
Hammer Elementary	212	740	6	1	27
Hester Elementary	226	664	3	4	75
Los Alamitos Elementary	401	881	10	4	7
Lowell Elementary	285	677	3	7	88
Mann (Horace) Elementary	227	618	1	3	78
Olinder (Selma) Elementary	345	589	1	1	75
Randol (James) Elementary	274	846	9	9	24
Reed Elementary	309	801	8	5	30
River Glen School	392	750	6	6	55
Schallenberger Elementary	304	764	7	6	46
Simonds Elementary	389	907	10	8	7
Terrell Elementary	258	749	6	6	55
Trace (Merritt) Elementary	428	671	3	4	62

	Number of Students Included in the 2004 API	2004 API Base	2004 Statewide Rank	2004 Similar Schools Rank	Percentage of Disadvantaged Students
SAN JOSE UNIFIED					
Elementary Schools					
Washington Elementary	402	563	1	1	87
Williams Elementary	460	934	10	6	2
Willow Glen Elementary	332	701	4	2	48
High Schools					
Downtown College Prep	230	641	4	10	72
Gunderson High	695	625	4	4	42
Leland High	1,297	829	10	7	6
Lincoln (Abraham) High	1,217	693	6	6	33
Pioneer High	1,027	734	8	6	17
San Jose High Academy	738	600	3	3	57
Willow Glen High	863	652	5	6	41
Small Schools					
Middle College High	14	718 *	8 *	N/A	0
ASAM Schools					
Gunderson Plus (Cont.)	13	354 *	B *	B	54
Leland Plus (Cont.)	13	527 *	B *	B	8
Pioneer Plus (Cont.)	14	377 *	B *	B	50
Willow Glen Plus (Cont.)	12	403 *	B *	B	50
SANTA CLARA UNIFIED					
Elementary Schools					
Bowers Elementary	243	745	6	2	59
Bracher Elementary	245	757	6	10	59
Braly Elementary	172	772	7	5	38
Briarwood Elementary	242	737	6	3	55
Haman (C. W.) Elementary	191	716	5	2	41
Hughes (Kathryn) Elementary	294	724	5	2	49
Laurelwood Elementary	331	863	9	4	10
Mayne (George) Elementary	258	716	5	7	67
Millikin Elementary	241	992	10	10	7
Montague Elementary	219	727	5	4	52
Pomeroy Elementary	343	728	5	3	46
Ponderosa Elementary	296	834	9	8	32
Scott Lane Elementary	279	686	4	5	73
Sutter Elementary	223	791	8	3	18
Washington Elementary	233	830	9	1	6
Westwood Elementary	262	739	6	3	40
Middle Schools					
Buchser Middle	848	710	6	5	40
Cabrillo (Juan) Middle	867	703	6	5	45
Peterson Middle	1,183	774	8	6	32

	Number of Students Included in the 2004 API	2004 API Base	2004 Statewide Rank	2004 Similar Schools Rank	Percentage of Disadvantaged Students
SANTA CLARA UNIFIED					
High Schools					
Santa Clara High	1,132	731	8	9	30
Wilcox (Adrian) High	1,317	721	8	6	32
Small Schools					
Wilson Altern. (K-12)	94	480 *	1 *	N/A	21
SARATOGA UNION ELEMENTARY					
Elementary					
Argonaut Elementary	404	940	10	7	1
Foothill Elementary	303	948	10	8	1
Saratoga Elementary	337	952	10	10	1
Middle Schools					
Redwood Middle	920	920	10	10	1
SUNNYVALE ELEMENTARY					
Elementary Schools					
Bishop Elementary	409	735	6	7	63
Cherry Chase Elementary	243	903	10	6	6
Cumberland Elementary	291	848	9	2	18
Ellis Elementary	310	776	7	6	50
Fairwood Elementary	195	815	8	9	52
Lakewood Elementary	353	751	6	8	51
San Miguel Elementary	279	753	6	9	63
Vargas Elementary	314	740	6	4	49
Middle Schools					
Columbia Middle	838	696	5	4	48
Sunnyvale Middle	923	801	9	5	25
UNION					
Elementary Schools					
Alta Vista Elementary	243	875	10	4	3
Athenour Elementary	266	820	8	2	14
Carlton Elementary	223	856	9	4	8
Guadalupe Elementary	221	911	10	8	3
Lietz Elementary	237	783	7	5	29
Lone Hill Elementary	177	825	9	5	10
Noddin Elementary	353	867	10	7	14
Oster Elementary	200	838	9	9	14
Middle Schools					
Dartmouth Middle	790	813	9	7	12
Union Middle	777	820	9	4	5

SAN MATEO COUNTY
2004 ACADEMIC PERFORMANCE INDEX
(API) BASE

	Number of Students Included in the 2004 API	2004 API Base	2004 Statewide Rank	2004 Similar Schools Rank	Percentage of Disadvantaged Students
BAYSHORE					
Elementary Schools					
Bayshore Elementary	97	678 *	3 *	N/A	69
Middle Schools					
Robertson (Garnet J.) Intermed	201	737	7	10	67
BELMONT-REDWOOD SHORES					
Elementary Schools					
Central Elementary	201	866	10	3	1
Cipriani Elementary	158	795	8	1	4
Fox Elementary	214	830	9	3	3
Nesbit Elementary	169	696	4	1	18
Sandpiper Elementary	305	887	10	2	0.5
Middle Schools					
Ralston Intermediate	779	812	9	2	4
BRISBANE					
Elementary Schools					
Brisbane Elementary	128	765	7	1	13
Panorama Elementary	145	706	5	1	41
Middle Schools					
Lipman Middle	228	764	8	7	35
BURLINGAME					
Elementary Schools					
Franklin Elementary	275	878	10	2	3
Lincoln Elementary	207	883	10	5	1
McKinley Elementary	178	813	8	5	20
Roosevelt Elementary	169	828	9	2	10
Washington Elementary	153	813	8	4	10
Middle Schools					
Burlingame Intermediate	848	822	9	2	4

	Number of Students Included in the 2004 API	2004 API Base	2004 Statewide Rank	2004 Similar Schools Rank	Percentage of Disadvantaged Students
CABRILLO UNIFIED					
Elementary Schools					
El Granada Elementary	292	733	6	5	44
Farallone View Elementary	288	753	6	1	24
Hatch (Alvin S.) Elementary	357	697	4	3	49
Middle Schools					
Cunha (Manuel F.) Intermediate	805	752	7	5	31
High Schools					
Half Moon Bay High	831	705	7	4	24
Small Schools					
Kings Mountain Primary	25	935 *	10 *	N/A	4
ASAM Schools					
Pilarcitos High (Cont.)	13	397 *	B *	B	38
HILLSBOROUGH CITY ELEMENTARY					
Elementary Schools					
North Hillsborough (Elem)	207	953	10	9	0
South Hillsborough (Elem)	173	936	10	8	0
West Hillsborough (Elem)	224	959	10	10	0
Middle Schools					
Crocker Middle	456	930	10	10	.5
JEFFERSON ELEMENTARY					
Elementary Schools					
Anthony (Susan B.) Elementary	452	702	4	7	63
Brown (Margaret Pauline) Elementar	204	750	6	6	57
Colma Elementary	218	733	6	9	78
Columbus (Christopher) Elementary	196	704	4	3	59
Edison (Thomas) Elementary	288	797	8	4	38
Garden Village Elementary	220	742	6	5	51
John F. Kennedy Elementary	262	729	5	2	58
Roosevelt (Franklin Delano) Elemen	241	753	6	7	42
Tobias (Marjorie H.) Elementary	231	789	8	2	35
Washington (George) Elementary	183	789	8	10	73
Webster (Daniel) Elementary	297	782	7	4	40
Westlake Elementary	279	709	5	1	54
Woodrow Wilson Elementary	288	723	5	3	65
Middle Schools					
Franklin (Benjamin) Intermedia	534	711	6	5	47
Pollicita (Thomas R.) Middle	517	657	4	4	53
Rivera (Fernando) Intermediate	463	731	7	6	38

231

	Number of Students Included in the 2004 API	2004 API Base	2004 Statewide Rank	2004 Similar Schools Rank	Percentage of Disadvantaged Students
JEFFERSON UNION HIGH					
High Schools					
Jefferson High	892	612	3	3	49
Oceana High	449	739	8	4	10
Terra Nova High	1,028	720	8	4	12
Westmoor High	1,305	721	8	3	31
ASAM Schools					
Thornton High (Cont)	47	318 *	B *	B	9
LA HONDA-PESCADERO UNIFIED					
Elementary Schools					
Pescadero Elementary	168	703	4	7	70
Small Schools					
La Honda Elementary	55	835 *	9 *	N/A	11
Pescadero High	51	678 *	6 *	N/A	53
LAS LOMITAS ELEMENTARY					
Elementary Schools					
Las Lomitas Elementary	213	927	10	10	3
Middle Schools					
La Entrada Middle	540	913	10	10	1
MENLO PARK CITY					
Elementary Schools					
Encinal Elementary	337	886	10	4	3
Laurel Elementary	134	908	10	8	6
Oak Knoll Elementary	383	911	10	8	4
Middle Schools					
Hillview Middle	636	877	10	7	5
MILLBRAE					
Elementary Schools					
Green Hills Elementary	209	812	8	3	13
Lomita Park Elementary	165	789	8	9	41
Meadows Elementary	251	817	8	1	7
Spring Valley Elementary	222	838	9	2	9
Middle Schools					
Taylor Middle	855	811	9	2	13

PACIFICA SCHOOL DISTRICT	Number of Students Included in the 2004 API	2004 API Base	2004 Statewide Rank	2004 Similar Schools Rank	Percentage of Disadvantaged Students
Elementary Schools					
Cabrillo Elementary	432	847	9	3	7
Linda Mar Elementary	139	750	6	2	19
Ocean Shore Elementary	233	848	9	1	8
Oddstad Elementary	210	798	8	2	11
Sunset Ridge Elementary	312	757	6	3	40
Vallemar Elementary	421	861	9	5	11
Middle Schools					
Ingrid B. Lacy Middle School	633	745	7	2	24
PORTOLA VALLEY					
Elementary Schools					
Ormondale Elementary	156	940	10	10	4
Middle Schools					
Corte Madera Elementary	346	929	10	10	2
RAVENSWOOD CITY					
Elementary Schools					
Belle Haven Elementary	560	589	1	3	92
Costano Elementary	346	635	2	8	90
East Palo Alto Charter (Elem)	282	721	5	10	82
Edison-Brentwood Academy	215	598	1	5	95
Flood (James) Elementary	208	736	6	10	62
Green Oaks (Kindergarten)	210	489	1	1	98
Willow Oaks Elementary	415	580	1	2	93
Middle Schools					
Chavez (Cesar) Academy (Elem)	476	539	1	2	95
Edison-McNair Academy	536	629	3	9	91
High Schools					
East Palo Alto High School	181	504	1	3	84
ASAM Schools					
Forty-Niner Academy	111	539	B	B	86
REDWOOD CITY					
Elementary Schools					
Adelante Spanish Immersion (Elem)	320	702	4	4	55
Clifford Elementary	578	783	7	2	23
Cloud (Roy) Elementary	465	839	9	6	11
Fair Oaks Elementary	295	602	1	5	98
Ford (Henry) Elementary	327	708	5	1	40
Garfield Charter (Elem)	529	598	1	2	90
Gill (John) Elementary	211	764	7	10	56

	Number of Students Included in the 2004 API	2004 API Base	2004 Statewide Rank	2004 Similar Schools Rank	Percentage of Disadvantaged Students
REDWOOD CITY					
Elementary Schools					
Hawes Elementary	244	682	4	7	75
Hoover Elementary	602	657	3	8	94
North Star Academy (Elem)	479	967	10	10	12
Roosevelt Elementary	264	696	4	5	64
Selby Lane Elementary	443	678	3	7	79
Taft Elementary	362	590	1	2	86
Middle Schools					
Kennedy (John F.) Middle	923	667	4	4	58
McKinley Institute of Technology	328	643	3	5	67
Small Schools					
Aurora High	56	469 *	1 *	N/A	79
Orion Alternative	94	800 *	8 *	N/A	30
SAN BRUNO PARK					
Elementary Schools					
Allen (Decima M.) Elementary	305	741	6	8	55
Belle Air Elementary	292	707	5	9	72
Crestmoor Elementary	141	848	9	7	11
El Crystal Elementary	133	779	7	7	22
John Muir Elementary	265	817	8	5	17
Portola Elementary	139	757	6	1	25
Rollingwood Elementary	164	788	8	5	23
Middle Schools					
Parkside Intermediate	584	710	6	2	31
SAN CARLOS					
Elementary Schools					
Arundel Elementary	174	856	9	2	1
Brittan Acres Elementary	212	822	8	1	3
Charter Learning Center	191	860	9	1	0
Heather Elementary	173	848	9	1	8
White Oaks Elementary	200	876	10	4	2
Middle Schools					
Central Middle	527	808	9	1	4
Tierra Linda Middle	470	854	10	6	4
Small Schools					
San Carlos High School	66	638 *	4 *	N/A	18

SAN MATEO UNION HIGH	Number of Students Included in the 2004 API	2004 API Base	2004 Statewide Rank	2004 Similar Schools Rank	Percentage of Disadvantaged Students
High Schools					
Aragon High	1,067	763	9	4	8
Burlingame High	953	780	9	4	4
Capuchino High	799	691	6	9	19
Hillsdale High	892	688	6	2	15
Mills High	1,073	793	10	4	6
San Mateo High	964	720	8	6	18
ASAM Schools					
Peninsula High (Cont.)	57	539 *	B *	B	32
SAN MATEO-FOSTER CITY ELEMENTARY					
Elementary Schools					
Audubon Elementary	278	842	9	1	7
Baywood Elementary	307	894	10	9	9
Beresford Elementary	128	727	5	4	32
Brewer Island Elementary	318	921	10	5	2
Fiesta Gardens International Eleme	255	721	5	2	40
Foster City Elementary	463	880	10	2	4
George Hall Elementary	235	752	6	7	39
Highlands Elementary	273	878	10	6	11
Horrall (Albion H.) Elementary	326	688	4	7	70
Laurel Elementary	285	839	9	9	19
Meadow Heights Elementary	171	835	9	7	19
North Shoreview Elementary	178	720	5	4	53
Park Elementary	196	726	5	3	45
Parkside Elementary	280	755	6	5	35
Sunnybrae Elementary	258	708	5	4	48
Turnbull Learning Academy	164	550	1	1	95
Middle Schools					
Abbott Middle	769	758	8	5	27
Bayside Middle	704	686	5	3	48
Borel Middle	821	762	8	2	24
Bowditch Middle	936	867	10	5	5
SEQUOIA UNION HIGH					
High Schools					
Carlmont High	1,360	740	8	7	16
Menlo-Atherton High	1,416	673	6	5	29
Sequoia High	1,122	599	3	5	45
Woodside High	1,352	665	5	7	37
ASAM Schools					
Redwood High (Cont.)	17	409 *	B *	B	24

SOUTH SAN FRANCISCO	Number of Students Included in the 2004 API	2004 API Base	2004 Statewide Rank	2004 Similar Schools Rank	Percentage of Disadvantaged Students
Elementary Schools					
Hillside Elementary	194	655	3	1	42
Junipero Serra Elementary	240	784	7	1	31
Los Cerritos Elementary	214	755	6	9	61
Martin Elementary	265	685	4	7	82
Monte Verde Elementary	298	830	9	1	25
Ponderosa Elementary	245	791	8	5	24
Skyline Elementary	286	785	7	2	30
Spruce Elementary	291	733	6	10	74
Sunshine Gardens Elementary	204	718	5	3	48
Middle Schools					
Alta Loma Middle	782	721	6	2	24
Parkway Heights Middle	721	637	3	2	60
Westborough Middle	663	782	8	6	23
High Schools					
El Camino High	986	723	8	6	12
South San Francisco High	1,096	686	6	8	30
WOODSIDE					
Elementary Schools					
Woodside Elementary	314	902	10	10	6

SAT SCORES

Many four-year colleges and universities use the Scholastic Assessment Tests to help them assess the abilities of prospective students. High SAT scores are usually an indication of an affluent, well-educated community; therefore these scores should not be used to judge the effectiveness of individual schools. However, high scores and a large percentage of students taking the test probably indicate that these schools have an academic and social environment that values academic success, a wide range of advanced level classes, and many students who work hard in their classes because they plan to go to a competitive college.

In recent years, the emphasis on SAT scores for college admissions has been widely debated. In response to some of the criticism, the College Board has changed the test, eliminating the section on analogies and adding a 25 minute writing sample. The new test, given for the first time in March 2005, contains more grammar questions and the math section includes material covered in second year algebra classes. While the old SAT was primarily an aptitude or intelligence test, the new one measures what knowledge students have mastered and thus is more curriculum centered. Because it now contains three parts—math, critical reading, and writing--the highest possible score on the new SAT is 2400 instead of 1600. (The results of the 2005 tests were not yet available at the time this book went to print.)

Despite the changes in the test, critics of the test continue to point out that the widespread use of SAT preparatory classes, which can cost thousands of dollars, creates a disadvantage for students whose parents cannot afford to pay for these classes. They also worry that the new, more curriculum-driven exam will increase the gap between poor and middle-class students because of the huge disparity in the quality of the nation's schools. Those who defend the SAT as an important predictor of success in college point out that because of widespread grade inflation, admissions officers need some standardized measure of applicants' academic achievement. While some competitive colleges give students the option of taking other tests (e.g., the ACT) and others require the SAT II exams which are subject specific, most competitive universities continue to rely on SAT scores to help give them a more complete picture of applicants' abilities.

You can find SAT scores for years after 2004 on The California Department of Education's website http://data1.cde.ca.gov/dataquest. This site also provides information about performance on the ACT and Advanced Placement exams.

MEAN SAT SCORES FOR
SAN MATEO COUNTY HIGH SCHOOLS

HIGH SCHOOL	% of takers in '04	'04 Verbal	'04 Math	'03 Verbal	'03 Math
NATIONAL	N/A	508	518	507	519
STATE	35%	496	519	494	518
ARAGON	62%	543	577	538	573
BURLINGAME	67%	521	557	520	554
CAPUCHINO	32%	483	512	497	497
CARLMONT	53%	533	560	535	555
EL CAMINO	36%	466	503	466	516
HALF MOON BAY	43%	536	536	540	541
HILLSDALE	52%	510	544	491	538
JEFFERSON	26%	431	451	406	427
MENLO-ATHERTON	55%	550	558	554	564
MILLS	70%	540	589	521	579
OCEANA	44%	477	499	472	504
PESCADERO	44%	NA	NA	NA	NA
SAN MATEO	53%	546	578	536	571
SEQUOIA	34%	489	511	492	521
S. SAN FRANCISCO	40%	480	515	466	516
TERRA NOVA	46%	507	522	515	541
WESTMOOR	38%	462	511	480	532
WOODSIDE	49%	488	491	498	496

MEAN SAT SCORES FOR
SANTA CLARA COUNTY HIGH SCHOOLS

HIGH SCHOOL	% of takers in '04	'04 Verbal	'04 Math	'03 Verbal	'03 Math
NATIONAL	N/A	508	518	507	519
STATE	35%	496	519	494	518
BRANHAM	54%	522	530	511	519
CUPERTINO	67%	548	623	529	608
DEL MAR	35%	498	508	497	516
DOWNTOWN COLLEGE PREP	20%	448	496	NA	NA
FOOTHILL	8%	477	500	536	546
FREMONT	60%	492	546	480	520
GILROY	38%	502	494	486	493
GUNDERSON	36%	464	493	448	480
GUNN	90%	607	642	611	656
HILL	37%	439	485	421	463
HOMESTEAD	72%	566	618	560	615
INDEPENDENCE	35%	462	509	455	493
LEIGH	52%	534	559	535	552
LELAND	78%	551	603	553	608
LICK	12%	441	472	430	441
LINCOLN	45%	538	522	536	524
LIVE OAK	38%	511	529	522	558
LOS ALTOS	75%	553	586	551	594
LOS GATOS	76%	586	610	570	590
LYNBROOK	94%	595	656	587	660
MILPITAS	56%	489	540	488	543
MONTA VISTA	88%	590	666	587	675
MT. PLEASANT	48%	462	488	452	488
MTN. VIEW	73%	563	594	567	603
OAK GROVE	34%	489	511	483	513
OVERFELT	25%	412	456	417	456
PALO ALTO	83%	608	630	606	633
PIEDMONT HILLS	61%	498	538	486	530
PIONEER	49%	528	542	520	534
PROSPECT	37%	538	550	496	536
SAN JOSE ACADEMY	38%	482	499	502	516
SANTA CLARA	46%	480	499	485	512
SANTA TERESA	44%	515	525	497	517
SARATOGA	89%	621	659	615	657
SILVER CREEK	44%	461	509	455	500
WESTMONT	44%	521	546	528	556
WILCOX	52%	476	524	500	536
WILLOW GLEN	36%	477	483	485	494
YERBA BUENA	33%	431	491	418	489

Source: California State Department of Education

SCHOOL DISTRICTS THAT HAVE PASSED PARCEL TAXES AND GENERAL OBLIGATION BONDS SINCE 1996

San Mateo County Districts That Have Passed Parcel Taxes SINCE 1996

Belmont-Redwood Shores
2004: 10 yr. $96 tax to improve programs, retain teachers, & maintain small classes

Brisbane
2005: 6 yr. $96 tax to fund small classes; reading, math & art teachers
1999: 6 yr. $72 tax to fund small classes; reading, math & art teachers

Burlingame
2004: 6 yr.$104 tax to maintain small classes & programs
2003: 8 yr. $76 tax to retain teachers, small classes, programs
1997: 8 yr. $40 tax to maintain class size & programs.

Hillsborough
1988: passed an ongoing parcel tax that increases with ADA and inflation, currently $445

Las Lomitas
2001: 6 yr. $196 tax to maintain small classes and programs; technology
1995: 6 yr. $98 tax to maintain class size & programs

Menlo Park
2003: Open additional $170 tax (total $485) to maintain small classes & teachers, increases each year according to CPI index
2000: Open $315 tax to reduce class size and support art, music, and technology
1995: 8 yr. $76 tax to maintain class size & programs

Portola Valley
2004: 10 yr. $210 tax to retain programs & staff

Ravenswood
2004: 5 yr. $98 tax to recruit & train teachers & fund teachers

San Carlos
2003: 8 yr. $75 tax for small classes & programs

San Mateo - Foster City
2003: 7 yr. $75 tax for programs & small classes

Woodside
2001: 8 yr. $196 tax for programs, small class sizes and salaries

San Mateo County Districts That Have Passed Bonds

Belmont
1997: $12 million to add classrooms & fix schools

Brisbane
2003: $11 million to renovate & upgrade

Burlingame
1997: $6 million to reopen school and modernize.

Cabrillo
1996: $35 million for construction, new sites & renovation

Hillsborough
2002: $66.8 million to modernize & expand

Jefferson HSD
2001: $52 million for construction & renovation
1995: $30 million to improve programs & modernize

Menlo Park
1995: $22 million for construction & renovation

San Mateo County Districts That Have Passed Bonds

Pacifica
1997: $30 million for renovations and new labs at middle schools

Portola Valley
2001: $6 million for renovation & construction
1998: $17 million for technology, renovation & facilities

Ravenswood City
2000: $10 million to modernize & improve technology
1996: $6 million to renovate sites & improve technology

Redwood City
2002: $22 million to construct & improve facilities
1997: $44 million for new classrooms

San Bruno Park
1998: $30 million for repairs, technology & classrooms
1996: $600,000 for renovations & seismic retrofit

San Carlos
1997: $22 million for safety, construction & renovation

San Mateo HS
2000: $137.5 million for repairs, renovation and safety

San Mateo - Foster City
1997: $79 million for expansion & renovation

Sequoia
2004: $70 million to modernize & expand facilities
2001: $88 million for construction & renovation
1996: $45 million to upgrade & modernize schools

South San Francisco
1997: $40 million for technology & repair

Woodside
1999: $5.2 million for classrooms & modernization

Santa Clara County Districts That Have Passed Parcel Taxes Since 1995

Alum Rock
2004: 5 yr. $100 tax to repair, improve facilities

Cambrian
2004: 4 yr. $63 tax to maintain small classes and programs
2001: 4 yr. $63 to reduce class size, improve programs, retain teachers

Campbell HS
2004: 5 yr. $85 tax to reduce class size, restore programs

Cupertino
2004: 6 yr. $98 tax to retain small class size and programs

Fremont
2004: 6 yr. $98 tax to maintain programs and staff

Loma Prieta
2004: $150 to renew Gann limit
2000: 4 yr. $150 tax to maintain programs
1996: 4 yr. $150 tax to maintain programs

Los Altos Elem.
2002: 4 yr. $597 tax for teachers, programs, small class size
1997: 4 yr. $264 tax to maintain small classes; repair facilities

Santa Clara County Districts
That Have Passed Parcel Taxes Since 1995

Los Gatos Elem.
2002: Open tax of $290 to maintain small classes, support services, science instruction
1998: 4 yr. $250 tax for teachers' salaries and small classes

Mountain View Elem.
2004: 5 yr. $75-$600 tax (based on lot size) to retain small classes & programs

Oak Grove
2002: 4 yr. $68 tax for repairs, modernization, services
1998: 3 yr. $68 tax for repairs and equipment

Palo Alto
2005: 6 yr. $493 tax to maintain small classes and restore programs
2001: 4 yr. $293 tax to attract teachers & maintain programs

Santa Clara County Districts That Have Passed Bonds

Berryessa
1999: $48 million to upgrade and modernize facilities

Campbell Elem.
2002: $75 million for renovation & construction
1999: $95 million for modernization and facilities

Cupertino
2001: $80 million for new facilities, renovation and repair

East Side
2002: $298 million for security, safety & technology
1999: $80 million for repair and modernization

Evergreen
1997: $60 million 7for construction & improvements

Franklin - McKinley
2004: $30 million for repair, construction, facilities
2001: $18 million for construction, upgrading, and safety
1996: $18.3 million for new elementary school and renovations

Fremont
1998: $144 million for safety and repairs

Gilroy
2004: $69 million for renovation and construction

Lakeside
1998: $1.45 million for repairs and new classrooms

Los Altos Elem.
1998: $94.7 million for construction, wiring, renovation

Los Gatos Elem.
2001: $91 million to renovate, modernize, and improve safety

Los Gatos - Saratoga HS
1998: $79 million for modernization, safety & repairs

Loma Prieta
2002: $4.9 million for construction & improvements

Luther Burbank
1997: $1.8 million to modernize and maintain small classes

Milpitas
1996: $64.7 million for new construction & renovations

Santa Clara County Districts That Have Passed Bonds

Moreland
2002: $35 million for construction & improvements

Morgan Hill
1999: $72.5 million for construction & renovation

Mt. Pleasant
1998: $12 million for repairs and seismic upgrades

Mountain View Elem.
1998: $36 million for small classes and repairs
1996: $34 million to renovate schools

Moutain View - Los Altos HS
1995: $58 million for renovations & improvements

Oak Grove
1995: $75 million to improve facilities & technology

Orchard
2002: $40 million to acquire & construct facilities
2000: $16 million for classroom construction, science & technology

Palo Alto
1995: $143 million for school modernization

San Jose
2002: $429 million for construction & improvements
1997: $165 million for classrooms and programs

Santa Clara
2004: $315 million for repairs, safety, & facilities
1997: $145 million to renovate schools and build high school science wings

Saratoga Elem.
2002: $19.9 million for construction & improvements
1997: $40 million to renovate schools, add classrooms & multi-use rooms for elementary schools, and add library & computer center at middle school

Sunnyvale
2004: $120 million to construct & improve facilities
1996: $34 million to renovate & repair facilities

Source: EdSource

PUBLIC SCHOOL DISTRICT
EXPENDITURES PER STUDENT
2003-2004

Santa Clara County

Alum Rock	$7146	Luther Burbank	$7006
Berryessa	$6227	Milpitas Unified	$6251
Cambrian	$6490	Montebello	$9317
Campbell Elem.	$6520	Moreland	$6446
Campbell H.S.	$6431	Morgan Hill Unified	$6201
Cupertino	$6127	Mt. View-Los Altos HS	$9913
East Side Union HS	$7347	Mt. View-Whisman.	$7100
Evergreen	$6055	Mt. Pleasant	$7211
Franklin-McKinley	$7205	Oak Grove	$6779
Fremont Union HS	$7381	Orchard	$6814
Gilroy Unified	$6934	Palo Alto Unified	$10,497
Lakeside	$10,533	San Jose Unified	$7683
Loma Prieta	$7079	Santa Clara Unified	$7539
Los Altos	$7744	Saratoga	$6803
Los Gatos	$7408	Sunnyvale	$7576
Los Gatos-Saratoga. HS	$8166	Union	$6629

San Mateo County

Bayshore	$6,086	Pacifica	$6,228
Belmont/Redwood Shores	$8,070	Portola Valley	$12,350
Brisbane	$7,333	Ravenswood	$9,072
Burlingame	$6,532	Redwood City	$7,720
Cabrillo Unified	$6,431	San Bruno Park	$6,356
Hillsborough	$10,432	San Carlos	$6,599
Jefferson Elem.	$6,285	San Mateo HS	$9,269
Jefferson HS	$7,056	San Mateo-Foster City	$6,721
La Honda-Pescadero	$11,951	Sequoia HS	$9,390
Los Lomitas	$11,054	South San Francisco	$6,252
Menlo Park	$9,643	Woodside	$13,164
Millbrae	$6,395		

Source: http://www.ed-data.k12.ca.us

WEBSITES

The following websites offer far more information than this book can possibly provide. Many of the sites give similar information and some link with each other. Parents should recognize that while these sites can give them volumes of information about specific schools, especially public schools, none of them can measure the true essence of a school—the feeling of the environment; the accessibility and leadership qualities of the principal; the warmth, passion, and commitment of the faculty; and the level of support from parents and the community at large.

Rather than spending days and days poring over all the statistics available through these websites, parents should use some basic information available in this book and on these websites to narrow down their options and then spend time visiting school campuses and talking to current parents.

Websites That Provide Information about California Public Schools

www.cde.ca.gov
California's Department of Education website provides API scores, STAR scores, and demographic information. It also links up to many other websites that provide information about the state's public schools and education policies.

www.cde.ca.gov/board
This section of the site describes the state's content standards by grade level and subject: English-language arts, math, history, and science. It also provides information about the high school exit exam that students, starting with the class of 2006, must pass before graduating.

http://data1.cde.ca.gov/dataquest
This part of the Department of Education's website provides data by county, district, and school on SAT, ACT, and Advanced Placement exams. This site also gives API and STAR reports.

www.ed-data.k12.ca.us
This website, established as a partnership of four entities, including the California Department of Education and EdSource, provides extensive information about every public school in California:

- Results of STAR tests, standards-based augmented tests, and API scores;
- Ethnic breakdown of the student and teacher population;
- Class size;
- Percentage of fully credentialed teachers.

Profiles for high schools include:
- Percentage of graduates eligible for UC/CSU admissions;
- SAT scores;
- Dropout rate.

It also has a feature that allows you to compare districts based on specific characteristics such as average class size and revenue limit funds per student.

www.greatschools.net

GreatSchools, a nonprofit organization, offers comprehensive online school information on elementary, middle and high schools. It provides information about public, private and charter schools in all 50 states and detailed school profiles for many states including California.

Profiles include information about achievement, curriculum, special programs, school demographics, and parent reviews. The site also includes articles about current education issues, explanations of how schools work, and advice to parents about interacting with their child's schools. The site has a "The School Finder," feature that allows you to compare a list of public schools based on test scores, class size, diversity, and distance from your home.

www.sccoe.org

Through the Santa Clara County Office of Education parents can obtain school report cards, school and district websites, maps, and information about interdistrict transfers.

www.schoolwisepress.com

This site publishes annual school reports, which you can find in many libraries. In addition, the company helps school districts publish their own schools' annual accountability reports. Its free, public Web site provides extensive information about schools, current educational policies, and hot-button issues in education. You can also find comparative rankings of schools by county and school level in the "compare" area of the School Wise Web site.

www.schoolmatch.com

School Match is a school research and database service firm that rates schools using "auditable" data. The site sells reports on individual districts and accredited private schools throughout the country.

www.smcoe.k12.ca.us

The website for the San Mateo Office of Education links users up with all districts and public schools in the county.

Websites Providing Information about Private Schools

www.acsi.org
The website for the Association of Christian Schools International provides information about member schools throughout the world. Clicking on California will give a list of member schools in the state and in some cases connect with websites for individual schools.

www.cais.org
The website for the California Association of Independent Schools lists member schools according to vicinity, enrollment and level, and type (i.e., elementary or secondary, coed or single gender). The list also links users to school websites.

www.dsj.org
The website for the Department of Education for the San Jose Diocese, which oversees Catholic schools in Santa Clara County, provides a listing for all the elementary and secondary schools in the diocese. It also links users to school websites.

www.sfarchdiocese.org
The website for the Archdiocese of San Francisco lists Catholic schools in San Francisco, Marin, and San Mateo counties and connects to some school websites.

INDEX

ORDER FORM FOR

PARENTS' GUIDE TO SCHOOL SELECTION
in Santa Clara and San Mateo Counties
Sixth Edition

The Pratt Center
Four Main Street, Suite 210
Los Altos, CA 94022
Phone: (650) 949-2997
Fax: (650) 949-2442

Number of books	Total
1	$24.02
2	$45.93
3	$67.85
4	$89.76
5	$100.88
10	$178.07
20	$310.84

10% off orders of 5 or more.
20% off orders of 10 or more.
30% off orders of 20 or more.

Listed prices already include discount.
Costs include shipping, handling and sales tax.

Number of copies:_____

Amount enclosed: $_____

Name _____

Phone _____

Address _____

Email _____

City _____

State _____   Zip _____